Chasing
the Tigers

Chasing the Tigers

A Portrait of the New Vietnam

Murray Hiebert

KODANSHA INTERNATIONAL
New York • Tokyo • London

Kodansha America, Inc.
114 Fifth Avenue, New York, New York 10011, U.S.A.

Kodansha International Ltd.
17-14 Otowa 1-chome, Bunkyo-ku, Tokyo 112, Japan

Published in 1996 by Kodansha America, Inc.

Library of Congress Cataloging-in-Publication Data

Hiebert, Murray.
Chasing the tigers : a portrait of the new Vietnam / Murray Hiebert.
p.   cm.
Includes index.
ISBN 1-56836-139-4 (hc)
1. Vietnam—Economic conditions.   2. Vietnam—Economic policy.
I. Title.
HC444.H53   1996
338.9597—dc20   96-32800

Maps by Jeffrey L. Ward

Printed in the United States of America
96   97   98   99   00   B/BER   10   9   8   7   6   5   4   3   2   1

For Linda and our children,
Ann and Jonathan

Contents

◆ ◆ ◆

List of Illustrations

◆ ◆ ◆

To the Reader

◆   ◆   ◆

The sources for most of the information and quotations in this book are from interviews with Vietnamese people and foreign Vietnam-watchers between 1990 to 1994. Full names, such as that of business-man Vuu Khai Thanh, are real names. In some cases where I needed to protect a source or a friend I either used a one-word name such as Mai (which is a pseudonym) or a job description such as "official" or "journalist." In instances where I depended on books or articles I have used notes to cite the source.

The currency references in this book are in U.S. dollars. The exchange rate for the Vietnamese currency in recent years has hovered at just over dong 11,000 = US$1.

For convenience I have used the metric measurement system common in Vietnam. A meter equals 39.37 inches. A kilometer equals five-eighths of a mile. A hectare is the equivalent of 2.47 acres, and a kilogram is 2.2 pounds.

Chasing
the Tigers

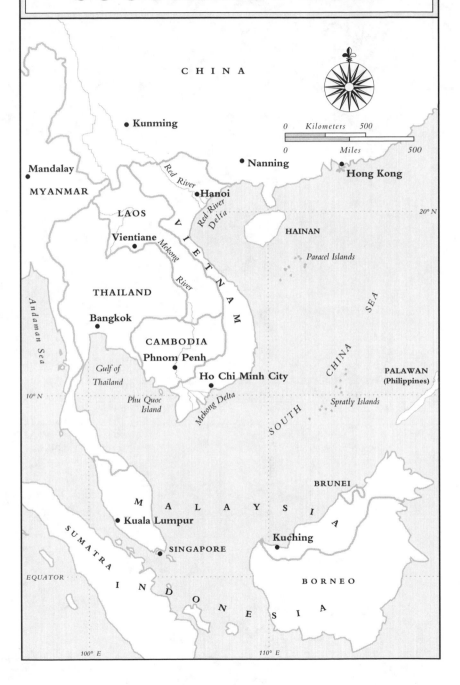

◆ SOUTHEAST ASIA ◆

CHINA

Kunming

Nanning

Hong Kong

Mandalay

MYANMAR

Red River

Hanoi

LAOS

Red River Delta

HAINAN

Vientiane

Mekong River

Paracel Islands

THAILAND

Bangkok

Andaman Sea

CAMBODIA

Phnom Penh

Ho Chi Minh City

SOUTH CHINA SEA

Gulf of Thailand

PALAWAN (Philippines)

10° N

Phu Quoc Island

Mekong Delta

Spratly Islands

BRUNEI

MALAYSIA

Kuala Lumpur

Kuching

SUMATRA

SINGAPORE

EQUATOR

INDONESIA

BORNEO

100° E

110° E

0   Kilometers   500

0   Miles   500

20° N

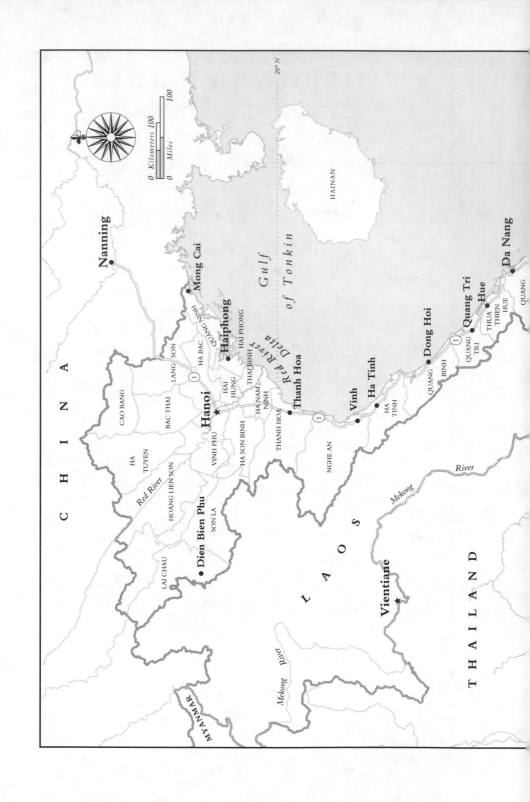

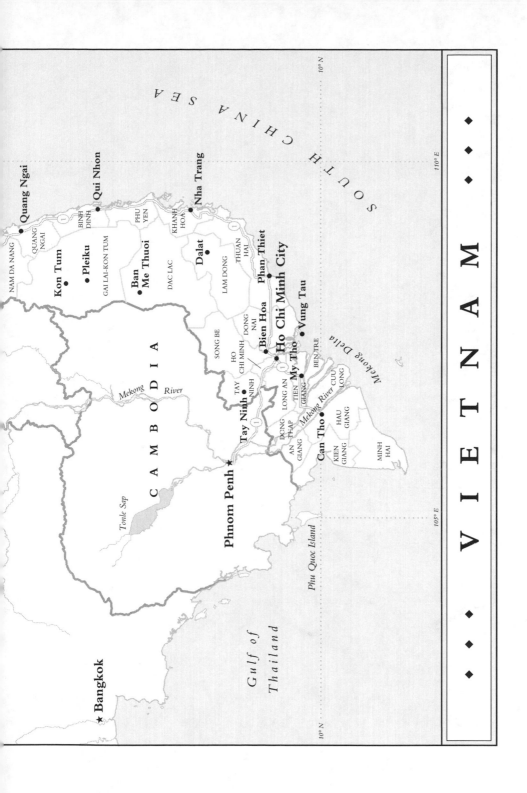

Introduction

Vietnam Awakes

◆ ◆ ◆

In 1978, after gung-ho Communist rulers had shut down the last of the capitalists in what had been known as Saigon, Vuu Khai Thanh was desperate to join tens of thousands of his ethnic Chinese compatriots in the boat people exodus from Vietnam. "All my family had gone," the former soldier in the U.S.-backed South Vietnamese army said of his eleven brothers and sisters. "I wanted to leave very badly, but I didn't find an opportunity." But in the topsy-turvy world of Vietnam Thanh soon found a new opportunity. With a healthy dose of faith in the Communist Party's 1986 economic reforms and help from his siblings in Canada and the United States, Thanh has turned two small, rubber sandal–making cooperative workshops into the multimillion-dollar Binh Tien Imex Corporation (Biti).

Today the soft-spoken forty-eight-year-old son of a Chinese herbalist presides over one of Vietnam's most prominent private companies. In 1993 his company sold $15 million worth of shoes and sandals, making it the country's largest producer and exporter of footwear. After Washington lifted its economic embargo against Vietnam in early 1994 Biti became the first Vietnamese firm to open an office in the United States. Like many other ethnic Chinese companies in Asia, Biti is a family-run business, with Thanh and his wife controlling nearly three-quarters of its shares. One of Thanh's top deputies is his younger brother, Vuu Danh. Danh fled the country in 1978, but fifteen years later sold his New York office supply company and returned home. Vietnam, says Danh, is where the opportunity is now.

Vuu Khai Thanh is one of many who are firing up impoverished Vietnam with an entrepreneurial flare reminiscent of the ethnic Chinese who helped jump-start the economies of several of Vietnam's thriving neighbors. A few years ago he formed a joint venture with a Taiwanese firm to produce sandals; he is now preparing to diversify into property development and marketing of household appliances. It is ironic that all of this capitalist activity should be going on in Communist Vietnam (even more ironic, Thanh's suburban Ho Chi Minh City office building used to serve as a Communist Party training school). But since 1986, when Vietnam's leaders launched their free-market reforms, the success that Thanh and Danh have enjoyed is indicative of the remarkable turnaround occurring all over Vietnam today.[1]

Businessmen, once repressed, are again investing in small enterprises. Shops in Hanoi and Ho Chi Minh City are lined from floor to ceiling with color television sets and video players from Japan and South Korea. Newly imported motorbikes—costing more than ten times the average per-capita income of $200 a year—clog city streets. A construction boom has erupted throughout the country. Peasants are replacing thatch-and-mud huts with brick houses, and Hanoi's new elite is building fancy new villas around idyllic West Lake. International property developers are lining up to build new office towers and hotels to cash in on a thriving real estate market. Agriculture is also booming, despite the fact that as recently as 1988 Vietnam had appealed for international aid to avert starvation in rural areas. Freed from their cooperatives, farmers are producing record harvests, making Vietnam the world's third-largest rice exporter, behind Thailand and the United States. As a recent visitor observed, Vietnam seems "like seventy-two million Rip van Winkles trying to make up for lost time."[2]

"Another dragon awakes!" "A tiger cub is born!" trumpet Vietnam's enthusiasts. Current conventional wisdom in the international marketplace is that Vietnam is poised for economic take-off and is only a few decades away from emulating Asia's four tigers—Hong Kong, Taiwan, Singapore, and South Korea—whose economies doubled in size every eight years between 1960 and 1985. By dismantling farm cooperatives, encouraging private enterprise, and opening the country to foreign investors, Vietnam's leaders have taken the first steps toward transforming one of the world's poorest nations. Although ravaged by decades of war with France, the United States, Cambodia, and China, as well as international isolation and failed Communist policies, Vietnam is reviving itself with remarkable speed. The country still has much ground to gain—it continues to suffer from widespread poverty, unemployment, and declining education and health services—just to catch up with neighbors such as Thailand and Malaysia, whose economies were roughly akin to Vietnam's in the 1950s. Yet in only a few years the former "sick man" of Asia has achieved impressive rates of growth, reined in hyperinflation, and sharply increased exports.

As for the Vietnamese themselves, most seem anxious to replace the reminders of war (and communism) with the trappings of modernization and economic development. In Hanoi the wreckage of an American bomber, long a reminder of U.S. brutality during the war, has been removed from Lenin Park to make way for a luxury hotel. B-52 Boulevard has been renamed Truong Chinh Street after a famous Vietnamese ideologue who, although best known for orchestrating the Communist Party's brutal land reform program in the 1950s, ultimately played a key role by urging his colleagues to launch their drive toward a market economy. More than half of Vietnam's population has been born since the war ended, and the new generation is far more intent on studying English and making money than reliving history.

Not everyone has gotten rich since the Communist Party began its free market reforms; for millions of peasants in remote areas of the countryside, life remains extremely difficult. For them, the slick billboards, glittering karaoke bars, satellite dishes, and cellular phones of the cities are still a world away.

Another remarkable change among many Vietnamese is in political outlook. The Communist Party continues to rule, but Vietnam is no longer Communist in any meaningful sense. The party has jettisoned its socialist dogma and is struggling to attract the same capitalists it once fought to oust from the country. Even the keepers of Communist orthodoxy have joined in the national preoccupation with making money. The central committee, the 161-person body that sets Communist Party policy, operates the An Phu trading company to fund its activities. The army runs factories and construction companies, while the security police—the organization charged with stifling any dissent—owns the Pacific Company, which operates a chain of hotels, some of which have the country's liveliest discotheques.

Although police still arrest anyone who poses a threat to the Communist Party's sole grip on political power, the country's rulers no longer try to manage every detail of people's lives. Strict social controls on where people live, work, and shop have crumbled. Neighborhood committees no longer tell people what to wear or criticize them for listening to the BBC. Shopkeepers and taxi drivers feel free to grumble openly about corrupt or incompetent officials. Even members of Vietnam's parliament, the National Assembly, have begun to grill government ministers about wasteful or inefficient projects. Journalists, as well, no longer simply print the party line; they expose corrupt officials. A new breed of writers, many of them war veterans such as Bao Ninh and Duong Thu Huong, churn out novels exposing the Communist Party's earlier excesses and challenging its glorification of the victory over the Americans, even though the government still keeps tight reins on what publishing houses can print. A new generation of contemporary Vietnamese painters such as Dang Xuan Hoa and Truong Tan have abandoned socialist realism and are experimenting with new styles, making them popular with foreign collectors. Buddhist pagodas and Christian churches are full again—even though some of their leaders are in prison for clamoring for "too much" freedom.

Indeed, it seems that almost anything goes as long as people don't challenge the Communists' grip on power. As Australian National University senior fellow David Marr observes, "For the past five years or so, the Vietnam Communist Party has essentially struck a bargain with the populace: Find new economic space for yourselves and leave us in control of politics."[3]

From the Dark Years to *Doi Moi*

In April 1975, when North Vietnam's Communists marched into Saigon and clinched victory over the South and the Americans, Nguyen Thi Ngoc Tram was fourteen. She grew up in Tuy Hoa, a desolate little city on the coast of central Vietnam, where her father served as an officer in the South Vietnamese army. As the Communists mounted their final offensive of the war, Ngoc Tram and her family fled south, arriving in Saigon a few days ahead of Hanoi's Russian-built tanks.

A few weeks later, Ngoc Tram's father was bundled off to a remote reeducation camp. Like roughly two hundred thousand other military officers, civil servants, politicians, religious leaders, intellectuals, and artists, he was forced to do hard labor on a near starvation diet. Without her father's salary Ngoc Tram's formerly middle-class family had to struggle to survive. "The situation of our family was very difficult," she recalls. "We sold all of our belongings, only keeping a reed mat and a bed to sleep on." Her ready smile betrays the fact that she lost several teeth during those years, as the family could not afford such luxuries as dental care. Her mother supported the family by selling secondhand clothes—which she bought from other struggling families who needed money to feed themselves—on the black market. As new arrivals in the city and dependents of an officer from the ousted regime, Ngoc Tram's family was not eligible for the subsidized rice rations, cooking oil, cloth, and other cheap commodities provided to people who worked for the new Communist rulers.

Eventually the family, which had lived in a large French-style villa during the war, managed to rent a ten-square-meter apartment for Ngoc Tram, her mother, and her younger brother. The apartment consisted of one dimly lit room and a tiny, decrepit bathroom, with a kerosene burner for cooking just inside the front door.

Ngoc Tram was allowed to continue studying until she finished high school in 1979 but was rejected when she applied to college as well as for jobs. "In the beginning, we faced a lot of discrimination because of my father." Her father survived his stint in reeducation camps and was released in 1980, but like many others he had aged beyond his years and had become cynical and bitter. He died a year later at the age of sixty-three.

Ngoc Tram and her family could have suffered a worse plight. Hundreds of thousands of Saigon residents were shipped off to "new economic zones" at this time, as the new Communist authorities attempted to defuse urban overcrowding and unemployment by moving people to poorly prepared "virgin land" or malaria-infested jungles. She is one of many who consider the first decade after the 1975 Communist victory to have been the "dark years." Although the Communist leaders had pledged that every family would have a refrigerator, a television, and a radio within ten years of the country's reunification, in fact most of their policies proved disastrous. Far from the socialist paradise these leaders promised and envisioned, life in Vietnam became miserable for millions during this period, when the country was already suffering from underdevelopment, wide-scale destruction, and the abrupt loss of American aid.

Private businesses became scarce and were shut down entirely in the 1978 "socialist transformation" campaign. In the countryside peasants were pressed to join farm cooperatives and to sell their rice at low prices to fund Hanoi's drive toward developing heavy industry. Production nose-dived, inflation soared, and exports lagged far behind imports. Vietnam became a drab place where even shoddy goods from local factories or the Soviet Union were in short supply. Even civil servants, for whom life was generally better, had dismal experiences. "Life was so bad," one official remembers. "Our incomes were very low and we had to stand in long queues for several kilograms of food. We worked hard and got nothing."

Harsh living conditions, rigid social controls, and war with neighboring Cambodia and China prompted large numbers of desperate

Vietnamese to flee the country. By the early 1980s nearly one million had left, including some two hundred fifty thousand ethnic Chinese who fled across Vietnam's northern border into China. Thousands of boat people fled to Hong Kong and neighboring Southeast Asian countries, often on tiny, overcrowded fishing boats ill equipped for a sea voyage; many were fleeced by officials of their gold and valuables as they left.

Fearing that they would be inundated with a flood of refugees, Thailand and Malaysia at times would turn new arrivals away from their shores. Some boat people fell into the hands of pirates who robbed them, raped the women among them, and rammed their boats. Thousands did not survive their flight, dying from exposure or drowning during tropical storms.

Popular dissatisfaction, even within the Communist Party, finally forced leaders to reverse the dogmatic policies that had kept Vietnam among the ranks of the world's poorest countries. Economic stagnation, inflation, and domestic discontent had worsened considerably by the mid-1980s, and at a landmark Sixth Congress in 1986, party leaders decided to embark upon several important economic reforms: They opened up the country to foreign investors, abolished internal trade barriers, and untied many of the fetters on local capitalists.

One extremely important move, Directive 10 of 1988, dismantled Vietnam's inefficient farm cooperatives and returned land to the farmers. The next year the Communist Party removed most of the remnants of central planning: They abolished price controls, phased out subsidies to money-hemorrhaging state enterprises, devalued the exchange rate, boosted bank interest rates, and sharply curtailed the state monopoly on foreign trade. Equally important, the withdrawal of Hanoi's remaining occupying force from Cambodia in 1989 convinced most countries to end Vietnam's economic isolation. This movement toward a more open society and economy, known as *doi moi* in Vietnam, has made the second decade of Communist rule much more agreeable—though by no means perfect—for a great number of Vietnamese.

After years of unemployment, Ngoc Tram was finally admitted to a two-year training program for kindergarten teachers in 1984. She graduated two years later and landed a job at a state-run kindergarten (not coincidentally around the time the Communist Party launched its reforms). Her life improved again in 1991 when her kindergarten introduced tuition fees for its nearly five hundred students. Since then her salary has increased to approximately $45 per month, which has allowed her to save enough to buy a secondhand 50-c.c. Honda motorbike that she uses to commute to work. Her mother has passed away, but she still lives in the same tiny apartment with her brother (who works for a private company producing lacquer furniture). The two of them have managed to add a color television set and a video player to their crowded living space.

Thanks to the reforms, life in Ho Chi Minh City has become livable again. "My life has changed a lot during the last two or three years," Ngoc Tram admits. "Now my life is stable. I no longer want to leave."

Bright Future

Enthusiasts see almost no limits to Vietnam's economic potential. While some economists and journalists continue to bemoan deficiencies in the economic system, foreign investors exude confidence: They are betting their capital that economic common sense will prevail in Vietnam as it did in the other booming economies of Asia. They point to the ingenuity and determination that carried the country through decades of war and years of hard-line Communist rule, as well as its literate, youthful labor force, its disciplined Confucian culture, and its location within the world's fastest-growing economic region. Their enthusiasm is not surprising. After decades of war and socialist mismanagement the Vietnamese have embraced market economics with a vengeance. A spirit of enterprise has replaced the rigid state plans, internal police checkpoints, and long queues for poor-quality rice that characterized Vietnam before its leaders abandoned hard-line communism.

Although there is much opportunity in Vietnam, the country still faces some rather daunting hurdles along the road to becoming Asia's newest "tiger." It is imperative that the country's nominally Communist leadership complete the reform process it began in 1986 and avoid what Harvard economist Dwight Perkins calls the "twilight zone" between central planning and the free market.[4] Furthermore, Vietnam must mobilize billions of dollars to build and repair an infrastructure that was never advanced to begin with and that was shattered and neglected during years of war. Domestically, Vietnam must complete its legal framework, simplify foreign and domestic investment procedures, and train more managers to guide the economy in the transition to a market system.

The country has only limited quantities of oil and other natural resources, its forests are rapidly disappearing, and its farmland is already three times as densely populated as that of neighboring countries. Like other Asian "tigers," Vietnam will have to rely more on its human resources than its other assets.[5]

The conditions in Vietnam today are not unlike those in Taiwan and South Korea in the 1950s, just before they hit their respective economic growth spurts. Observers of the East Asian "miracle" are convinced that Vietnam has what it takes to follow in these countries' footsteps and emerge as the region's next economic powerhouse. Indeed, Vietnam is already "chasing the tigers."

1

Asia's Youngest Tiger Roars

◆ ◆ ◆

Sprouting Like Mushrooms

Two decades ago Tran Xuan Lap was a young electrical engineer in Hanoi's air defense forces, the unit charged with protecting the skies over the Vietnamese capital from American bombers. One of his unit's best-known exploits—the 1967 downing of a bomber piloted by John McCain, today a U.S. senator—is commemorated with a stone plaque at the edge of idyllic Truc Bach Lake, where thousands of Hanoi residents come to relax on weekends and holidays.

Not long after the war ended Lap was transferred to a military college, where he helped train new recruits on how to protect Vietnam's air space in case of future war. He stayed there until 1991, when the collapse of aid from the crumbling Soviet Union, Hanoi's longtime patron, convinced his cash-strapped commanders to pursue more earthly pursuits. Like everyone in Vietnam these days, it seems, Lap started doing business. Today he runs the air defense unit's Ha Long Company, a growing network of thirteen enterprises whose activities range from operating guesthouses and coal mines to assembling television sets and sewing garments. Lap, today a middle-aged lieutenant colonel who sweeps his frizzy hair across his forehead to cover a balding pate, refuses to disclose how much his company earns. All he says is that Ha Long paid more than $200,000 in taxes in 1992.

Lap does not seem to have bothered much changing his life style

17

to fit his new job. He shows up at his run–down office near the air force museum in the suburbs of Hanoi in a baggy, brown uniform that hides his bulging middle. He has not hired a secretary, so our meeting is constantly interrupted by his staff running in and out seeking the boss's advice. Ha Long Company is only one of a growing number of business-for-profit ventures run by Vietnam's armed forces. According to defense ministry figures, by the end of 1993 they operated over three hundred enterprises, employing roughly seventy thousand troops, or about one-eighth of the country's active duty soldiers. In 1993 these companies had a turnover of nearly $164 million and netted the government $11 million in taxes, according to the official Vietnam News Agency. In addition, military enterprises exported $90 million in coal, rubber, coffee, and manufactured products.[1]

Still, like most of the military's enterprises, Ha Long's X19 Garment Factory (which produces military uniforms and men's dress suits) is small, technologically backward, and barely profitable. One problem is finding good managers. "Many of my cadres fought well during the war, but they're not good at doing business," the affable Lap complains. But the soldier-turned-businessman's biggest headache is the shortage of capital to fund expansion and modernization. To get around this problem Lap is seeking foreign partners. Ha Long recently struck a deal to sell computers for a Taiwanese firm and hopes this will lead to a joint assembly plant in Vietnam.

Because the armed forces are one of Vietnam's biggest landowners, Ha Long's most lucrative projects in the coming years undoubtedly will involve property development. Lap says he is talking to a business group from China's Hainan Island about building a hotel on exotic Ha Long Bay in Vietnam's far northeastern corner. He is also looking for a foreign partner to help build a luxury hotel on Hanoi's Truc Bach Lake.

By the end of 1993 the army had obtained sixteen licenses worth $147 million for joint ventures with foreign companies, and ten other applications were in the pipeline. Hong Kong & Shanghai Hotels, best known for its Peninsula Hotels, is building with the military a fifteen-story hotel on the banks of the Saigon River in Ho Chi Minh City. Just down the river, Singapore's Keppel Corporation is helping the navy upgrade the Ba Son Shipyard to build and repair ships.

But it is not only the once-formidable army that has been experimenting with capitalism since the country's socialist planners began loosening their iron grip on economic activity. Entrepreneurs seem to be sprouting up, as the Vietnamese say, like mushrooms after the rain.

In Khe Sanh, one of the bloodiest battlefields of the war, a growing number of American tourists are besieged by local bounty hunters trying to sell old dog tags, shell casings, and cigarette lighters left behind when U.S. soldiers abandoned the base in 1968. (Actually, most of these artifacts have been faked by enterprising capitalists.) Visitors to Cu Chi, the elaborate two-hundred-kilometer tunnel network near Ho Chi Minh City from which Communist infiltrators launched attacks during the war, are offered an opportunity— for $1 a bullet—to fire AK-47s, the Russian-made assault rifles once used by anti-American guerrillas. Having figured out that old battlefields attract tourists, Vietnam's Institute of Military Science and the Quang Tri provincial government are planning to restore several listening posts along the demilitarized zone (DMZ) that divided Vietnam at the seventeenth parallel for two decades. These electronic listening posts along the DMZ (dubbed the "McNamara Line," after the former American defense secretary) were used to monitor the infiltration of North Vietnamese troops into the south during the war.

In the cities it seems that the front of every house has been turned into a shop selling everything from bicycle parts to imported clothes, tea and fruit drinks, and *pho*, Vietnam's spicy noodle soup. Old men sit on street corners offering to pump air into the tires of an increasing array of bicycles and motorcycles for the equivalent of a few pennies.

In recent years some two dozen barbers have appeared on Quang Trung Street, in the run-down but still elegant French-built section of Hanoi. Ensconced on the sidewalk along a crumbling concrete wall and sporting tattoos, yellow dyed hair, and single golden earrings, they offer basic haircuts for less than thirty cents; a shave or an ear cleaning is extra. Their equipment may be basic, but the Quang Trung barbers provide Hanoi's increasingly fashion-conscious men an alternative to the one-style army cut of the state-owned shops that long dominated the market. Some have brightly colored posters offering the latest punk cuts, popular in neighboring Thailand. Only one of the barbers has a genuine—albeit aging—barber's chair, which he has to take home each night. The others use an assortment of rattan or wooden chairs.

Capitalism's Roller Coaster

All of this wheeling and dealing stands in stark contrast to the austere place Vietnam had become following the 1975 Communist victory. As the sun rose over the Saigon River on March 24, 1978, truckloads of armed soldiers and policemen took up positions in the business districts of Ho Chi Minh City in a zealous assault against the last remnants of capitalism. Thousands of youth volunteers wearing red armbands began searching shops and houses in Cholon, the city's Chinatown, and making an inventory of the goods to be confiscated by the government.[2] Within hours thirty thousand families—many of them ethnic Chinese—lost their means of making a living. Less than two weeks later the south's currency was abolished, rendering useless any cash the rich may have had remaining. The death knell of capitalism prompted tens of thousands of disgruntled refugees to flee Vietnam, and was soon followed by a stepped-up drive to force the south's peasants into farm collectives.

Flush with revolutionary euphoria, Hanoi's Marxist victors sought to emulate their former Soviet patrons by developing heavy industry at the expense of agriculture. Production was based not on the demands of the market but on detailed plans formulated by bureaucrats in the state planning commission. Factories did not have to bother with efficiency: the state supplied their raw materials, marketed their products, and paid their workers' salaries.

But the much-touted leap to large-scale socialist production never took place. Instead, the country, already suffering from underdevelopment, decades of wartime destruction, and the abrupt loss of foreign aid, staggered from one economic crisis to the next. The economy grew only 0.4 percent per year between 1976 and 1980, lagging far behind population growth, which surged at an annual rate of 2.3 percent. Rice output per capita fell due to passive resistance from farmers, bad weather, and fertilizer shortages. Mounting food shortfalls caused rising dissatisfaction in southern cities where people were already hard hit by the lack of consumer goods following the withdrawal of the Americans.

Vietnam remained an enclave of poverty at a time when the rest of Asia was prospering. Vietnamese officials often blamed the war and the American trade embargo for the country's miserable economic performance. But Hanoi's ideologically inflexible leaders were equally responsible for not giving people incentives to boost output. The escalation of hostilities with Cambodia's Khmer Rouge regime increased the burden on Vietnam's empty coffers and provoked China to end its economic assistance. Hanoi's invasion of Cambodia in 1978 then prompted the international community to impose economic sanctions on Vietnam, forcing it to increase its dependence on the Soviet Union.

By the end of the 1970s growing economic malaise had convinced the Communist Party that it had to do something if it hoped to hold on to power. In 1979 Hanoi—following China's example—introduced an agricultural "contract system" under which farmers could keep any output over a contracted amount. Enthusiastic peasants responded by boosting production roughly one million tons per year over the next four years.

Despite Hanoi's experiments with piecemeal reforms, production continued to stagnate and prices soared out of control. Finally, in 1986, the Communist Party was forced to admit that its centrally planned, collectivized economy could not boost the country's living standards. Over the next few years its leaders responded by letting go of the reins of central control, abandoning farm cooperatives, and unleashing capitalists eager to take advantage of the country's industrious labor force and natural resources.

Land was returned to private farmers, a new foreign investment code was promulgated, and the state monopoly on trade was ended. In addition, price controls were lifted, the currency was allowed to float, subsidies for state companies were abolished, and interest rates on bank deposits were increased. As it pulled out the last vestiges of its occupying army from Cambodia in the late 1980s, Hanoi also began mending diplomatic fences with its neighbors.

It was not long before these moves began to make a difference. Farm output hit historic highs, privately owned workshops started blossoming, shops filled up, and foreign investment began flowing in. The economy has averaged a healthy 8 percent growth each year since the reforms began in earnest, but Vietnam still has a very small economy: Its total output in 1995 was only about $20 billion. The government's goal is to maintain 8 percent growth through the 1990s and double per-capita income from $200 to $400 by the year 2000. If Vietnam achieves this goal it will have caught up with the standard of living enjoyed by Thailand in the mid-1960s. Thailand, of course, has not stood still in the meantime; its output today is seven times that of Vietnam.

Through Hanoi's moves to control money supply, inflation was reduced from a staggering 680 percent in 1986 to just 5.2 percent in 1993, before ballooning to nearly 15 percent the following year and leveling at 13 percent in 1995. After fluctuating wildly in the early 1990s, the country's currency has stabilized, while its 1995 hard currency exports hit $5.3 billion, more than ten times the 1986 level.[3]

Vietnam often gets high marks for its efforts to liberalize its economy. "Vietnam is on the right track," Callisto Modavo, chief of the World Bank's East Asia division, told aid donors at a meeting in Paris in late 1994. "It has the right vision and is producing results."[4] Many international aid donors seemed to agree, having pledged $1.86 billion worth of soft loans and grants for Vietnam in 1994 and another $2 billion in 1995 and $2.3 billion in 1996. Indeed, Vietnam's performance is remarkable for a country that suffered a loss of approximately $1 billion in Soviet aid after 1989 and faced a continuing American trade embargo for an additional four years. Surprisingly enough, Hanoi undertook its first reforms without financial assistance from either the World Bank or the International Monetary Fund (IMF) because Washington blocked such help.

Much of the credit for the country's early economic accomplishments must be attributed to the hard work of millions of peasants and workers whose energies were unshackled by the Communist Party's reforms, but some of the success was due to sheer good luck: A Vietnamese–Russian joint venture, Vietsovpetro, began pumping oil from the White Tiger (Bach Ho) field off the southern coast just as Soviet aid dried up. The U.S. decision in 1993 to stop opposing international loans to Vietnam and to lift the American trade embargo in 1994 provided another shot of adrenaline. Credits from the World Bank and the Asian Development Bank are expected to help boost Vietnam's tattered social and physical infrastructure. Better roads and more reliable supplies of electricity will make it easier for private investors to tap the country's diligent work force.

"The first $3 billion in infrastructure development will encourage more foreign investors," says John Brinsden, the Vietnam representative of Britain's Standard Chartered Bank, which has opened a branch in Hanoi. "We'll see a snowball effect once they know a bridge won't collapse or that they'll have a hospital for their expatriate staff."

Reversing the Dominos

All of this good news has fueled optimism that Vietnam will emerge as the next Asian tiger, completing the reversal of the old domino theory, which held that all of mainland Southeast Asia would go Communist if the Americans lost in Vietnam. "There is growing evidence that the Vietnamese economy is in the early stages of a boom," crowed a government report prepared for a donors' conference in late 1993, "perhaps similar to what a number of other countries in the region have been experiencing in recent years."[5] Some enthusiasts predict Vietnam will replace China within the next year or two as the fastest growing economy in Asia. Economic growth hit 9.5 percent in 1995 and was expected to reach 10 percent in 1996.

No one doubts Vietnam's tremendous potential. Its people are its single most important resource. The work force is young, educated (literacy stands at an impressive 88 percent) and has a reputation for hard work. The Vietnamese have already demonstrated their organizational skills and discipline during decades of war, and the country has a surplus of engineers, thanks to earlier aid from the former Soviet bloc.

Vietnam's location provides another advantage. Lying on the edge of the South China Sea gives the country easy access to the world's markets and to the region's most important shipping lanes. Geographical proximity to Asia's high-performing economies already has encouraged companies from Taiwan, Hong Kong, South Korea, Singapore, and Japan to shift their factories to Vietnam to benefit from lower wages, much as they moved to Thailand, Malaysia, and Indonesia a decade ago. This proximity also is beginning to facilitate the flow of foreign capital to Vietnam and will make it easy for the Vietnamese to imitate their neighbors' successful strategies.

Vietnam shares the 2,500-year heritage of Confucianism with many of the region's economic champions, including China. The Confucian social system—which emphasizes not the individual but his or her obligation to fit into the larger scheme of things—long looked down on commerce, ranking businessmen on the lowest rung of the social ladder. Still, in recent decades the Confucian-influenced societies of Asia have whipped the rest of the world in economic performance. One reason is undoubtedly the emphasis of Confucianism on education, which has created the region's dynamic human capital. Even though Vietnam's education system has languished somewhat during the past decade, the country's illiteracy rate is still lower than that in many richer nations. A second factor may be the Confucian emphasis on discipline and self-restraint. Many observers believe this accounts for the stunning 30 percent savings rates in Asia, used to build the new shops and factories that have fired up the region's economies. Like their neighbors, Vietnamese are expected to begin saving once their incomes increase.

Vietnam also has some natural resources, oil and natural gas being the most important. Vietnam's proven oil reserves in 1994 stood at 1.2 billion barrels, and its gas reserves are estimated at 3.7 trillion cubic feet. Yet much of the country's hydrocarbon potential lies in an offshore seabed claimed by China, and clashes could erupt if Vietnam tries to exploit it. Petroleum experts believe Vietnam will triple its oil output to over 300,000 barrels a day by the beginning of the next century. These reserves could help develop the country's crippled infrastructure, but they are not large enough to significantly boost the country's income, as they did in nearby Malaysia, where the reserves are five times bigger. Vietnam also has sizable coal reserves (variously estimated at between five hundred million and 2.3 billion tons), considerable iron ore, and a large hydroelectric potential.[6]

The country's land and forests, however, are already critically overtaxed. With more than nine hundred people per square kilometer of farmland (or only one-tenth of a hectare per person), Vietnam is three times more densely populated than neighboring China or Thailand. Serious deforestation in Vietnam over the past quarter century has caused its forest cover to shrink from 40 percent of the land area to just over 20 percent today. "All in all Vietnam has a very large population relative to its resources," a 1993 World Bank report warns, "which means two things. First, the country will have to develop on the basis of human resources rather than natural resources. Second, it will be a major challenge to preserve the fragile resource base in the face of population pressures."[7]

Vietnam's population density means it cannot expand the amount of farmland under cultivation to absorb its surplus work force. The destruction of its forests means it cannot fund its development drive by exporting timber, as Thailand and Malaysia did. Furthermore, Vietnam will need to invest some of its limited resources in rehabilitating its degraded environment and protecting it from growing population pressures. To reduce rural poverty and halt deforestation, Vietnam must rely on foreign and local investors to generate jobs in light industries such as textiles, garments, computer software development, and information technology management. Much like the densely populated city states of Hong Kong and Singapore that have limited natural resources, Vietnam will need to develop labor-intensive, export-oriented industries in order to prosper.

Asia's Economic Miracle

What are the chances that Vietnam, with its mix of assets and liabilities, will catch up with its high-flying neighbors—South Korea, Taiwan, Hong Kong, Singapore, Malaysia, Thailand, and Indonesia?

In 1993 the World Bank published a study of the successful Asian economies that have grown faster since the 1960s than those of any other region of the world.[8] Although the authors did not find a single "East Asian model" of development, they did underline some common themes: Each of these countries maintained a stable economic environment and invested in people by supporting the development of education and health care; they also provided a reliable legal framework to protect investors and encouraged a competitive climate for private entrepreneurs. They inspired high levels of savings, invested heavily in infrastructure projects such as roads and ports, and gave technocrats autonomy to manage the economy without political interference. The report's authors found that most of these countries promoted agriculture during the early stages of development and opened their doors to foreign ideas, technology, and investment. This was soon followed by an import-substitution strategy that was gradually overhauled to encourage the export of manufactured goods.

How does Vietnam fare in comparison to the East Asian miracle economies? Like its neighbors, Vietnam began its reforms by trying to boost agriculture and encourage import-substituting industries. It also opened itself up to foreign investment, although investors complain that they are hobbled by too many regulations and licensing requirements. Hanoi has started promoting exports, but one-quarter of its foreign earnings still come from only two items, both of which are natural, not manufactured, resources: crude oil and unprocessed agricultural products. The country's manufactured exports reach only about $8 per capita, half the level of Bangladesh and less than 3 percent of Thailand's output.

To shift its economy into overdrive, Vietnam needs to more actively promote manufactured exports. Its powerhouse neighbors found this to be the key to absorbing surplus labor and to increasing foreign exchange earnings to pay for new technology. In addition, Hanoi must bolster foreign trade by streamlining its complex system of trade permits, import licenses, and tariffs. Although they have begun to overhaul the archaic banking system, domestic savings must double from its current level of 17 percent if Vietnam hopes to generate the levels of investment that propelled its neighbors.

"Vietnam's economy is at a crossroads," argues Dwight Perkins, director of the Harvard Institute for International Development, which has been advising Vietnam since 1989. "How Vietnam completes the reform process now under way will determine whether the nation's economy will take off and begin to catch up with its East Asian neighbors." Perkins, an expert on China's economic reforms, says that in order to sustain its present high rates of growth Vietnam needs to pull itself out of "its current half way house in what we call the twilight zone between planning and the market."[9]

Two top priorities are the completion of the country's legal system and the overhaul of the state's role in the economy. Although the government has made a good start in drafting new laws, investors too frequently crash through the remaining cracks in the legal framework. Vietnam is desperately short of civil servants with the skills in management, banking, law, and accounting needed to complete the march to the free market. At the same time, Perkins adds, the government needs to end its socialist-style "regulatory mind-set" that often makes it difficult for private entrepreneurs to set up businesses.[10]

A third priority cited by businessmen—both domestic and foreign—is the need to upgrade the country's crumbling transportation infrastructure and power distribution network. Only 13 percent of Vietnam's 105,000 kilometers of often bone-jarring roads are paved. Roads in the north were damaged during the war and those in the south have not been maintained since the fighting ended. Highway One, the country's north-south artery, has only a single potholed lane in each direction and is shared by bicycles, ox carts, motorbikes, cars, buses, and transport trucks. Farmers in the south take over part of the highway for drying their rice. At least one-third of Vietnam's bridges need major repairs or should be replaced. Many share their one lane with a decrepit railroad track. The country's two major ports—Saigon in the south and Haiphong in the north—are inefficient and their equipment is run down. Haiphong's harbor needs to be dredged to remove silt that blocks the entry of large vessels.

Energy poses another hurdle, particularly in Ho Chi Minh City, where the demand for electricity is growing at the rate of 10 percent per year. Hanoi loses a quarter of its electricity supply because power lines, many of which are dangling haphazardly from city lamp posts, have not been maintained. The entire country has an installed electricity capacity of a mere 3,500 megawatts, only half the capacity of nearby Malaysia, whose population is less than one-third that of Vietnam's.

Hanoi claims that it plans to invest $4 billion by the turn of the century to boost power generation. It is looking for another $3.4 billion to upgrade the nation's highways and ports, and has approved $4 billion to expand Ho Chi Minh City's Tan Son Nhat airport, projects that will mean opportunities worth billions of dollars for foreign contractors. Firms from South Korea, Taiwan, Hong Kong, and Singapore are expected to dominate the bidding.

Vietnam's social infrastructure—quality education and health care—has also suffered since the 1980s. Approximately half of the children under six years old suffer moderate to severe malnutrition.[11] The population continues to surge 2.2 percent a year, prompting some to fear a Malthusian disaster in the making. Poorly paid teachers are being lured to more lucrative jobs, and growing numbers of students are dropping out of ill-equipped schools to help their parents run small, family workshops or farms. Vietnam must reverse these trends before it can catch up with its neighbors, who based their successful development on an educated, healthy population.

Foreign donors are beginning to help Vietnam tackle some of these infrastructure problems. The World Bank and the Asian Development Bank are expected to supply some $600 to $700 million a year in soft loans for projects such as refurbishing Highway One, modernizing the capital's electricity grid, upgrading the port in Ho Chi Minh City, training teachers, and improving school buildings. Japan, United Nations agencies, and other bilateral donors will push the aid level to approximately $2 billion a year. Actual disbursements have been slow, however. In 1995 Vietnam was expected to spend only an estimated $500 million of the aid money pledged. Spending has been slowed by red tape and the lack of technocrats to manage aid projects.

The World Bank, the Asian Development Bank, and U.N. organizations are working with the government to ensure that these credits are used on projects that can be completed quickly, yield high rates of return, and provide significant numbers of jobs. These international financial institutions are also training technocrats and managers to set priorities and formulate and execute projects.

British economist Adam Fforde, a leading expert on Vietnam's economy, compares the country to a "tiger on a bicycle." Fforde points out that the Vietnamese tiger has managed to "pedal surprisingly fast" since the Communist Party launched its de-Stalinization drive, but adds that the challenge now is to begin "motorizing the bicycle as the tiger grows in strength."[12]

The trick for Vietnam, according to Perkins, Fforde and other experts, will be to fine-tune its policies in order to build on its initial success. Like its flourishing neighbors, Vietnam cannot rely on miracles to usher in a new era of prosperity, but instead must allocate its limited physical capital and human resources to the most productive investments. Vietnam will have to boost its standard of living the old-fashioned way: by working for it.

2

Roots of the Nation

◆ ◆ ◆

In the Shadow of China

Street names in many countries carry some significance, and Vietnam is no exception; but in Vietnam they encapsulate the nation's history of struggle to survive. One of Hanoi's main east-west arteries is named after the Trung sisters, who staged a revolt against Chinese domination nearly two thousand years ago. In Saigon—now renamed after Ho Chi Minh, the leader of Vietnam's fight to oust the French colonial rulers and reunify the country—the street linking the main business district to Cholon bears the name of Tran Hung Dao, who withstood a fierce Mongol invasion from the north in the thirteenth century. Thousands of other thoroughfares are named after Ba Trieu, Ngo Quyen, Le Loi, Phan Boi Chau, and other heroes and heroines of Vietnam's struggles for independence.

Most of Vietnam's cities have religious shrines that pay homage to those who fought off foreign invaders. These landmarks are daily reminders of the Vietnamese people's 2,500-year history, a saga dominated by foreign occupation, internal rebellion, the search for territory, and the battle to build and defend a nation on a narrow stretch of land on the southeastern edge of the Asian continent. The centuries of struggle for independence have played a major role in shaping the Vietnamese character.

Vietnam today is slightly smaller than the state of California, but its population of seventy-four million makes it the world's thirteenth most populous nation. Owing to its rugged topography most of the ethnic Vietnamese, who make up 89 percent of the population, live on only one-fifth of the country's land area. Vietnam's farmland supports more than nine hundred people per square kilometer, making it more than three times as densely populated as nearby China and Thailand, and most of Vietnam's people, rice production, industrial output, political power, and cultural activity are concentrated in two relatively small areas: Hanoi and the Red River delta in the north, and Ho Chi Minh City and the Mekong delta in the south. These two plains are joined by a narrow, mountainous strip of land—more than a thousand kilometers long but in some places only fifty kilometers wide. Most of the country's ethnic minorities live in the highlands of the center and in the mountains of the far north. The country's long configuration not only creates different weather patterns, but also makes communication and political integration difficult.

Vietnam's location also played a key role in its history. The South China Sea (called the Eastern Sea by the Vietnamese) and the Gulf of Siam form its long, 2,200-kilometer border in the east and south—a very strategic location along the main sea-lanes linking the Indian and Pacific oceans. Over time, the sea brought not only traders but devastating typhoons, pirates, and foreign invaders to Vietnam, and interestingly, because Vietnam had no wheeled transport until the mid-nineteenth century, the sea (along with the country's rivers) long served as the people's main arteries of transportation and communication.

The Truong Son mountains stand to the west and beyond them are Laos and Cambodia. Vietnam's long, narrow shape makes it difficult to defend and has prompted modern Vietnamese rulers to try to extend their defensive zone by forming alliances or suzerain-vassal relations with these two smaller neighbors. To the north lies colossal China, whose common land and sea borders have meant that Vietnam has had more contact with the Chinese than any other country in Southeast Asia. Vietnam has profited enormously from its exposure to China's rich civilization but also has faced constant threats from Chinese expansion and hegemony.

Although scholars continue to debate its origins, what we know as Vietnam began in the fertile Red River delta of the north. According to some accounts, indigenous residents—including distant relatives of people from the islands of the Pacific and Southeast Asia—were living in the hills of the Red River delta several millennia ago when much of present-day northern Vietnam was still covered with water. Then some four or five thousand years ago, people, cultural ideas, and languages from southern China began moving into Vietnam and other parts of Southeast Asia and mixing with the local cultures.

The dominant language of Vietnam provides some hints about the diverse influences on its people: It is distinct but has borrowed much of its syntax from Mon-Khmer (which is linked to modern Cambodian) and inherited its tonal character from Tai (which is associated with contemporary Thai). The infusion of Chinese words—which, according to some estimates, make up half of the language's business vocabulary and as much as three-quarters of its scientific and political terms—took place over the last 1,500 years.

Archaeologists have uncovered in Vietnam simple stone tools that appear to have been used at least 200,000 years ago. Other archaeological evidence has been uncovered indicating that villages of several hundred inhabitants were cultivating rice and raising animals in the area as far back as the third millennium B.C. Archaeologists excavating on the fringes of the Red and Ma River deltas of northern Vietnam have found elaborate bronze drums, weapons, and tools of the Dong Son culture dating back more than 2,500 years. Archaeological digs in Vietnam have discovered a culture that shared many traits with other Southeast Asian countries, including houses built on stilts, boat-shaped coffins, and the custom of chewing betel nut, a mild stimulant.

According to popular Vietnamese mythology, Vietnam was founded by Hung Vuong, the first emperor of the Hung dynasty, which is believed to have ruled the kingdom of Van Lang from 2879 to 258 B.C. Hung Vuong, it is said, was the oldest of the one hundred children of Lac Long Quan, a dragon lord of the sea, and Au Co, a mountain princess. In the middle of the third century B.C., An

Duong Vuong, the chieftain of a neighboring state, ousted the last king of the Hung dynasty and created the new kingdom of Au Lac. A popular legend, reflecting early Vietnamese belief in the supernatural, claims that a golden turtle helped An Duong Vuong build a new capital at Co Loa, near present-day Hanoi, but his kingdom was short-lived. In 208 B.C., Au Lac was conquered by a military commander from southern China who incorporated it into a new kingdom called *Nan Yueh* in Chinese, or *Nam Viet* (meaning southern Viet) in Vietnamese. In 111 B.C., after the Han dynasty unified China, this region—renamed *Giao Chi*—became a province in the Chinese empire.

It was not long before the Vietnamese rebelled against Chinese attempts to tighten their administrative control and introduce new taxes. One of the most celebrated uprisings was lead by Trung Trac, the wife of a Vietnamese nobleman, and her sister, Trung Nhi, in 39 A.D. The Trung sisters failed but remain immortalized as heroines. Other revolts broke out from time to time in the Red River delta, creating new folk heroes, but the Vietnamese did not succeed in casting off the yoke of their northern neighbors until 939, after the ruling Chinese dynasty of that day had begun to disintegrate.

Although the Chinese exerted immense influence over them, the Vietnamese managed to avoid being assimilated. Yet while resisting China's occupation, Vietnam inevitably absorbed many elements of Chinese culture, making it the only nation in Southeast Asia with close cultural affinity to China. This often makes it hard for foreigners to characterize the Vietnamese. "If you look at the Vietnamese from Bangkok, they look very Chinese," observes historian David Marr of Australian National University. "But if you look at them from Quangzhou [China], they look very Southeast Asian."

Vietnam's elite adopted Buddhism, Taoism, and other elements of the Chinese Confucian social and political philosophy, a hierarchical social system in which emperors rule under a "mandate from heaven." A person's obligations to the emperor and to one's parents provide the foundation for the Confucian social order, and if people violate this moral order, chaos follows. Vietnamese leaders also introduced a Chinese-style administrative system run by scholar-officials required to pass rigorous civil service exams and study Chinese classics. In the countryside, however, where most of Vietnam's population lived, the Chinese had only limited influence.

Regardless, it is wrong to conclude—as foreign scholars long did—that Vietnam is little more than a miniature version of China. Instead Vietnam, like Korea, adapted many classical Chinese concepts to create its own distinct culture. "Vietnam and China are only similar on the surface," argues Vu Minh Giang, the Russian-educated dean of Hanoi University's history department. "Inside, the structure is quite different," he says, adding, "it's easy for the Vietnamese to be influenced by other cultures, but they always adapt [foreign ideas] in their own way." Giang points out that Chinese society was "vertically" organized from the emperor to the scholar-officials and on down to the common people. In Vietnam, however, the social structure was "horizontal," he argues. "The Vietnamese emperor was always afraid of the people." The Chinese emperor was almost always richer and controlled larger amounts of land than his Vietnamese counterpart.

Like Japan and Korea, China was highly centralized, while Vietnam, like many of its Southeast Asian neighbors, was decentralized. "In Vietnam, every village is like a country with its own conventions and rules," Giang insists. The Vietnamese borrowed Chinese characters to write their language but adapted them to fit their own phonetic system.

The Vietnamese state began to take shape under the succession of dynasties that followed independence from China in the tenth century. Over the next thousand years the Vietnamese managed—except for a two-decade stint in the 1400s—to fight off renewed annexation attempts by Chinese rulers, although almost all Vietnamese emperors paid tribute to China in exchange for a degree of independence.

Not long after the Vietnamese had reclaimed their independence they found themselves in conflict with the Hindu Kingdom of Champa to the south, which had been heavily influenced by merchants and Brahman teachers from India who had visited the region as early as the second century A.D. During the ensuing several hundred years Vietnam's history was punctuated by repeated dynastic conflicts, domestic rebellions, wars with its neighbors, and a determined territorial expansion toward the south.

The Ly kings (1009–1225) first established the capital in Hanoi, calling it *Thang Long*, or Soaring Dragon, and launched the "march south," which eventually put the Vietnamese in conflict with their Cham and Khmer neighbors. Buddhism and the construction of pagodas flourished under the Ly kings, who also introduced a Chinese-style civil service examination system and expanded the dike system to hold back the flood waters of the Red River. In 1044 Emperor Ly Thai Tong seized the Cham capital in central Vietnam in response to a Cham attack. In the twelfth century a three-way conflict erupted when the Khmer ruler in the far south launched a series of sea and ground attacks against Vietnam and Champa.

The Tran dynasty (1225–1400) is best known for defending the country against foreign invaders. In 1287 Tran Hung Dao repelled the third in a series of invasions by Kublai Khan's dreaded Mongol armies from the north by using iron-tipped stakes to trap their naval vessels as the tide receded on the Bach Dang River. The Tran rulers also introduced a new tax system, extended the administrative system from the provincial level down to the village, and expanded the water control system in the Red River delta. Tran Hung Dao's successors in the fourteenth century fought repeated wars with Champa in what today is central Vietnam. Contact with the Cham and later the Khmer (another Indianized civilization in the Mekong delta in the far south whose ancestors had built the magnificent temple complex at Angkor between the ninth and fourteenth centuries) increased Vietnam's exposure to Indian culture and to Buddhist ideas, which served to balance Chinese influence.

With the decline of the Tran kings, China's Ming dynasty in 1407 seized control of Vietnam, again briefly turning it into a Chinese province. Much of China's cultural impact on Vietnam today stems from this period. The Ming rulers replaced Buddhism with Neo-

Confucianism and insisted, among other things, that women wear pants, men stop cutting their hair, and all people give up chewing betel nut and lacquering their teeth. Le Loi, one of the country's most revered heroes, rescued Vietnam from the Ming emperors in 1428 and established the Le dynasty, which reigned until 1786. The Le kings revamped Vietnam's administrative system, introduced paper money two hundred years before it was used in Europe, and formulated a new legal code that in contrast to Chinese law gave women near equality with men.

At the same time, Vietnamese settlers continued migrating south, setting up new villages that often co-existed peacefully with neighboring Cham settlements. But in 1471 the Le rulers defeated Champa, thereby extending Vietnam south of the present-day city of Danang.

The Le dynasty soon weakened, however, and in the sixteenth century the country became engulfed in a bitter rivalry among three different families: the Mac, the Trinh, and the Nguyen. For most of the next three centuries Vietnam was troubled by internal conflict and partitioned into north and south.

By the middle of the sixteenth century, Hoi An, near the present-day city of Danang, had become a bustling entrepôt trading center as increasing numbers of Portuguese, Dutch, and English ships stopped at its port en route to China, Japan, and other countries in Southeast Asia. Jesuit missionaries arrived in 1615, and by the end of the seventeenth century, had converted more than 100,000 Vietnamese to Catholicism even though Christianity was outlawed.

Despite the conflicts among the ruling families, by the middle of the eighteenth century the Vietnamese succeeded in ousting the Khmer from the Mekong delta and extended Vietnam's borders to roughly what they are today. But tensions between the clans made it increasingly difficult for them to rule, and they began to face growing numbers of local rebellions. The most celebrated revolt—the Tay Son rebellion, led by three brothers from central Vietnam—ousted the ruling families, and in 1786 reunified the country for the first time in two centuries. As they gained control of the countryside, the

Tay Son rebels pledged a series of millenarianist reforms, including promises to punish oppressive landlords and redistribute their land to the poor.

In 1802, however, with help from French missionaries and mercenaries, a new leader, Nguyen Anh, who took the name Gia Long, seized control and reversed many of Tay Son's reforms. He built a new capital in the central city of Hue, modeling it after the Forbidden City in Beijing, and reintroduced a Neo-Confucian administration. The Nguyen rulers introduced new taxes and increased forced labor to build palaces and roads, which gave rise to another round of peasant discontent.

Colonialism, Communism, and War

The biggest threat to the Nguyen emperors eventually came from a new source: France. French Roman Catholic missionaries were converting growing numbers of Vietnamese, creating fear among the rulers that Christian villages would spawn rebellion. When the government began persecuting Christians, French missionaries pressed Paris to intervene. They were joined by French traders and diplomats who warned that France's European rivals were far ahead in the race for a colonial foothold in Asia.

French warships attacked the central city of Danang in 1858, and over the next three decades France gradually crushed the remaining resistance and imposed control over the whole country. Paris divided Vietnam into three administrative zones—north, center, and south—and imported thousands of French administrators to run their new colony. They also made these three territories part of a larger Indochina federation, including Cambodia and Laos. The French injected some new elements into Vietnam's economy, which had changed little since the seventeenth century, when Dutch merchants had first come to trade silk. The French installed a telegraph system, built a railroad network, opened a few coal and tin mines in the north, and established rubber plantations in the south. They also constructed major irrigation systems in the Mekong delta, expanding the land under rice cultivation and helping the country become a leading rice exporter.

One of the most notable developments during French rule was the reform of Vietnam's writing system. Classical Chinese had become the formal written language of Vietnam during China's occupation, although Vietnamese remained the language of the countryside where the majority of people lived. But in the early twentieth century, under pressure from nationalists, a Vietnamese script—a system using the Roman alphabet to write the language phonetically, first developed by Catholic missionaries in the 1600s— was adopted as the language of administration.

Even more important, French colonial rule brought abrupt changes to traditional Vietnamese society. As the emperor lost power to foreign administrators, the country's traditional village social structure, headed by a council of notables with wide-ranging independent power, began to erode. A small but powerful class of wealthy landowners—often controlling hundreds of tenants—began to emerge, particularly in the southern delta. The emergence of a cash economy, the increasing emphasis on private property, and growing disparities between the rich and the poor created tensions within the traditional village structure.

Some of the country's scholar-gentry cooperated with the French but most did not. Many intellectuals struggled with questions such as whether Vietnam could benefit from cooperating with the colonialists, and what the Vietnamese had to do to survive in the modern world. One of the best-known scholars in the anti-colonial movement was Phan Boi Chau, who traveled to Japan in 1904 to seek financial backing for a Vietnamese uprising and to investigate the results of Japan's modernization program. The Japanese defeat of Russia the following year fired up Chau's hopes for Vietnamese independence, which he thought could be achieved through armed rebellion. But Chau's endorsement of violence was not supported by all scholar-activists. Phan Chu Trinh visited Japan two years later and concluded that the best way for Vietnam to gain independence was through nonviolent reform and an emphasis on education.

Like many other Western colonialists, the French did little overall to modernize the economy of Vietnam, viewing it primarily as a cheap source of raw materials and a market for their industrial products. Paris gave vast amounts of land to French colonial settlers, exacerbating the already critical problem of landlessness among peasants. By 1939 more than 80 percent of the rice-growing land in the south was controlled by less than one-quarter of the landowners. Nearly 60 percent of the farmers were landless and forced to work on large plantations.[1] Heavy taxes, forced labor on public works projects, and exorbitant interest rates on credit made life even harder for peasants. Social services also declined.

In 1930 Ho Chi Minh, the son of a poor scholar from central Vietnam, who had spent nearly two decades in France, the Soviet Union, and China, presided over a conference in Hong Kong that unified three separate Communist movements into the Vietnamese Communist Party. One of the leading planks of the new party included the ouster of the French and the establishment of an independent Vietnam. The formation of the Vietnamese Communist Party coincided with growing unrest in the country, prompted in part by economic hardships created by the Great Depression. The most famous uprising took place in 1930 in Nghe An and Ha Tinh provinces, in north-central Vietnam, where demonstrators burned government buildings and markets.

The Communists spent the next decade trying to survive, responding to political changes in France, and recruiting new members from among Vietnam's intelligentsia. Following the Nazi defeat of France and the Japanese takeover of Vietnam at the beginning of World War II, Ho established a Communist-led united front—called the *Viet Minh*—to launch the struggle for independence.

When Japan surrendered in 1945, Viet Minh cadres seized control of government installations. On September 2, at a massive rally in Hanoi, Ho read Vietnam's independence declaration, parts of which were based on the American Declaration of Independence. But the

French soon returned and attempted to reestablish their control over the country—until 1954, when they were defeated at Dien Bien Phu by guerrilla forces lead by military strategist Vo Nguyen Giap. A peace accord in Geneva temporarily divided Vietnam in two at the seventeenth parallel, pending nationwide elections scheduled for 1956.

Sharp rifts surfaced between Vietnam's nationalists over how the country ought to develop and modernize, making further internal conflict inevitable once independence had been achieved. Some wanted to replace traditional society with Marxism; others hoped to develop closer ties with the West while maintaining traditional values. Both sides agreed that they needed to strengthen the country's economy but chose different paths toward modernization.

Over the next two decades Vietnam not only experienced a civil war, but also became a focal point of the cold war between the world's superpowers. South Vietnamese President Ngo Dinh Diem, backed by the United States, which wanted to contain communism, refused to prepare for the elections, which were never held. And in the late 1950s North Vietnam—with aid from its Communist allies in China and the Soviet Union—started to support a liberation struggle in the south.

War had begun in Vietnam and intensified as Washington began bombing the north and in 1965 committed American combat troops to fight in the south. The United States remained until the 1973 Paris peace agreement ended direct American involvement in Vietnam. Yet fighting between Vietnamese forces continued until April 30, 1975, when Communist tanks crashed through the gates of the presidential palace in Saigon.

With the defeat of the Americans Vietnam was reunified for the first time in almost a century, although the legacy of three decades of war and internal division would continue. Flush with their military prowess, the country's new rulers rushed to introduce their Marxist-Leninist utopia and sought to unite neighboring Cambodia and Laos into a socialist bloc drawing on the idea of an Indochina federation picked up from the French in the 1930s.

Some 200,000 supporters of the ousted regime spent years in reeducation camps, where they were forced to do hard labor and were indoctrinated with the country's new ideology. Hundreds of thousands of others were sent to open new economic zones in remote rural areas with few tools or supplies. Over the next decade more than a million desperate refugees fled Vietnam on rickety, overloaded fishing boats. Another 200,000 crossed the border into China.

The country's newly acquired peace did not last long. Soon the Khmer Rouge in Cambodia, exploiting racial antagonism created during centuries of Vietnamese encroachment on Khmer territory, began mounting attacks across Vietnam's southwestern border. In December 1978 Hanoi retaliated by invading Cambodia and ousting the Chinese-backed Pol Pot regime. Angered by Vietnam's growing alliance with the former Soviet Union, China responded by launching a brief attack across its southern border into Vietnam. Hanoi's occupation of Cambodia prompted a decade of international economic isolation that continued until the last Vietnamese troops were withdrawn in 1989.

3

The Vietnamese

◆ ◆ ◆

James Luang is bullish about his Vietnamese work force. "The skills of the workers here are the best in Southeast Asia," enthuses the Taiwanese manager of Lac Ty Company, a joint venture factory in Ho Chi Minh City producing canvas shoes for export. "The Vietnamese learn fast. They're better than workers in Indonesia, Thailand, or Malaysia," he claims. Luang is one of a growing number of foreign investors attracted to Vietnam by its inexpensive, disciplined labor force. "People here are skillful and intelligent like the Taiwanese," the articulate, American-educated businessman says, paying the Vietnamese what he clearly regards as his highest compliment. "Our customers like our products. They think they've found a gold mine."

Vietnam is a nation of amazing diversity. What is often held true in one part does not hold true in another. One thing most businesses and investors agree on, however, is that the country has a young, motivated work force, with an immense ability to learn and the capacity for surprising bursts of collective effort.

As in many other Asian countries, the foundation of the Vietnamese universe is the family rather than the individual. The family plays a large role in shaping one's social identity, as depicted by popular writer Nguyen Huy Thiep in a recent short story, "Fired Gold." In a scene that might seem a bit odd to non-Asian readers, the nineteenth-century Vietnamese emperor Gia Long alludes only indirectly to Nguyen Du, the beloved poet who crafted the epic *Tale of*

43

Kieu. "I already know this man," the emperor says. "His father is Nguyen Nghiem. His older brother is Nguyen Khan." That is to say, even Vietnam's greatest poet was nobody without his family.[1]

In the Confucian tradition, inherited from China, Vietnamese emphasized not the individual but rather his or her duty to fit into the larger scheme of things, a duty that included loyalty of subjects to the emperor, obedience of sons to their fathers, and fidelity of wives to their husbands. It was imperative for families to produce a male heir to continue the family line and to take care of the spirits of his parents after death.

Early in their lives Vietnamese learned their proper role in a complex social order that fostered dependence and conformity rather than independence and individuality. Relationships were carefully defined and specific terms characterized each person's position within the family. Even today, for example, a brother is not simply a brother but an older brother or a younger brother; an uncle is not merely an uncle but father's older brother or mother's younger brother, and so on. A person's position within the family is determined by his or her age and gender. The young respect the elderly.

The burden of social conformity falls hardest on women, who traditionally have been considered inferior to men, as in the saying "ten daughters aren't worth one son." Yet Vietnamese women have never been subjugated like their counterparts in China. In Vietnam women have long played key roles in the rice-growing cycle and served as the first village traders. Within the family, Vietnamese often joke, the wife is the minister of interior and head of the treasury, while the husband serves as minister of foreign relations.

A family group includes not only those who are living but also a long line of ancestors and those who are not yet born. Many Vietnamese believe their ancestors remain active in the world beyond to assist or punish their descendants. To venerate the departed soul, surviving relatives organize elaborate ceremonies before the family altar on death anniversaries and at Tet, the lunar New Year. Tet is the most important celebration of the year, something akin to Americans trying to compress Christmas, New Year's, Thanksgiving, and everyone's birthday into one giant holiday. The extended family in the past consisted of grandparents, parents, children, and grandchildren living together in one house. But Vietnamese researchers such as sociologist Pham Bich San believe that the nuclear family has gained importance since the fifteenth century, when private land ownership began to replace commonly held land in the Red River delta. Many of the family's traditional functions were taken over by the army, party officials, and cooperatives following the Communist victory, but the role of the family has been resuscitated by the Communist Party's reforms, and the family has reemerged as the dominant economic unit, particularly in the countryside, where nearly four-fifths of Vietnam's population lives.

Many Vietnamese have attributes that often surprise or perplex foreigners. It often seems that Vietnamese are most comfortable in a familiar group. A foreigner traveling around Vietnam invariably will be asked where he is staying and with whom, and if he answers that he is staying alone in a hotel, he will be told that he must be very lonely. Most Vietnamese don't like to eat alone either. Perhaps because of this Vietnamese seem less concerned with privacy. Those who spend time in Vietnam's hotels experience chambermaids charging into their rooms without knocking, even early in the morning and despite Do Not Disturb signs. The Vietnamese live in such crowded conditions that privacy is almost impossible. Lovers who want to be alone are forced to escape to parks.

People in Vietnam often say that they are taught as children to regard any demonstration of inner feelings as a sign of weakness or a "loss of face," and indeed, Vietnamese behavior cannot be understood without attempting to understand this concept. As in China, Japan, and other Asian countries, face is the core of one's being. The concept of saving face is an unwritten set of rules by which people try to avoid damaging another person's self-respect or prestige, particularly in public.

Westerners are sometimes struck by the indirectness of the Vietnamese language, in which meanings are frequently implicit and hidden between the lines. Vietnamese seldom confront a problem head on, as Westerners commonly do. Like other Asians, the Vietnamese often deliver their main point after a long introduction or a story, whose meaning completely depends on its context. Rarely does a Vietnamese get down to business without first drinking tea with his interlocutor.

At times it can be difficult even for Vietnamese to decipher what is truly being said. For example, it is not uncommon for the Communist Party's censors to approve a novel, short story, or movie and then pull the plug several weeks later after intellectuals point out that the work could be interpreted as an attack on the party. One friend who had studied in the former Soviet Union remembers being frustrated when he returned to Hanoi. "People would say something to me and I would have to think back a few months earlier to what I had said to understand the implied meaning of what I was being told. Or someone would put a picture or poem on my desk and I'd have to try to understand what it meant."

Not surprisingly, foreigners have an even harder time understanding what Vietnamese are saying. American anthropologist Shaun Malarney, a fluent speaker of Vietnamese, relates the following: While traveling in central Vietnam, his driver declared that he would not be able to continue the trip because he had to go to a wedding the next day. Malarney, who liked the driver, was disappointed but told him he was sure that he would be able to find another ride, perhaps by hitchhiking, with another car heading north. The next day Malarney told his Vietnamese assistant he regretted that his driver had to go to this wedding. The assistant was puzzled. "He didn't have to go to a wedding," he told Malarney. "I guess you haven't been in Vietnam long enough." The driver, his assistant explained, was uncertain whether the anthropologist wanted him to continue on the trip, so to provide a face-saving out he said he had to go to a wedding. Apparently, the driver would have continued the trip if Malarney had read his signal correctly and coaxed him to go on.

Foreigners may be surprised at how difficult it can be to get a

direct answer. Gathering information about the Vietnamese economy, for example, is difficult because many statistics are still considered to be state secrets. Once when I wanted to include the figure
for Vietnam's foreign currency reserves in an article, my assistant
called an economist friend who helped us whenever he could. "I've
never thought to ask that question," he responded—clearly implying
that I should understand he would get into trouble if he gave us the
figure.

As a foreign journalist in Vietnam I was expected to apply for
permission to the foreign ministry's press department for most interviews and all travel outside of Hanoi. My "handlers" at the foreign
ministry would never directly refuse any of my requests. Instead I
would be told that a certain visit was "not convenient at that time"
or that they "still haven't heard back" from the person I had asked to
interview. Once an official told me jokingly that "the computer still
hasn't answered." After a few weeks of vague replies, I was supposed
to understand that a request was being rejected. Interestingly
enough, despite this tradition of indirect, implicit communication in
Vietnam, the younger generation of urban Vietnamese—who are
more and more influenced by the West—have a tendency to be more
direct and straightforward. This inevitably leads to conflicts and mis-
understandings between generations and reflects the great change
that has rocked Vietnam and will continue to do so.

Despite the indirect style and concern about "saving face," Vietnamese are surprisingly free in showing their emotions. It is common, even in the north (where people are generally more reserved
and subdued than in the south), to come across emotional explosions
such as women hawkers clawing at each other over the same space
on a sidewalk, or two men throwing punches following a minor
fender-bender on the country's chaotic roads. The Vietnamese also
can be brutal in their criticisms of each other. People commonly
refer to an overweight friend—say Phuong—as "Fat Phuong," and
men will openly advise a casual female acquaintance about what she
should do to lose weight. Any foreigner who has tried to learn
Vietnamese (an intricate language with six tones) undoubtedly has

been criticized for speaking so much more poorly than someone else.

The role of laughter in Vietnamese society may also perplex Western residents. In addition to reacting to a humorous situation, Vietnamese often laugh or grin in the face of embarrassment, misfortune, or adversity. One day while I was driving through an intersection near my office in Hanoi a young woman on a bicycle overloaded with vegetables darted out from behind a parked vehicle directly into my path. I slammed on my brakes and managed to avoid hitting her, but she toppled over from fright. Not expecting me to stop so suddenly, a motorcycle coming down the street to my right banged into my car. As I got out of the vehicle, I noticed that the woman was laughing as she struggled to pick up her unwieldy bicycle. I expected the man on the motorcycle to begin shouting at me, but he too rode off, grinning from ear to ear without saying a word. My encounter ended without any apparent bad feelings. But in other instances, serious problems have erupted among coworkers or between a boss and his employee whenever a foreigner mistakenly interpreted the smile of a Vietnamese as a sign of disrespect or arrogance.

Despite strict order within families, the Vietnamese seem to be less orderly away from home. In an effort to avoid tax collectors, more shopkeepers in Hanoi and Ho Chi Minh City seem to be selling from baskets or mats spread out on the street than from stalls inside the formal market. Businessmen regularly boast to foreign journalists that they falsify receipts and cheat on their taxes.

Traffic, particularly in Hanoi, is a driver's nightmare, even though Vietnam is still decades away from the gridlock of Bangkok or Jakarta. People riding motorcycles or bicycles seem to dart out of nowhere with little apparent respect for any rules.

Perhaps nothing makes observers more bullish about Vietnam's long-term prospects than the people's astonishing capacity to overcome barriers of all kinds. Not long after the economic reforms, for example, a real estate boom erupted in the country. This happened despite the fact that according to Vietnamese law all land still belonged to the state and could not legally be sold. Sellers quickly discovered that they could get around the law by erecting a small shack of sorts and then selling the rights to use the land under it. "We don't bother with the law," a real estate agent in Hanoi told me. "We hire specialists to fix our papers."

Vietnamese have an age-old tradition of setting off firecrackers at Tet to chase away evil spirits. In early 1995, however, the government banned firecrackers, considering them to be a growing safety hazard and a waste of the country's limited resources. Within a few weeks merchants had found a way to get around the ban: They began marketing the recorded sound of exploding firecrackers on tape and video cassettes. Some Vietnamese joke that the spirits may not respond to the noise in the absence of smoke.

Vietnamese resourcefulness never ceases to amaze foreign residents. Just after dawn one morning, a guard in our apartment building rang the doorbell and said he needed one of my business cards. I was too sleepy to ask why he wanted it. A couple of hours later I got an urgent phone call in my office from an unidentified caller pleading with me to come to the Hanoi People's Committee, or city hall, immediately. Uncertain about what was going on, I asked Kathleen Callo, a dynamic Reuters journalist, to go with me. We got to the People's Committee office on Hoan Kiem Lake within ten minutes. People were milling about the building, but nothing unusual seemed to be going on. We waited around for nearly an hour, but no one approached us, so we left.

Just before noon, the caller phoned back to my office insisting that he had to see me immediately. We agreed to meet in a coffee shop just down the street. I soon realized why Anh, a short, intense man in his early forties, was so anxious. Police, he said, were planning the next morning to bulldoze his house, which was located in the western suburbs of Hanoi near the Mai Dich cemetery, where the country's deceased senior leaders are buried. Anh and some anxious neighbors who faced the same fate had demonstrated at the People's Committee headquarters that morning. They wanted foreign journalists to witness their protest, but as soon as the protesters arrived paranoid police had whisked them to the back of the five-story marble building so out of place among the low, French-colonial structures clustered around the lake—which is why we had not seen them.

Anh showed us a copy of the deed to his land, complete with an official red stamp. He said the police had come to his neighborhood the previous night informing him and his neighbors that the papers granting them land-use rights were invalid. Apparently they had been illegally issued by corrupt village officials. The police told them they would be back in thirty-six hours to level the illegally constructed brick houses. Anh and many of his neighbors had invested their life savings in the new houses. Desperate not to lose everything they protested by sending a letter to the National Assembly, demonstrating at city hall, and contacting foreign journalists.

Callo and I weren't sure who was right, the house owners or the police, but we were intrigued that the conflict was being played out in the open. Following Vietnam's procedures for foreign journalists, we sent letters to the foreign ministry's press department requesting meetings with the responsible Hanoi housing officials. Late that same afternoon we visited Anh's neighborhood in my car, which had license plates identifying its owner as a foreigner. The next day Anh called back to give us a progress report. The police had not come back and his house was still standing. Officials had told him that soon they would hold a meeting with neighborhood representatives to discuss how to resolve the conflict. He had been successful. In the months that followed I occasionally bumped into Anh around Hanoi. Each time he would run up, energetically pump my hand, and profusely thank us for having saved his house. I have no idea how much impact we had on the survival of Anh's neighborhood. What really impressed me was that Anh had the ingenuity and courage to complain—even to foreign journalists, whose phones were tapped and whose movements were monitored by the security police.

"Every Tree Has Its Own Leaf"

Even though the Communists struggled for decades to stamp out faith in the supernatural, the Vietnamese expend a lot of energy appeasing the gods and checking their zodiac calendars. Almost no one gets married, starts a business, or builds a house without checking first with an astrologer, geomancer, or fortune-teller. The news weekly I write for, Dow Jones & Company's *Far Eastern Economic Review*, rented office space in Hanoi from the Vietnam News Agency, the official mouthpiece of the country's Communist government. I never got used to the fact that on the last day of every month its accounting department burned incense on a small altar in a corner of its office. "It helps our clients pay their bills on time," one of the accountants explained, surprised that I might find their ritual the least bit unusual.

The *Review*'s office assistant, Tran Le Thuy, an energetic Westernized woman in her late twenties, always checked whether the dates and times we planned to travel were auspicious. Once, after a fortune-teller had told her that we needed to depart on a trip before dawn, she left her house at 4:30 A.M. and stood on the dark street waiting two hours for our car to arrive. The fact that she had left her house meant that she had begun her trip on time, thereby averting possible disaster.

The determined curiosity of the Vietnamese can perplex a foreigner who, walking down the street, often feels like Alice in Wonderland. Everyone seems to stop what they are doing to stare and mutter a comment about how tall or fat or white the foreigner is. Mothers will poke their children and point at the strange passerby as if he or she were a new arrival from outer space. Early one morning, in the days before metered taxi cabs arrived in Hanoi, I had to take a *cyclo* (a three-wheeled bicycle taxi) to my office across town. I hailed a muscular driver in his early thirties dressed in shorts, a tattered T-shirt, and rubber flip-flops. We negotiated a price, and I was just settling down for the five-kilometer trip across town when the interrogation started.

"Where are you from?" he asked. It was still early and I had not been able to have either a shower or a cup of tea because the electricity and water in my apartment had been cut off by a severe rainstorm during the night, so I tried to ignore him.

"You're British, right?" he said, answering his own question.

"No," I responded.

"But the license plate on your car begins with 'zero one.' That's for British people."

"Aha," I mumbled, still hoping to avoid a drawn-out conversation. I did not feel like explaining that I am a Canadian citizen but that the car had been registered by my wife Linda, an American who was working for a British relief agency.

"Why do you wear a seat belt when you drive your car?" he continued. I remained silent but was beginning to wonder how this man, who I did not remember meeting before, knew so much about me.

"You have a daughter who likes dogs," he added, maneuvering his vehicle through Hanoi's streets, which were becoming increasingly crowded in the morning rush hour. "She walks her dog every day."

"How come you have a Japanese son?" he persisted, making a small slip that lessened my suspicions that he worked for the ministry of interior's security apparatus, which monitors the activities of foreigners. My son is ethnically Korean, but presumably to a Vietnamese he could look Japanese. After this first strange encounter I saw the *cyclo* driver dozens of other times. His beat apparently included my neighborhood. He might have moonlighted for the police, but more likely, he simply engaged in the popular Vietnamese practice of gawking at foreigners while waiting for customers.

Even though their history is punctuated by repeated struggles to free the country from foreign domination, the Vietnamese are fascinated by foreigners. Despite repeated invasions and occupations, most Vietnamese demonstrate little xenophobia. Students will often stop a foreigner on the street, hoping to practice speaking English. Shopkeepers and casual acquaintances will invite strangers into their houses for a chat and endless cups of tea.

Foreigners who have spent time in Vietnam probably would agree that the Vietnamese are at the same time charming and tough, discreet and somewhat evasive, ambitious and sometimes quarrelsome, more sentimental and poetic than analytical, and that they are resilient and proud, generally cheerful and optimistic about life, able to work under difficult circumstances, frequently set in their ways, yet pragmatic and resourceful. Still, no generalization about a country and its characteristics can hold true for all its people, and any description of the Vietnamese must necessarily be vague and imprecise, particularly now, when the country is modernizing at break-neck speed. "Every house has its own view; every tree has its own leaf," the Vietnamese say when describing their diversity. As American historian Keith Taylor points out, "The Vietnamese have incredible variety in how they look at the world. What you say about the north won't work in the south to describe how people think about economics, religion or the family. It's a waste of time to strive after the holy grail"—a clear reference to efforts by some scholars to fit Vietnamese culture into neat categories.

The South Runs, the North Reigns

All ethnic Vietnamese share a common language, customs, and national identity, but over the centuries significant (though often overstated) psychological, social, and political differences have emerged among the north, center, and south. "Northerners are uptight, traditional and conservative," says an overseas Vietnamese businessman who was born in the south, migrated to Australia, and now has returned to do business in both Hanoi and Ho Chi Minh City. "Southerners are easygoing and loud-mouthed. Northerners are very proud, very calculating. Northerners are like the British, while Southerners are like Australians."

Southerners have a reputation for being more direct in their speech. "Northerners like to talk about their problems in a roundabout way and avoid controversial points," argues Tran Bach Dang, an independent-minded intellectual who headed the Communist Party in Saigon during the war. "In the south, we like to be outspoken, regardless of whether we're right or wrong." People from the north are considered thrifty, while Southerners often are compared to an apocryphal prince from Bac Lieu in the far south who, while riding on the train, lit his cigarettes with paper money to impress his fellow passengers.

Environmental differences account for at least some of these contrasting attitudes toward life and money. Peasants in the Red River delta of the north have been preoccupied with water—too much in the rainy season and too little in the dry season—since the first settlers began farming the region more than two thousand years ago. Such conditions forced them to live in tightly organized communities and cooperate to build an intricate network of dikes to protect their fields and villages against floods. The water supply in the Mekong delta of the south is more predictable, allowing a much looser social structure to develop. The Tonle Sap, a giant lake in Cambodia, absorbs excess water during the monsoon rains and supplies additional water during the dry season.

Life is most difficult for farmers in central Vietnam, where the soil is poor and the rainfall irregular. "The strictest people come from the center," an official in Hanoi observes. "It's hard for them to make a living, so they're always appointed bookkeepers, tax-collectors, or put in charge of warehouses."

Peasants in the north build brick houses as soon as they can afford it to protect their families against the region's harsh winters and frequent typhoons. In the south, which has a moderate tropical climate and few natural calamities, even wealthy farmers are content with thatch or wood huts. "Farmers in the north need to save because they'll be hit by typhoons, floods, and cold weather," says Nguyen Khac Vien, a French-trained medical doctor in his eighties. "In the south, it's easy to grow rice or catch fish, so farmers don't have to worry so much about money. If a northern farmer catches a fish or raises a chicken, he takes it to the market to sell," continues Vien, a longtime social commentator and frequent critic of the

Communist Party. "If a Southerner catches a fish or raises a chicken, he buys a bottle of wine and invites his friends over for a feast."

Wealth and weather, however, are not the only reasons houses in the south differ from those in the north. Southerners point out that the Mekong delta lacks a rockbed on which to construct heavy brick houses, and the area lacks wood fuel with which to fire clay bricks. Climate has also produced subtle differences in food. Dishes in northern Vietnam are generally oilier and less spicy than dishes in the south. Southern food is sweeter and uses more indigenous fruits and vegetables. Meals throughout the country are accompanied by *nuoc mam*, Vietnam's pungent fish sauce.

The configuration of villages also differs between the north and south. Farm dwellings in the Red River delta are tightly clustered in villages surrounded by bamboo hedges, whereas houses in the south are randomly scattered along the Mekong River's tributaries. According to Vietnamese observers, this has played a key role in shaping the different worldviews of peasants in the two halves of the country. "In the north, the bamboo hedge determines the village," notes Tran Van Giau, eighty-five, a retired southern historian and longtime Communist activist. "It keeps villagers in and outsiders out. If you have no fence, you have no limitations. People who produce a lot are more liberal than those who live inside a bamboo hedge."

The north also is much more densely populated than the south. The Red River delta averages 1,045 people per square kilometer, compared with only 369 in the Mekong delta. An Giang province in the south, for example, has approximately 220 square meters of farmland per person, nearly twice the 128 square meters of Hai Hung province in the Red River delta. As a result, Northerners generally have to work harder to survive.

Population pressures in the Red River delta prompted the Vietnamese to begin migrating south in the eleventh century, but they did not gain full control over today's central Vietnam until five hundred years ago, and over the far south until three centuries after that. Many of the first to leave the north were those without land, political exiles, or criminals. "As they moved south, they left behind much of their heritage," says Tran Quoc Vuong, a prominent Hanoi archaeologist and historian. "The influence of Confucianism and China weakened." Moreover, the migrants adopted many cultural traits from the Cham and Khmer, who had been influenced by India rather than China. "Hanoi had no seaport—it was the capital of the peasantry," adds the balding, bright-eyed professor. "The Cham and the Khmer were open to the sea, so the new arrivals became more open-minded. The march south brought people much closer to Southeast Asia. In the north, people always have one eye looking back," he says, referring to Vietnam's giant Chinese neighbor.

These regional differences were reinforced by foreign influences beginning in the second half of the nineteenth century. The French administrators divided the country into three regions, colonizing the south outright and ruling the north and center as protectorates. This meant that the south, ruled according to French law, enjoyed more political freedom than the other two regions. The south also experienced more Western influences.

In the wake of the French defeat in 1954, Vietnam became the center of the cold war struggle between capitalism and communism in Southeast Asia. The south had a free market and was heavily influenced by the United States, while the north lived under a hard-line Marxist regime allied to the former Soviet Union and China. The Vietnam War also prompted wide-scale population movements within the country, even though it remained politically divided. Roughly 900,000 Northerners fled south as refugees in the mid-1950s to escape communism, while others came as soldiers in the decade after 1964 to fight for national reunification. At the same time, up to one hundred thousand Southerners opposed to American intervention moved north under the Communist Party's orders to escape persecution. All of this resulted in unusual political configurations. The north's premier, Pham Van Dong, was born in the center; its president, after the death of Ho Chi Minh in 1969, was Ton Duc Thang, who came from the Mekong delta. Among the south's prominent leaders, Ngo Dinh Diem was born in the central

Vietnamese city of Quang Binh, and Nguyen Cao Ky was a refugee from the north.

The migration continued after the war ended in 1975, as thousands of Northerners headed south to help establish Hanoi's political control or to seek economic opportunity. The arrival of northern administrators and carpetbaggers accentuated many of the long-standing animosities between north and south. Numerous bureaucrats "came with the instinct of the victorious," says one European businessman, who has long worked in Vietnam. "Many of the regulations they imposed were not adapted for the conditions in the south, and Southerners didn't like it," he observes, referring to the "socialist transformation" policies in the late 1970s that caused the economy of the south to nosedive. "National concord has been a problem since reunification," adds a Ho Chi Minh City journalist, who also had worked as a reporter in the city during the war. The years since the war ended are "not enough to forget and normalize relations."

Many Southerners believe that the government in Hanoi is still staffed largely by Northerners who have a typically northern outlook on national affairs. Some observers speculate that greater economic prosperity in the south with Ho Chi Minh City growing at a rate of 15 percent a year (nearly twice the national average), could prompt growing resentment against the north's domination of national politics and lead to increasing demands for a stronger voice in setting the national agenda.

Will these frictions result in chaos, future clamoring for a redivision of the country, or even civil war? Most analysts do not think so. For one, the ethnic forces so pivotal in the breakup of the former Soviet Union do not divide Vietnam. The fact that nearly 90 percent of the population is ethnic Vietnamese mitigates this possibility. "We have learned that if Vietnam is divided, we can't defend ourselves against our neighbors," argues one official from the south working in Hanoi. He says that the north needs the south's rice surplus, while the south needs the north's coal, minerals and its market for consumer goods. He warns that if Hanoi is not careful it could face future political discontent in the south. "The south's living standard is higher, so their demand for democracy is greater," he insists. "If Hanoi puts too much pressure on the south, maybe the people will resist."

In an effort to reduce regional tensions the Communist Party is careful to balance its top positions among representatives from different parts of the country. For instance, Do Muoi, the party chief, is from the north, President Le Duc Anh was born in central Vietnam, and Premier Vo Van Kiet comes from the south. The country's top leaders also represent a careful balancing of interests within the Communist Party. Anh represents the military and security apparatus, while Kiet speaks for those who support faster economic reform and a more rapid opening to the outside world. Muoi, who straddles these two poles, is backed by many of the country's technocrats.

Other recent political appointments have reflected an attempt to balance additional social and racial interests. In 1991 Nong Duc Manh, a member of the Tay ethnic group, was the first ethnic minority leader ever elected to the Communist Party's ruling politburo. His promotion, Vietnam specialist Carlyle Thayer argues, was prompted by Hanoi's recognition that minorities need to be included in the country's political decision-making process if Vietnam hopes to avoid the ethnic antagonisms that have ravaged such former Communist nations as the Soviet Union and Yugoslavia.[2]

Women also have been given at least a token political role. Truong My Hoa, a southern activist during the war, became the first woman to reach the Communist Party's upper echelons in 1991 when she was appointed to the nine-member secretariat, which runs party affairs on a day-to-day basis. Another woman, Nguyen Thi Binh, who had served as foreign minister for the southern Communist movement during the war, was named vice president.

Ho Chi Minh City is often described as the engine firing up Vietnam's economic recovery. One reason is that, thanks to U.S. aid during the war, the south's infrastructure is as much as thirty years ahead of the north's. Also the south has more "business" experience. "It's easy for Southerners to adapt to a free-market economy," says

Dang, the southern intellectual. "They were born in a capitalist atmosphere. It's more difficult for Northerners who suffered in agricultural cooperatives for thirty years. The Southerners threw out the cooperatives after three years." Many credit the south with rescuing the country from hard-line communism. "The south saved this country from the Pol Pot shock," a northern sociologist argues, alluding to the brutal Maoist policies in neighboring Cambodia under which up to a million people are believed to have died. "The north brought the country two good things—it defeated the French and the Americans. But the south saved Vietnam in two ways—from land reform and from collectivization."

Ho Chi Minh City and its surrounding provinces never fully implemented Hanoi's "socialist transformation" policies and allowed many small private producers to continue operating after 1978. In addition, many of the recent economic reforms that have been introduced nationwide were tried in the south first. Ho Chi Minh City, for example, was the first to experiment with piecework salaries to boost sluggish production. Much of the impetus for Vietnam's economic reforms came from southern leaders, especially Kiet and Nguyen Van Linh, who were leaders in Ho Chi Minh City in the late 1970s and early 1980s before they were transferred to Hanoi. Linh, who launched the reforms when he headed the Communist Party from 1986 to 1991, was born in the north but has spent most of his adult life in the south. Deputy Premier Phan Van Khai, who is being groomed to replace Kiet as premier, also comes from the south.

Northerners have also played a key role in the south's economic resurgence. Some of them fled the 1954 Communist takeover in the north and became a major force in the southern economy during the war. "The fixed idea that northerners don't know how to do business just isn't true," argues Ho Chi Minh City journalist Ly Quy Chung. "They need time to learn, but after that they'll catch up. I think the distance between the north and the south will become narrower over the next few years." Although foreign investors flocked to Ho Chi Minh City first, it has not always proven to be a capitalist paradise. "Many foreign businessmen see Saigon as the El Dorado, but you can easily be misled in Saigon," a French businessman observes. "They appear to speak in a straightforward manner and then . . . [pretending to bite off his fingers]. It's more difficult to get into the north, but it's easier to get into trouble in the south."

Differences in history and geography between north and south have created different relationships with the outside world. The north is developing tighter commercial ties to the booming southern provinces of China, while the south is establishing closer economic links to Singapore, Hong Kong, Taiwan, South Korea, Japan, and the West.

There exist religious differences as well. The north practices a mix of Confucianism, Taoism, and Buddhism, and almost every village has its own folk religion, commemorating a local hero, god, or goddess whose spirit is believed to protect local residents from misfortune. By contrast, Buddhism is much stronger in the center and the south, regions where Confucianism is weaker and fewer village folk religions have emerged.

The north practices mainly Mahayana Buddhism from China, while the south has included elements of Theravada Buddhism from Sri Lanka. This mixture of Buddhist traditions in the south allowed for messianic Buddhist cults to flourish, such as Hoa Hao—a group that frequently clashed with both the pro-American and Communist governments. At the same time, Buddhists from the center and south are more politically active than their northern counterparts. Monks from the center captured international headlines in the 1960s by immolating themselves to protest abuses by the U.S.-backed regime during the war. More recently, several Buddhist monks in central and southern Vietnam have been arrested after clamoring for greater freedom from government interference.

Although the Communist Party in the south was the first to experiment with economic liberalization, many Southerners complain that their region is politically more conservative than the north. "The economic reforms and new discos give the feeling of big change in Ho Chi Minh City," a southern painter notes. "But in political life there have been no important changes. Maybe they think they must hold the city more secure politically when they open the economy," he suggests, alluding to the country's leaders. One dynamic young official, who hails from the center but has spent most of his life in Hanoi, agrees. "The south is economically open, but politically closed," he observes. "Southerners are seen as collaborators with the former regime, and Ho Chi Minh City is politically less stable than Hanoi. The top leaders in the south have to be more careful and prove to Hanoi that they are firm in upholding security interests and the political line."

Dang, the southern intellectual, thinks the differences in political style may have deeper roots, arguing that the north is more intellectually vibrant owing to its long tradition of scholar-officials. He believes the different pace of life between the two regions today contributes to the distinctive intellectual styles. "Southern intellectuals only talk about things which are close to their daily life and the economic situation," says Dang. "They don't talk about questions of freedom, political pluralism, or a multiparty system. But in the north the economy is still at a standstill, so they have time to drink tea and talk about the major issues affecting Vietnam."

Others think the difference is due to the fact that Hanoi gives Northerners more intellectual freedom. The southern artist argues that the majority of the intellectuals in the north are "Communist Party members or have lived under communism for a long time, so the party gives them the right to criticize. If I talked like that, they'd say I was trying to work against the regime." He may be right; southern dissidents do seem to be treated more harshly than Northerners. Duong Thu Huong, a fiery Hanoi novelist arrested in 1991 for attacking the Communist Party and calling for greater political openness, was released after seven months. But in Ho Chi Minh City the medical doctor Nguyen Dan Que was sentenced to twenty years in prison for a similar offense.

In 1994 Doan Viet Hoat, leader of a southern group called Freedom Forum that had circulated antigovernment leaflets, was sentenced to fifteen years. A year later Hoang Minh Chinh, a northern dissident and former party official, was given a twelve-month term for "abusing freedom and democratic rights to violate the interests of the state." Officials in Hanoi often make statements indicating that they consider Ho Chi Minh City to be ideologically suspect. In a hard-hitting speech prior to the Communist Party Congress held in mid-1996, General Secretary Do Muoi warned that the city had become a "fertile ground for hostile forces," which were "politically destabilizing, economically sabotaging, and culturally polluting." Muoi did not identify the "hostile forces," but observers thought they included not only dissidents calling for more political liberalization but also businessmen not adequately dedicated to the country's "socialist orientation."[3]

Yet many observers believe that if the Vietnamese government is to face a political threat in the future it will come from the north rather than from the south. "One of the lessons the Vietnamese Communist Party drew from the former Soviet Union is that its greatest challenge will come from within the party. The party's biggest force is in the north, not in the south," one official said, alluding to the fact that only 1 percent of the south's population has joined the party, compared to 9 percent in the north.

Other differences can be seen in the country's media and in the arts. Several Ho Chi Minh City newspapers have begun printing in color and regularly publish articles criticizing corrupt officials or exposing social problems such as the declining quality of education or the growing incidence of prostitution; most Hanoi papers are more cautious and less informative. On the other hand, many of country's most innovative and daring artists, such as movie director Luu Trong Ninh, musician Tran Tien, or writer Nguyen Huy Thiep, come from the north. "There are very few good writers in the south," a literary critic in Hanoi says, arguing that Northerners are better known for their poetry and colorful language. "Southern novels are mainly romantic love stories. They don't have deep social analysis like in the north."[4]

Despite all these apparent differences between the north and south, the Vietnamese are alike in their ability to survive. Foreigners in Vietnam are often amazed at how urban residents manage to live so well—let alone keep body and soul together—when their official salaries remain so low.

Take the family of Nguyen Viet Huynh, a forty-nine-year-old Hanoi electrician. Huynh earns less than $20 a month repairing equipment at the state-owned Thang Long Knitting Factory in Hanoi. His wife, Dao Thi Thanh, a congenial woman whose girlish face belies her forty-seven years, works in the state-owned Hanoi Bus Assembly Enterprise, which assembles passenger buses using parts imported from abroad. Thanh earns a little over $10 a month. Their combined salary is enough to provide about one-third of the estimated $90 they need to cover the family's basic living expenses. Roughly 80 percent of this amount is spent on food, while utilities and their two children's school fees each cost an additional $9. On paper, this leaves the family with no money for clothes or medical emergencies.

Like most city dwellers, both parents are forced to moonlight to make ends meet. "It's hard for foreigners to understand how we survive," Huynh observes. "You see that our salaries are very low, yet we manage to live in a decent manner," he says, referring to the family's middle-class life style that includes a Honda motorbike, a refurbished kitchen, a Russian-made refrigerator, and a new color television set. "We're all forced to find our own ways to get by."

Huynh finds extra jobs repairing, installing, and selling electrical equipment in his spare time. Not long ago he went to Ho Chi Minh City, where he helped his sister set up a furniture-building workshop. "Some months I earn several million dong on the side, but other months I earn nothing," Huynh explains. Thanh, meanwhile, sells imported parts for vehicles in her free time, using the wide-ranging connections and experience she has gathered at the factory where she has worked for the past dozen years. "If we have extra money, we live better that month," Huynh says.

Despite all they have been through in recent decades—war, the Communists' drive toward socialism, and years of grinding poverty—many Vietnamese maintain unwavering optimism that life will get better.

4

Red Capitalists

◆ ◆ ◆

The First Tycoons

In a dilapidated shed in the southern suburbs of Hanoi, a dozen workers are hunched over a clanky drying machine busily turning over squares of compressed noodles. As the squiggly dried pasta plops onto a plastic sheet at the far end of the noisy contraption, other workers, squatting on tiny stools, scoop the mountain of instant-noodle bricks into huge bags. A handful of *cyclo* drivers, soaking wet from the spring rain, hang around waiting to load their pedicabs for a trip to the market.

Much of Vietnam's economic future lies in small and often chaotic workshops like the one run by the Food Technology Company. With flour imported from Canada and China, its two hundred employees—working around the clock in three shifts—produce seven tons of instant noodles each day for a population that is learning to eat on the run.

The workshop was set up in 1992 by Le Quang Khai, a thirty-nine-year-old mechanical engineer with a high forehead and a sparse mustache. Like many other members of Vietnam's new breed of entrepreneurs, Khai was a state employee until the late 1980s, when the Communist system began to crumble. He had spent more than a decade working in the ministry of transport's machinery design department. Khai designed and produced the noodle factory's equipment himself for $100,000 after studying a $1 million Japanese model. He earned the startup capital between 1989 and 1991 while working in Moscow, where he and his older brother ran a trading company that imported clothes from Thailand, Poland, and Vietnam. "In this period, it was easy to make money in the Soviet Union," he says.

By 1994 Khai and his brother, a computer expert who continues managing their import business in Moscow, had saved enough to invest another $100,000 in a joint-venture instant-noodle factory in Poland. Khai also was talking to a Chinese company from Shanghai about building a $1 million joint-venture paint plant in the Vietnamese capital. Khai says his biggest problem has been marketing in a country where until a few years ago the state held a tight monopoly on distribution. To get his products into the country's market stalls, Khai has set up a network of sixty agents around northern Vietnam. In 1993 Khai's noodle sales reached $545,000. He says he faces some competition from southern producers, but his biggest challenge comes from eight other noodle factories around Hanoi.

One of Vietnam's most successful entrepreneurs is Le Van Kiem, whose shy, constantly humble expression is betrayed by his Rolls-Royce (the first in the country), his fleet of six Mercedes-Benz sedans, and his diamond-studded watch. Kiem's company, Huy Hoang, which runs two modern factories in the suburbs of Ho Chi Minh City, employs over three thousand people and produced garments worth $28 million in 1995, up from only $5 million five years earlier. About two-thirds of the garments were sold in Europe.

But garments are only one of Kiem's money-spinners. Since the multilateral lending institutions resumed their credits in 1993, Kiem has set up a construction firm to compete for the multimillion-dollar road and port projects that Vietnam plans to build with loans from the World Bank and the Asian Development Bank. One of Huy Hoang's biggest projects was a $1 million contract to build a roundabout at a busy Ho Chi Minh City intersection. Kiem also made a foray into property development by building luxury housing for expatriates in Ho Chi Minh City and in the thriving port city of Vung Tau. He is bidding on other projects, including one to upgrade

Highway One, the country's main north–south artery. Kiem expects his group's turnover in 1996 to reach $80 million, double its 1995 level.

Kiem, fifty, had not been groomed to go into business. He was born in Hue, in central Vietnam. His father was a railroad engineer and a professional boxer, while his mother was a descendant of Vietnam's former royal family. In 1947, during the war to oust the French colonial administration, his father took him—he was then only a baby—to Hanoi, where he grew up and studied civil engineering.

After the U.S.-backed Saigon government collapsed in 1975, Kiem went to the south, along with thousands of other Hanoi-appointed bureaucrats. He served as the deputy director of a state-owned road construction company. Kiem, who now calls himself "a socialist capitalist," liked the dynamism of Ho Chi Minh City and decided to stay.

In 1979, when the Communists took their first steps toward a free market economy, Kiem seized his opportunity. Using $1,000 of his mother's savings, he set up a small family workshop producing animal feed and colored powder for construction. Three years later he quit his government job and went into business full time. He invested his earnings in several new ventures until he had saved enough to build a state-of-the-art factory producing jackets and shirts for export. He renamed the company Huy Hoang, or "Glory," after his son, who is studying in Australia. He hopes to be able to list Huy Hoang when Ho Chi Minh City sets up its fledgling stock exchange, now not expected before 1997.[1]

Not all of the entrepreneurs in Vietnam today are newcomers like Kiem. In early 1993 the government quietly informed Nguyen Thi Nu, a feisty sixty-seven-year-old grandmother who sweeps her gray hair back in a bun, that it was planning to return the Duc Tan Floor Tiles factory to her. The country's Communist rulers had confiscated the factory, which she founded in 1960, at the height of their collectivist fervor in the late 1970s. But more than a year after initiating the proceedings to return the factory, officials were still reviewing the assets of Vietnam's biggest tile company. "I may have to pay money to get it back," says Nu. On the wall behind her desk is a huge color photograph depicting the visit of Premier Vo Van Kiet, who came to Duc Tan shortly after officials promised to return it to her. Kiet, one of the architects of the Communist Party's reforms, had never fully implemented Hanoi's plans to stamp out capitalism when he served as mayor of Ho Chi Minh City in the late 1970s.

Government officials have not bothered explaining to Nu why she must pay to get the factory back, although they likely based their decision on the fact that Duc Tan is turning a profit. In 1993 it doubled its output to 8.5 million tiles. The increase was partially due to rising demand resulting from the construction boom that has engulfed the country in the wake of the reforms. Still, much of the credit for Duc Tan's success goes to Nu. Communist officials retained her as manager even after they took over the factory.

Duc Tan is not the only company being returned to its previous owner. Two other Ho Chi Minh City firms—the Lien Huong Fish Sauce Factory, which produces the pungent condiment Vietnamese eat with almost every meal, and the Pham Hiep Rubber Company, which manufactures car tires—have already been returned to their founders. But the original owners did not get back everything they had lost: some of their equipment had been sold to pay off debts incurred by the state-installed managers.

Despite the party's liberalization and the success of entrepreneurs such as Khai, Kiem, and Nu, many still complain that Vietnam lacks a capitalist-friendly environment. Private companies struggle to overcome hurdles that the Communist government initially put up to block private entrepreneurs. One of the biggest gripes is the underlying uncertainty surrounding private investment. "Many people still don't trust the government's policies, so they keep their money under the table," explains Kiem, who reserves much of his ire for local bureaucrats. "It's government policy not to discriminate between the state and private sectors," he points out, "but in reality the officials who implement the policies often don't treat us equally."

For example, he says it is much easier for a state company to get an export license than it is for a private competitor.

Nu is frustrated by the government's failure to rein in smuggling, estimated at anywhere from 10 percent to 25 percent of the country's annual import bill. Her Duc Tan tile factory has been hard hit by an invasion of smuggled tiles from neighboring China. Nu, who had more than a million tiles stockpiled in her warehouses in 1994, said she would have to lay off half the company's six hundred workers unless the government managed to slow the onslaught of untaxed foreign products. Nu, five of whose siblings fled abroad after the Communist victory, recognizes that she will have to invest in new equipment to produce high-quality tiles if she wants to compete with goods from China. But she is hesitant: "For the past nineteen years, I've had money to invest, but I haven't done it," she says. "I feel the legal system still isn't developed enough to insure my investment."

At least Nu has money to invest. Most entrepreneurs must rely on loans from family and friends to get started and are forced to rely on profits to expand. A 1992 survey of private entrepreneurs found that 42 percent cited lack of capital as the biggest problem holding them back. Nonetheless, the private sector's share of limited bank credit in Vietnam is rising quickly. It reached approximately 40 percent in 1994, up from only 30 percent the year before.[2] But according to a 1995 survey conducted by the State Planning Committee and Japan's Overseas Economic Cooperation Fund, private businesspeople who get credit typically pay over 20 percent interest on loans for capital investment, while state firms pay 9 percent or less. In addition, private firms have to put up collateral equal to one and a half times the value of their loan, but state-owned companies can secure loans with little more than letters of guarantee from their sponsoring government ministries.[3]

Because of these problems, economists warn that the government will have to do more to encourage domestic entrepreneurs and promote local manufacturing. As Vietnam's neighbors found earlier, a rapid surge in small and medium-size enterprises not only absorbs millions of unemployed rural workers but also boosts export earnings and provides access to the world's latest technology. "The biggest obstacle to becoming a real tiger probably lies in the fiercely ambivalent attitude of the Party and government towards a 'real' corporate private sector," argues economist David Dapice of the Harvard Institute for International Development. "Without private companies of more than princelings, it is hard to see how growth could be sustained for decades," he says, alluding to companies run by relatives of senior officials.

The World Bank, in its 1994 report, urged the Vietnamese government to "create a level playing field between public and private firms." To complete the transition to a market economy, the bank says, Hanoi needs to develop its legal framework, including contract, company, land, and bankruptcy laws.[4] The private sector currently accounts for roughly two-thirds of the country's total output. Private factories produce approximately 30 percent of industrial output nationwide, over 40 percent of which comes from Ho Chi Minh City, the economic hub. (If production of oil and electricity are excluded, private workshops account for over 40 percent of industrial output.)[5] The role of the private sector in agriculture, trade, and services is even bigger; economists believe it accounts for more than 90 percent of farm output, 70 percent of domestic trade and 60 percent of the country's transport services. (Precise statistics are not available in Vietnam. When I asked Hanoi economist Le Xuan Nghia if he trusted the government's figures, he threw his hands in the air and said, "Ask the gods.")

Most private economic activity is generated by small household units, employing only a handful of workers. By 1995 some 12,500 private firms had registered with the government. Others licensed by the government included 5,034 "limited" companies, 131 joint stock companies, and 270 "association" businesses. Roughly half of these firms are located in the Ho Chi Minh City area. The number of private companies is still very small, although the real figure is probably higher than the official number, since many businessmen avoid registering to evade the attention of tax officials. Precious few of these private companies have reached commanding heights, and all of them are in the south. Most are tiny outfits: the registered private firms have an average capital of only $12,500, while the average capital of "limited" companies reaches $63,000. A survey of private companies in Ho Chi Minh City found that 45 percent were losing money and another 20 percent were effectively bankrupt.[6]

The overall role of industry in Vietnam remains small, accounting in 1993 for only one-fifth of gross domestic production, one-tenth of the country's jobs, and 45 percent of its exports. (If the sale of unprocessed oil is excluded, the industrial share of exports is even smaller.)[7] Yet industry is one of the fastest-growing sectors of the Vietnamese economy, expanding more than 13 percent a year since the late 1980s. Although the private sector remains relatively weak, it has grown quickly and is expected to increase its influence over the next decade.

State Capitalists

The General Forwarding & Agency Company may not be so large or have a particularly glamorous name, but it holds a niche in Vietnamese history. In October 1993 the shipping outfit became the first state-owned firm to be privatized. The largest block of shares went to employees, making the company "more dynamic," says Do Van Nhan, who was elected managing director at the company's first shareholders meeting. "I see our staff working harder, because they want to make a profit for themselves." Two months later another small Ho Chi Minh City company, the Refrigeration Electrical Engineering Corporation, went private—or was "equitized," as Hanoi's Communist leaders prefer to call it. Several other companies began selling shares, usually to their employees or to those of controlling ministries. Prices for the most part were sharply discounted, and many of the buyers received concessional loans from the government to buy their shares.

Vietnam's experiment with privatization, announced with considerable hoopla in 1992, was launched to reduce the burden struggling firms put on limited state coffers, improve the efficiency of these companies, and mobilize private capital for production. But the campaign has been slow getting started; several of the companies nominated for privatization have dropped out. One obstacle is resistance from managers, workers, and state officials. Long protected under the socialist system, many fear they will lose their jobs or power if the company is privatized and required to make a profit. The country's poorly developed legal and accounting framework is another stumbling block: The country has no set rules or regulations helping officials to calculate procedures for privatizing a state firm. Finally, because Vietnam does not have a stock market, Vietnamese are not acquainted with the concept of buying shares.

Communist ideologues also fear that an end to large-scale state ownership poses a threat to the future of Vietnamese socialism. "Many decision makers are still confused about ideology," one official explains. "They think that privatizing state enterprises or allowing private land ownership means they are deviating from communism. This makes them confused." It took General Forwarding a full year to evaluate its assets—set at nearly $565,000—and get final approval for the sale from its owner, the ministry of transport. Some 42 percent of the company's shares were purchased by the firm's employees, 18 percent were retained by the ministry, and the rest were sold to ministry staff. No shares were left for sale to the general public.[8] "It took so long because we were the first case," explains Nhan. "No one, including government officials, knew how to go about privatization," he observed. "It was like people trying to find their way in the dark."

Vietnam's state sector is small compared to most other former socialist countries: Government enterprises employ only 7 percent of the country's work force, compared to 77 percent in Russia. Even so, state companies play an important role in Vietnam's economy. They contribute one-quarter of the country's total output, 70 percent of industrial production, and over half of the government's tax

revenue, but many state enterprises are inefficient outfits with ob-
solete equipment, poor management, a lethargic work force, and
mediocre products. According to Vietnamese economists, approximately 30 percent make money and only 40 percent break even.[9]
Despite this inefficiency, the government doesn't want to shut down
these money-losing factories because they provide hundreds of thousands of jobs.

By 1995 Vietnam had approximately 6,000 state enterprises,
down from an estimated 12,000 at the time that the pilot equitization scheme was announced three years earlier. Most of the companies that disappeared under the government's re-registration project
were small, unprofitable ventures belonging to provincial governments; some that vanished were integrated into larger enterprises,
while others were leased to private businessmen or sold to pay off
their debts.[10] Much of this privatization process, however, was spontaneous and unorganized. Economist Adam Fforde points out that
even many remaining state companies are no longer managed by
government ministries but have fallen "under de facto control of
managers or other private or quasi-private interests."[11]

Vietnamese technocrats hope that the number of firms volunteer-
ing for equitization will pick up once a few examples have proven
successful, although they have no intention of privatizing all state
enterprises. So far Hanoi has resisted calls to allow foreigners to buy
shares in state-owned enterprises to speed up privatization and provide another vehicle for foreign investment in Vietnam. Despite economic reforms, officials want the state to continue to play a leading
role in Vietnam's economy. In a draft report prepared for the Communist Party Congress held in mid-1996, leaders called for more
state control of the economy, insisting that reforms "must be accompanied by the strengthening of the role of state management along
the socialist line." The report added that state firms and cooperatives
are expected to increase their share of gross domestic product to 60
percent by the year 2020, up from an estimated 45 percent in 1996,
raising questions about the Party's commitment to allowing private
enterprises to develop into modern corporations.[12]

Some even talk of the state establishing large conglomerates—similar to the giant business groups called *chaebol* in South Korea, that have diverse corporate empires, including manufacturing, marketing, construction, and banking—to control key sectors of the economy. One entrepreneur who is being groomed for such a role is Nguyen Huu Dinh, the forty-six-year-old manager of the Saigon Jewelry Company, set up in 1989 with $50,000 worth of assets from the Ho Chi Minh City government. The balding businessman, who is constantly armed with a smile, moved quickly to establish a network of twenty-six shops around the country. The company's gold bars have become the favorite currency with which most big-ticket items—houses, cars, and motorcycles—are sold in the south. (Until a few years ago the exchange rate of the dong often fluctuated wildly, prompting sellers to quote prices in gold or U.S. dollars.)

Dinh's career was bolstered by the fact that he ended up on the winning side of the Vietnam War. He was born in central Vietnam but moved to Saigon in the early 1970s to study economics. Like scores of prominent Communist officials and business leaders in Ho Chi Minh City today, he was imprisoned for opposing the American military intervention. After the Communist victory, Dinh was hired to work for a state-run trading company. A few years later the friendships he made in jail paid off: He was picked to found the city's jewelry firm. Since then he has built an extensive business empire.

"Our goal is to develop in diversified fields," says Dinh. In 1992 he established the country's first finance firm, Saigon Finance Joint-Stock Company, of which the Saigon Jewelry Company holds two-thirds of the shares. The company controls 20 percent of two leading Ho Chi Minh City banks, and serves as the distributor for several top international brand names, including Canon and Olivetti. Dinh's company also operates a handful of small hotels and runs several enterprises producing jewelry and decorative stone for construction. Saigon Jewelry holds a 35 percent stake in the International Beverage Company, which began bottling Pepsi-Cola in Ho Chi Minh City hours after Washington lifted its trade embargo in February 1994.

"He's a one-man band," says a competitor who admires Dinh's achievements. He shows no signs of slowing down. To sharpen his skills, Dinh took evening courses at Ho Chi Minh City's Economics University and recently completed a degree in business management.

Despite the advantages of state enterprises, managers like Dinh continue to be frustrated with Hanoi's policies. Many complain that the government grants more favorable tax breaks to foreign-investment projects than to Vietnamese companies. For example, foreign firms pay a maximum profit tax of 25 percent while Saigon Jewelry is charged a whopping 45 percent. "After that I have little money left to reinvest," Dinh states, adding that "this doesn't allow us to become a powerful company." He also has to contend with more stringent accounting regulations than his private competitors. "We're expected to keep detailed accounts. But if a private company sells ten items, it can say it sold only one. To succeed in competition with the private sector, a state company needs to have much higher production." Dinh says a salary cap further limits his ability to compete for the most talented staff, whereas private firms and foreign investors face no such limits. Regardless of how much an employee earns for his company, Dinh is not allowed to pay more than $55 a month.

Dinh's can-do style distinguishes him from the previous generation of state-enterprise managers, who were mainly army veterans rewarded for their ability to blast American bombers out of the sky. "Not only have they changed their clothes and their cars and hired beautiful young secretaries, but they've also changed their style of working," Le Dang Doanh, director of a government economic think tank in Hanoi, says about the new breed of state-enterprise managers emerging in Vietnam. "They've contributed a great deal to Vietnam's economic reform."

State companies are evolving in a variety of configurations, and the once clear line between private and state capital is becoming fuzzy. In some cases, private and state firms team up in unofficial joint ventures. For instance, Thong Nhat Company, an energetic, family-operated chain of shops that sells construction materials in

Hanoi, has joined forces with a sleepy firm belonging to the ministry of science, technology and environment. "They have the right to import construction materials, but they have poor marketing skills," Nguyen Cong, one of Thong Nhat's owners, says of his partners. "So we use their legal position to import construction materials and pay them for this relationship."

In other cases, state employees are setting up dynamic new private firms while officially remaining on the government's payroll. One of these new entrepreneurs is Ha The Minh, thirty-seven-year-old director of the computer and communications department in the ministry of science. About two-thirds of the charming, Hungarian-trained engineer's time is spent doing digit signal processing research for the government. Minh spends the rest of his time running the HT & NT Company from a tiny, overcrowded storefront on Hanoi's Hai Ba Trung Street, just down from the magnificent French villas recently refurbished by the Australian Embassy. Minh and a research colleague borrowed $20,000 from relatives and friends in 1993 to set up the company and since then have supplied many of the computers being used by the foreign firms setting up shop in Vietnam. Minh refuses to disclose how many computers he sells—like most Vietnamese entrepreneurs, he is afraid of the tax man's watchful eye.

One of the reasons Minh launched his own firm was to raise funds to supplement the government's limited research budget. State funding for computer research in Vietnam in 1994 totaled $1.8 million, of which his institute received only $5,500. Minh used more than half this amount to import one computer software program from Singapore. As a result, he dips into his profits to fund some of his center's research projects. On paper at least, HT & NT is not legal. Government employees—particularly members of the Communist Party such as Minh—are not supposed to do business, but his boss turns a blind eye because he is afraid of losing Minh's skills. "My director wants me to continue doing research, so he allows me to do private business," Minh says. "He's a bit loose."

Many state employees have quit their government jobs and joined private companies, but others like Minh prefer to keep their feet in both the private and public worlds. He believes that government laboratories, even though poorly funded, give him more opportunities than the private sector to do broadly focused research. But what if Minh's boss or some other bureaucrat decides to ban his private business activities in the future? "I'll transfer my shares to my wife or to my mother," he says.

Like most Vietnamese businessmen, Minh is anxious that the government introduce policies bolstering economic development but is not particularly impatient for the Communist Party to end its monopoly grip on power. "Some people think the current government isn't good enough," he says, alluding to dissidents who demand a multiparty political system. "For me, if the government develops the economy, it can be accepted for a period of time. I'm satisfied with the present pace of political change," Minh says, adding that such reforms as the foreign investment law and the land law (which grants long-term user rights to farmers) have done a lot to boost Vietnam's economy. Reiterating a concern voiced by Vietnamese businessmen familiar with the current situation in the former Soviet Union he says, "One thing I don't want is political chaos."

Scams, Scandals, and Kickbacks

Each day hundreds of small wooden boats, many of them with cargo stacked so high that their oarsmen can barely look over the top, cross the Bac Luan River separating Chinese Dong Hung from Vietnamese Mong Cai. Porters stagger up the steep river bank with huge loads of twice their weight or more. They unload their wares in the Mong Cai shantytown that has sprung up since the frontier was unofficially reopened in 1989. Along dusty streets near a newly built market, hotel, and post office (that has a new digital microwave telecommunications system), merchants repack the beer, textiles, porcelain dishes, apples, and construction materials from China for distribution throughout Vietnam.

An informal network of middlemen, many using reinforced bicycles or the backs of their motorcycles, moves the goods south. As
the goods are transported, they spread prosperity along the newly
surfaced highway that until a few years ago was a potholed, one-lane
road. Two- and three-story brick houses seem to be sprouting up
everywhere, replacing the former thatch huts of this once impoverished region of Quang Ninh province, best known for its coal mines.

Since the world's two largest surviving Communist powers began
mending fences in the late 1980s, bulldozers in Mong Cai have
leveled the overgrown remains of China's devastating 1979 invasion
of northern Vietnam. Military units have cleared the land mines, and
construction crews have strung electricity lines and laid water and
sewer lines. Similar transformations are taking place in Lang Son,
Lao Cai, and other towns along Vietnam's northern border. The
rebirth of this remote mountainous region mirrors the phenomenal
changes taking place all across Vietnam. Vietnamese seem to be seizing every opportunity—including those that are illegal—to better
their lives. Much of the commerce along the Chinese border is in
fact smuggling. Some importers avoid passing through customs alto-
gether, but most simply pay bribes to get crooked officials to lower
the tariffs on their goods.

Many Vietnamese factories are threatened by the flood of cheap
goods into the country. One of these is Tran Hung Dao Engineering, named, ironically, after the legendary Vietnamese general who
repulsed invaders from the north in the thirteenth century. During
its heyday in the early 1980s the Tran Hung Dao plant produced
6,000 small engines a year and employed some 1,200 workers. But
soon after the Communist Party opened the country to foreign
competition in 1986, the factory, with its antiquated equipment and
outmoded products, began falling on hard times. Its difficulties increased once hustlers began smuggling cheaper Chinese-made engines into northern Vietnam. "We've almost closed our doors,"
laments factory director Nguyen Van Ton. Hundreds of similar plants
throughout Vietnam have been hard hit by the invasion of Chinese
goods. Many manufacturers of textiles, bicycles, electric fans, and

other light industrial products have already closed their doors or stand on the brink of bankruptcy.

Corruption is another problem. Almost daily, the country's newspapers chronicle the cases of officials accepting kickbacks from businessmen and workshops producing fake medicines, soft drinks, and other goods. Greed often seems to have gained the upper hand.

Perhaps the most celebrated case is that of Nguyen Van Muoi Hai, who was one of the first entrepreneurs to capitalize on the reforms launched by the Communist Party in 1986. He started the Thanh Huong Perfume Factory and became a success practically overnight selling perfumes and toiletry items. Within just a few years officials were touting him and his company as one of the brightest examples of free enterprise in the new Vietnam. He traveled around Ho Chi Minh City in a convoy of limousines, escorted by bodyguards on motorcycles with sirens. When he arrived at his destination, the outriders jumped off their motorbikes and formed two lines for their boss to pass through. "Welcome, general director," an aide would say, bowing as Muoi Hai passed through the door.[13]

He opened a chain of glitzy boutiques in hotels and in the Ho Chi Minh City airport to sell his products and regularly won awards for his fragrances. He appeared in slick television advertisements promoting his company's perfume and toiletries and was even featured in the government-controlled media, which added to his rags-to-riches image. Soon after this success he began offering investors incredible interest rates (up to 15 percent a month) in his new credit cooperative. People sold family heirlooms and queued up by the hour waiting to deposit money into his credit cooperative. A black market sprang up as investors sought to buy low numbers, allowing them to move to the front of the queue. Thousands of people, including many civil servants and pensioners, poured millions of dollars into the scheme.

Some journalists at *Youth*, a Ho Chi Minh City newspaper that began serious investigative reporting when Hanoi relaxed its controls on the press, were the first to suspect that Muoi Hai's success might be too good to be true. They noticed that one of his top deputies was the former director of a state enterprise who had been fired for corruption. The editors became even more suspicious when Muoi Hai barred their journalists from visiting his production plant. When the paper published an article raising questions about Thanh Huong, Muoi Hai sent a letter to the editors that they interpreted as a murder threat. Finally, in March 1990, the police arrested Muoi Hai, his wife, and four associates for "misusing their reputation to illegally take the property of other citizens." Investigators discovered that he did not even have a factory; he simply added water to imported perfume and rebottled it, peddling it under labels such as *Caresse*. They also discovered that he was not investing his deposits in production but rather was using them to buy luxury cars, houses, and jewelry for himself and his wife.

Muoi Hai had developed a classic pyramid scheme using money from new depositors to pay interest to those who had invested earlier, managing to avoid investigations by giving key officials free deposit certificates on which they could draw monthly interest payments. By the time Muoi Hai's business was shut down some 140,000 depositors had invested nearly $25 million, most of which he had squandered. In the end officials only managed to recover assets worth about $6.5 million.

The collapse of Thanh Huong prompted the largest public protests in Ho Chi Minh City since the 1975 Communist takeover. Hundreds of depositors staged demonstrations in front of city hall demanding that the government help them recoup their deposits. Nervous customers in other credit cooperatives panicked and rushed to withdraw their funds, causing at least two dozen other co-ops to collapse.

Muoi Hai was sentenced to twenty years in jail, but his imprisonment did not put an end to get-rich-quick schemes in Vietnam. A giant *hui* group (an informal credit circle) collapsed in Ho Chi Minh City in 1993, resulting in losses estimated at between $9.5 and $19 million. Many such scams are the result of gaping cracks in a regulatory system that allows abuses by greedy businesspeople and corrupt officials.

Vietnam's informal system of rule by people, rather than rule by law, sometimes results in conflicts between capitalists and bureaucrats—particularly at the local level, as I inadvertently found out. Because I wrote for a business magazine I tried to visit as many emerging companies as possible, and one firm I wanted to see was Haivinaco Limited, touted as the largest private company in the north. Located in the port city of Haiphong, Haivinaco produces exquisite porcelain pieces for export. The company is headed by Bui Xuan Hai, an energetic man in his early fifties. The foreign ministry insists on approving all travel and meetings by foreign journalists in Vietnam, so I sent a letter to the press department requesting a visit, which was quickly approved. However, officials of the Haiphong foreign office—who also need to sanction trips by foreigners— dragged their heels, telling my assistant that a visit was "not convenient at this time."

Several months later I tried again, and again, approval from the foreign ministry was prompt, but local officials refused to authorize my visit, telling my assistant that they were "too busy." I asked the foreign ministry to intervene, pointing out that the government undoubtedly would benefit from propaganda about one of Vietnam's more successful businessmen, yet the ministry responded that it could not order local authorities to let me come.

I called Hai and arranged to see him during his next visit to Haivinaco's showroom in Hanoi. He wasn't surprised that I had not been allowed to visit him in Haiphong. In painstaking detail Hai described how the same local officials who had blocked my visit had recently forced him to take them on a trip to Hong Kong, where he had to buy them new motorcycles and video cassette players. Hai went on to explain that the bureaucrats surely did not want a foreign journalist coming to Haiphong and inadvertently discovering their "extortion." "The central government supports renovation, but a lot of officials still struggle against change," the businessman explained. "Localities try to keep their privileges and many low-level officials use their positions to violate the law."

Of course, Hai's specific charges were impossible to verify, so about six months later I applied once more. This time, after again receiving authorization from the foreign ministry, I personally called the head of the Haiphong foreign office and told him that I was coming to visit Haivinaco in two days. "Vang . . . vang," he responded, which means something like "I hear you." The next morning the foreign ministry called to say that Haiphong could not host my visit. (Probably no one would have stopped me if I had simply set out for Haiphong, but officials could have made things difficult for me the next time I needed to travel.)

A few months later Vietnamese newspapers reported that Hai had been arrested. Although his crimes were not officially explained, according to reports in *Labor* newspaper, he was charged with "abusing his reputation to capture socialist assets" and "violating regulations on land management."[14] It would appear that he was charged with illegally gaining control over state-owned land. There is no way of knowing whether these charges are true or the result of a vendetta by an official who had not benefited enough from Hai's largesse.

Vietnam's Ethnic Chinese

Many of the most vibrant private companies to emerge in recent years have been set up by ethnic Chinese in Ho Chi Minh City's Cholon district. This bastion of Chinese enterprise had been devastated during the crackdown on capitalists in 1978. Today, Cholon's largest business group is the Viet-Hoa (Vietnamese-Chinese) Bank, established in 1992 by more than fifty shareholders, most of whom are ethnic Chinese.

This group was pulled together by sixty-two-year-old Tran Tuan Tai, a dynamic, portly businessman who is chairman of the bank's board. Like many graying men in Vietnam, Tai dyes his hair jet black, but this seems to be his only concession to vanity. He arrives at his office in a beat-up, ten-year-old Toyota dressed in a loose-fitting shirt and a frayed pair of pants. Throughout our interview he jumps up constantly—at times nearly tripping over bulges in his poorly fitting carpet—to answer one of four telephones or to bark orders through his open office door. Tai had operated half a dozen factories producing furniture, garments, and other products in southern Vietnam before the Communist victory in 1975. Afterward (except for a brief stint when he served as the buying agent for a state-owned import-export company), he was jobless for the next fourteen years. "I lived off the gifts of my relatives in France, Australia, and the United States," says Tai, who is believed to have been a millionaire before the Communists expropriated his factories.

In 1989, however, as the pace of economic reform gained momentum, Tai was able to set up a credit cooperative that he used as the platform from which to launch Viet-Hoa Construction Company. This company financed and constructed Cholon's five-story An Dong market, completed in 1993. Observers note that this nearly $5 million venture—the first significant investment project in Vietnam launched by a group of ethnic Chinese capitalists in the postwar period—symbolized the reemergence of the ethnic Chinese as an important force in Vietnam's economy.

The success of the market project convinced Tai to put together the Viet-Hoa Bank, one of Ho Chi Minh City's most vigorous middle-sized banks. Within two years it opened seven branches and eight gold shops around Cholon. Tai now is looking to expand to other parts of Vietnam and overseas. "These are the ones to watch," a competitor says of Tai and his fellow shareholders. The Viet-Hoa Bank was capitalized at $5.5 million and in 1994 held $19 million in deposits, largely from ethnic Chinese customers. Tai said the bank had loaned out four-fifths of its deposits, mainly for such construction projects as a new twenty-two-story commercial tower in Cholon, a market in the central highland city of Dalat, and a housing complex in Ho Chi Minh City.

During the past few years thousands of ethnic Chinese have resumed trading activities or have established workshops processing food, producing textiles and garments, or assembling electronic equipment. Researchers say Cholon's ethnic Chinese now control two-thirds of the small-scale industrial output and one-third of the trading activities in Ho Chi Minh City, even though they make up less than 10 percent of the city's population. In 1989, at the time of its last census, Vietnam had 960,000 ethnic Chinese, of whom approximately 80 percent were in the south. Nearly 380,000 ethnic Chinese lived in Ho Chi Minh City; Hanoi had fewer than 10,000, only a quarter of the number who lived in the capital up until the late 1970s.[15]

Some of the ethnic Chinese, refugees from the Manchu conquest of southern China, arrived in Vietnam in the last half of the seventeenth century and settled around the present-day southern towns of Bien Hoa, My Tho, and Ha Tien. A second wave of Chinese immigrants came during the French colonial period.

In 1956 the Ngo Dinh Diem government in Saigon banned ethnic Chinese from eleven types of business activities, but they still managed to dominate South Vietnam's wartime economy. Academics believe that they controlled four-fifths of the industrial output, half of the banking activities, 90 percent of wholesale trade, half of all retail business, and most of the rice trade.[16] Many of the ethnic Chinese lived in separate communities much like the Chinatowns in New York and San Francisco. They ran their own schools using a curriculum from Taiwan, operated their own hospitals, and worshipped in their own temples.

Separate Chinese business and cultural activities came to an abrupt halt in 1975, when the new Communist government closed private companies and took over private hospitals and schools. Hanoi's zealous 1978 campaign to smash the remaining vestiges of capitalism prompted tens of thousands of ethnic Chinese from the south to join the often-treacherous boat people exodus.

China, already angered by Hanoi's growing alliance with the former Soviet Union, condemned Vietnam for mistreating its "overseas Chinese" residents. As relations between China and Vietnam deteriorated, Hanoi became increasingly distrustful of the ethnic Chinese in the north, even though most of them had supported Hanoi's struggle against the United States. Many were forced to choose between moving to isolated "new economic zones" or fleeing to China. Most of those who stayed were stripped of their membership in the Communist Party and their children were barred from attending colleges. But it was not long before the Vietnamese Communist Party—apparently recognizing that it needed help from this dynamic minority to jump-start its economy—began to soften its policies toward ethnic Chinese. By 1986, when Hanoi abandoned doctrinaire socialism, ethnic Chinese once more were allowed to join the party, serve in the army, and attend universities. Two years later the ministry of education allowed schools to resume teaching in Chinese in areas with high concentrations of ethnic Chinese students.

The ethnic Chinese have resumed many of the activities in which they were involved prior to the Communist takeover, although they haven't quite recaptured the monopolies that they held during the war. Vietnamese observers say the government's earlier discriminatory policies have partially broken up the once tightly knit Chinese communities and forced them to seek greater integration in the larger Vietnamese community. The ethnic Chinese (at least two-thirds of whom are believed to have close relatives abroad) have played a key role in Vietnam's reintegration with the outside world. Even though Vietnam in effect was closed for a decade after the war ended, many ethnic Chinese managed to maintain links with Chinese communities in Taiwan, Hong Kong, and in Western countries.

Since the late 1980s these families have provided a major impetus for foreign investment in Vietnam. Businessmen from Taiwan, Hong Kong, and Singapore, which are largely populated by ethnic Chinese, have emerged as the most important investors in Vietnam, snaring licenses worth $7 billion, or nearly 40 percent of the total, by the end of 1995. In some cases firms from these countries have invested directly through their relatives in Ho Chi Minh City; in others they have turned to their kinsmen to help guide them through Vietnam's bureaucratic labyrinth.

Does all of this business activity mean that the ethnic Chinese have forgotten 1978? "We still think of what happened," admits Tai, whose Viet-Hoa group, in a joint venture with a Taiwanese firm, runs the Caesar Hotel, where many overseas Chinese businessmen stay when they visit Vietnam. "Now we're more daring than before, but we still haven't jumped into the market with both feet." He says most Chinese are waiting for the government to complete the regulations needed to police the domestic investment law passed in 1994.[17] Until then, Tai says, "we won't dare to invest in big projects, only medium-sized ones. We want to do more business, but we're still a bit timid."

5

The Hungry Earth

◆ ◆ ◆

Land of Hope

Perhaps nothing better exemplifies Vietnam's economic turnaround than agriculture. As recently as 1988, Hanoi appealed for international aid to avert starvation. Remarkably, only one year after the Communist Party's decision to abandon farm cooperatives and return land to its tillers, Vietnam emerged as the world's third-largest rice exporter, behind Thailand and the United States.

Such accomplishments are due to the hard work of small-time farmers like Nguyen Thanh Phan, whose sinewy, bronzed body reflects decades under the sun. Phan, forty-seven, cultivates 4,600 square meters of rice land fifteen kilometers south of the city of Can Tho, in the heart of the fertile Mekong delta. Phan grew up here, in the midst of vibrant green rice fields and towering coconut trees, during the war with the United States. His village experienced little fighting and he managed to avoid being drafted into the army because he was the only son of aged parents.

Not long after the war ended in 1975 the country's new Communist rulers began redistributing land in the Mekong delta and forcing farmers to join cooperatives, a move that none of his neighbors welcomed. "Many people wrote letters protesting collectivization," Phan says. Some even expressed their dissent by chopping down their fruit trees or slaughtering their draft animals. By 1979 overall rice production in the Mekong delta fell to six million tons a year—a full million tons less than when the country was still at war.[1]

One reason for the slump was that the new Communist rulers were investing primarily in heavy industry, which left little capital for agriculture; another was the fixed, artificially low farm prices, which gave peasants little incentive to produce. In addition, inputs such as fertilizer were in short supply and rarely arrived on time under the government's Soviet-style centralized distribution system.

Stagnant production and growing unrest prompted the Communist Party in 1981 to drop the cooperative "work point" system that paid people for showing up at work rather than for actually working. It was replaced with a "contract" system that allowed farmers to keep what they produced above a certain quota. Rice production rose for several years and then stagnated, at least in part because the state's prices again were too low to offer farmers much incentive.

As famine threatened in early 1988, the party abandoned its efforts to collectivize agriculture and granted peasant families long-term land tenure. Farmers such as Phan, who got back the land his father had tilled under the French, were given the rights to their plots for at least twenty years, without fear that a zealous bureaucrat would arbitrarily pass the land on to someone else. The government ended state subsidies as well and stopped forcing farmers to sell their rice to the state at fixed, low prices. It allowed the free market to drive up the price of rice and freed private merchants to provide fertilizer. Soon Phan's two crops were producing six tons of rice a year, up from four tons under the old co-op system. Much of this increase, Phan says, is due to the fact that he is working harder and investing more in his fields.

As agricultural output expanded, a new bustle and energy swept the Vietnamese countryside. Farmers began building pigpens, planting fruit trees, and buying bricks or wood to replace their old mud or thatch houses. For the first time, peasants started spending on consumer goods such as bicycles, watches, and televisions.

In 1992 Phan used some of his increased income to add a second room to the small wooden house where he lives with his wife and five of their six children. He also helped half a dozen neighbors to run an electricity line to their village and bought a new, varnished, ancestral altar to commemorate his father and mother, who are buried under whitewashed grave markers at the edge of his rice fields. A year later Phan planted scores of orange, tangerine, and mango trees along the irrigation canals skirting his fields. The trees will keep moisture in the soil and their fruit will boost his income. Once these trees begin producing he hopes to earn enough to replace the thatch roof on his house with tiles and to cement over his dirt floor.

Despite improving fortunes, Phan still has two major complaints. The first is that he can't receive credit to help him buy such inputs as seeds and fertilizer. Only one-third of the country's farmers nation-wide obtained bank credits in 1995; because banks lack capital, many of Vietnam's farmers were forced to turn to private money lenders who often charge interest rates of 10 percent or more a month.[2]

The second problem is low prices. Vietnamese farmers have be-come victims of their own success. As rice production soars, the price stagnates. With inflation pushing up the cost of other goods and services, the real incomes of farmers have fallen. In 1993, for example, grain prices dropped 3.5 percent, while the cost of con-sumer goods rose 23 percent.[3]

One reason the rice price stays low is that the government tightly controls exports to ensure adequate local supplies and prevent any domestic discontent. Middlemen and brokers make much of the profit from exports. State-owned companies that have a monopoly on rice exports do not have funds to buy the rice or warehouses to store it after the harvest. As a result, "margins between the farm gate and the border get spread out over a lot of people," says agronomist Vo Tong Xuan, vice rector of the University of Can Tho.[4]

Nonetheless, rice output has surged an average of nearly 9 percent a year in the Mekong delta since 1988, when the cooperatives were dissolved.[5] (Despite this surge in the south, the rest of the country has witnessed only a 2 percent annual increase, barely enough to keep up with the country's population growth.) Grain output na-tionwide hit 27.5 million tons in 1995, up from eighteen million tons seven years earlier, an increase that has made it possible for Vietnam to export 1.5 to 2.2 million tons of rice each year since the late 1980s. Rice now accounts for about one-tenth of the country's total export earnings.

The Red River Delta

Foreigners living in Vietnam—diplomats, businessmen, aid workers, and journalists—often have a fairly good idea of what is going on in the cities. That is where most expatriates live and have the freedom to talk to people. Few foreigners, however, have more than a rudimentary understanding about Vietnamese peasants. Part of the reason for this is the rules under which foreigners work in Vietnam.

As mentioned earlier, I needed to request permission from the foreign ministry for any travel outside of the capital. This was usually granted, and when I arrived in a province I would have to report to local officials who typically would appoint two "minders"—one undoubtedly received his salary from the ministry of interior's security apparatus, while the other was probably paid by the local government—to accompany me to all of my meetings.

Luckily, few of these minders tried to stage-manage my trips. Most would let me choose the village I wanted to visit and select the people I wished to interview, but they were always in the background, often prompting answers to my questions. Sometimes this made it impossible to speak frankly with people in the countryside. Other times I was surprised at just how candid Vietnam's independent-minded peasants could be, regardless of who was listening. For example, on a 1993 visit to Boi Thuy village in Nam Ha province, about eighty kilometers south of Hanoi, my "handlers" let me wander through the village and made no apparent effort to control individuals to whom I spoke. I spotted Tran Van Thanh, dressed in a pair of tattered black shorts, repairing a bamboo frame on which he was growing gourds to supplement his family's income. I stopped to chat with the disheveled, sixty-three-year-old farmer, and Thanh described how he, his wife, and their twenty-four-year-old son farmed only 1,620 square meters of land due to overcrowding in the Red River delta. (Thanh's two daughters have married and live with their husbands' families; one of his sons works in a tin mine near the Chinese border, and a third son was killed in 1982 during a border skirmish with China.) Thanh's plot occupies only three-fifths of the

2,800-square-meter average farmed by households in the Red River (according to a 1993 World Bank–sponsored living standards survey).[6] In contrast, the average household in the Mekong delta, where Phan farms, cultivates a whopping 11,084 square meters of land.

Thanh's family plants two rice crops each year, but that keeps them busy for less than 100 days, just over half the annual 180-day average worked by Vietnamese rural laborers.[7] In most years, Thanh's family produces only enough rice to feed themselves for nine months, sometimes less. Because Boi Thuy is only half a meter above sea level, the village's fields are flooded by the monsoon rains that arrive each June. When the flood waters came in mid-1992, it took a full week before the village's antiquated pumping station got enough electricity to begin draining the fields. By the time the water receded Thanh and 200 other farmers in the village had lost half of their autumn crops.

After Thanh and I had talked for a while about the hardships of farming in the Red River delta, I asked him how his life had changed under the Communist Party's recent reforms. "Nothing has changed," he responded. "We don't earn any more now than before." I was surprised not so much by his answer but by his willingness to utter such a politically incorrect statement in front of the officials who accompanied me. The minders, who had been quiet up to this point, suddenly swung into action. "Nothing has improved?" one of them challenged. "What about your house?" the other one prompted, referring to the farmer's relatively new brick house. "When did you build that?"

"Four years ago," Thanh said. "But I built the house with loans from my neighbors. I haven't paid them back yet."

Thanh obviously was not intimidated by the two young bureaucrats, so I decided to push the question further. "How has your life changed since the defeat of the French colonialists?" I asked. "It hasn't changed," he said about the Communists' four-decade rule in northern Vietnam. "I'm still very poor." Thanh's answer sent a twitter through a group of curious neighbors who had gathered to listen to our conversation. "Nothing has changed?" one of the minders asked with surprise. "You have your own land," the other pointed out. "You have schools and clinics." Thanh listened, saying nothing. "Tell him life has gotten better since liberation," one of my handlers urged, referring to me, the visiting foreigner. "Tell him you have independence, democracy, and freedom," he said. "Nothing is more precious than independence and freedom." After an awkward delay, Thanh repeated what he had been told to say but spoke without any feeling. Thanh was evidently more worried about the impact of the upcoming monsoons on his crop than about political ideals of independence and freedom.

Undoubtedly, life in Boi Thuy is not as difficult today as it was forty years ago. After all, thanks to the Communists, Thanh has a tiny plot of his own. After paying taxes he can keep his harvest rather than turn most of it over to a landlord, as people did under French colonial rule; and he has replaced his old mud shack with a brick house, even if he had to take out a loan to finance it. Still, as far as Thanh is concerned, life remains hard.

Finally, I asked him if he had ever thought of leaving his village and moving to the Mekong River delta, where there is more land and it is much easier to make a living. "I want to die in my native land, even if my stomach is hungry," Thanh insisted, reflecting a common Vietnamese desire to be buried near ancestors.

The Red River delta produces nearly one-quarter of Vietnam's rice, but that is barely enough to feed its dense population, even in good years. The northern delta, with its sixteen million people and 1.6 million hectares of land, is far less productive than the Mekong region, whose grain surplus has turned Vietnam into a major rice exporter. A government survey conducted in 1993 found that 72 percent of farmers in the Red River delta stated that their lives had improved since 1990; only 8 percent said their lives had gotten worse. (Nationwide, 52 percent of the farmers indicated that they were better off, 18 percent said their living standards had declined, and the remaining 30 percent reported that their lives hadn't changed).[8] Although food production in the Red River delta has risen sharply since the government abandoned farm cooperatives, its per-capita output in 1993 reached only 371 kilograms, just over half the 696 kilogram average in the Mekong River region.

The low-lying provinces of the Red River delta have a population density of roughly 1,045 people per square kilometer, almost three times the level of the Mekong River region. In Thai Binh province, along the coast, the level reaches more than 1,500 people, and because fields are so small in the Red River delta, most farmers are out of work at least half the year. To make matters worse, the Red River delta is hit each August and September by severe flooding that takes a heavy toll on agricultural output. The river and its tributaries do not have a natural reservoir such as the Mekong River's Tonle Sap Lake in Cambodia, which limits flooding by absorbing huge amounts of excess water during the monsoon rains.

To deal with flooding, the Red River delta's inhabitants have always turned to building dikes. The first dike was constructed two thousand years ago, and by the thirteenth century embankments had been extended all the way to the South China Sea. The dikes, however, prevent sediment from running onto the fields, causing the beds of the Red River and its tributaries to rise. As a result, the riverbeds in many areas have risen to levels two to three meters higher than the surrounding countryside, making it difficult to drain the fields during annual monsoon rains. After the government began collectivizing agriculture in 1960 it built more than two dozen massive drainage and irrigation systems that covered nearly one-third of the Red River delta. Yet much of the equipment in these stations is now old and breaks down often, while the archaic electricity distribution grid causes frequent power failures that delay water pumping.

Until a few years ago the Red River delta also had many small industrial enterprises producing low-quality carpets, textiles, and handicraft goods for the former Soviet Union, but with the collapse of the Soviet empire and Hanoi's decision to stop subsidies to financially ailing state enterprises, many of these workshops have been shut down. These closures have added to unemployment in the region and to the competition for land as people thrown out of work return to farming.

In spite of this, the rural economy of the Red River delta is undergoing dramatic changes. Many farmers are supplementing their incomes significantly with nonfarming activities. For example, Ninh Hiep, one of the delta's most prosperous villages, has become a major trading center that supplies many of the textiles and garments for Hanoi's markets. Other villages are producing ceramics or raising frogs, snails, and snakes for export to China.

Even with its dense population, the Red River delta still has the potential to provide more jobs. As director of Hanoi's Agriculture Science Institute Dao The Tuan argues, the delta's mild winters, for instance, could be exploited to produce vegetables such as tomatoes, potatoes, and onions for Asian countries whose winters are either too hot or too cold to grow these products.

In the 1980s the delta grew large quantities of fresh produce for Siberia but lost this market with the disintegration of the Soviet Union. To become a major producer of cash crops, however, the Red River delta needs to snare new foreign markets in such countries as Japan and Taiwan. The delta also needs to improve local packing facilities and upgrade its roads and ports to transport fresh produce quickly.[9]

Dynamics of Despair

Ly Seo Zung belongs among the ranks of those who have profited least from Hanoi's economic reforms: the country's ethnic minorities. The shy, fifty-seven-year-old Hmong grandfather lives in Ngay Phong Tru village, near the top of a steep mountain in the ruggedly beautiful Lao Cai province in northwestern Vietnam. Ly fled here with his family in 1979 as Chinese troops approached his village at the height of their invasion of Vietnam. In his old village, about twenty kilometers north of his new home, he used slash-and-burn farming techniques to grow corn on nearby mountain slopes.

At Ngay Phong Tru, Ly plants wet rice on a small plot in a valley down the mountain from his village. Illiterate and not sure how big his plot is, Ly says he produces enough corn and rice to feed his family for about nine months each year. The Hmong farmer raises a few chickens and a pig (which share the family's dark, dusty, one-room mud hut) to buy grain for the remaining months. Ly's home has neither running water nor a kerosene lamp to provide light at night. Behind the house one of his daughters is husking rice for dinner on a simple mill consisting of a log attached to a crude stand and a hollowed-out stump. With a sleeping baby tied to her back she lifts the log with her foot and lets it thump down onto the kernels of grain inside the stump, repeating this over and over for an hour until she has milled enough rice for the family's evening meal.

Ly has planted ten plum trees that he hopes will soon add to the family's income. The price he and the fourteen other families in his village get for their fruit, however, will be poor until their district gets better road links to markets in the Red River delta.

Owing to the difficulty of moving bulkier products to the market, some of Ly's neighbors have taken to raising opium poppies, even though it is illegal. (A police chief in nearby Sapa says some of the opium production, which has increased under the reforms, is for local consumption, but much of the crop is smuggled to China or overseas through Vietnam's airports.)

Ly at first is not sure how many children he has and takes a long drag on his bamboo water pipe while tabulating the total; he finally settles on ten. His four oldest children—a son and three daughters— are married and have moved in with their in-laws. The other six children still live with Ly. His oldest son attended school for five years in their old village. None of the others have been able to study because the closest school is nearly twelve kilometers away by foot, in the district town of Bac Ha. Despite Vietnam's impressive overall literacy figures, only one in ten Hmong—and only 3 percent of Hmong women—can read and write.[10] The village's biggest health problem is malaria, which plagued two members of Ly's family in 1992. The closest clinic is near the school, almost half a day's walk away. Life in Ngay Phong Tru is harsh by any standards. Still, Ly is glad he moved. "In our old village, we had no land," he says. "Here there's more opportunity to make a living."

Vietnam's fifty-three ethnic minority groups number just over eight million people, or approximately 11 percent of the country's population. The largest of these—the Tay, Hmong, Dao, Chinese, Khmer, Muong, Thai, and Jarai—each have from 100,000 to one million people. The half dozen smallest groups have less than 1,000 people each. Except for the Khmer, who farm in the Mekong delta, and the ethnic Chinese, who live mainly in Ho Chi Minh City and other lowland towns, most of the minority peoples live in the central highlands and in the northern mountain regions that make up three-quarters of Vietnam's land area.

Rapid population growth among the minorities, coupled with the migration of several million ethnic Vietnamese from the over-crowded deltas to the highlands since the late 1970s, have caused a critical land shortage in the highlands. The persistent search for food has led to the rapid destruction of the country's forests and a sharp decline in soil fertility, reducing the ability of minority farmers to eke out a living.

In an attempt to save what is left of Vietnam's dwindling forests, Hanoi instituted a policy to resettle migratory slash-and-burn farmers such as Ly. Since 1968 almost two million of the country's nearly three million shifting cultivators have been resettled, but, according to forestry ministry officials responsible for the project, this program has had only limited success. Of those resettled in fixed villages, roughly 70 percent continue to practice slash-and-burn farming, mainly because the government lacks the resources to build irrigation systems, roads, and schools to keep people from moving. And yet, experts warn, pressure on land in the highlands is so acute that Vietnam's hills can no longer sustain slash-and-burn farming. They say that land shortages are forcing shorter fallow cycles that do not give nature time to replenish the land.

Land scarcity also threatens what remains of Vietnam's forests. In Lao Cai province, where Ly lives, the forest cover by the late 1980s had fallen to 16 percent, down from 44 percent at the end of World War II, says Nguyen Huy Phon, deputy director of Hanoi's Forestry Inventory and Planning Institute. In the neighboring provinces of

Lai Chau and Son La, this figure had dropped below 10 percent. Deforestation has created nearly ten million hectares of barren hills in northern Vietnam, posing critical environmental risks. Phon blames several recent devastating flash floods in Vietnam's northern provinces for the destruction of mountain forests. Also, soil erosion and silting threaten the region's hydroelectricity dams and irrigation systems.[11]

Rural Vietnam's water supply is threatened as well, as farming families increase the indiscriminate use of chemical fertilizers and pesticides. The number of pesticides, many of them smuggled into the country from China, has exploded in recent years. So far the government has done little to educate farmers about correct pesticide usage and the possible side effects to their water supply. At the same time, thousands of small workshops have begun processing manioc or milling rice in the countryside, dumping huge quantities of untreated waste directly into rivers and streams. The most seriously affected areas are Ha Tay, Nam Ha, and Ha Bac in the north, and Ho Chi Minh City and Can Tho in the south.[12]

The country's wildlife is also endangered by too many people trying to live on too little land. Gibbons, leaf monkeys, slow lorises, and other species considered "extremely threatened" by the Convention on the International Trade in Endangered Species are for sale in Vietnam's markets and are smuggled to China, Hong Kong, and Taiwan for exotic restaurants or to be raised as pets. Environmentalists claim hunters have wiped out some two hundred species of birds over the past four decades.

Vietnam, like many neighboring countries, faces a dilemma: how to balance its economic development with the cost of environmental protection. Unlike many other countries in Asia, however, Vietnam does not have the luxury of developing first and worrying about its environment later. Vietnam has "very little environmental capital, such as forests, left to waste," warns David Dapice of the Harvard Institute for International Development. "Thailand could destroy its forests as its economy grew, but Vietnam's forests are already depleted," he observes. "Further neglect is not really an option."

Yet, Vietnamese environmentalists argue, there is a limit to what the country can do until it achieves a higher standard of living. "I often talk to farmers about the value of protecting mangroves and wildlife," says Le Dien Duc of Hanoi University's Center for Natural Resources Management and Environmental Studies. "They smile at me and say: 'Your talk is very interesting, but we're starving. We have nothing to eat.' "

Stuck at the Bottom

The autumn harvest has just been completed in Quang Thach village along the coast of north-central Vietnam, about two hundred kilometers south of Hanoi. Naked boys splash in a small stream, while water buffalo chomp on giant stacks of straw. Two women with flat rattan baskets are winnowing rice for dinner.

These idyllic scenes outside the front door of Dao Tam Tu's house do little to help this frail, seventy-one-year-old Vietnamese farmer forget that his family's life has not improved much under the Communist Party's economic reforms. Tu's 1,440-square-meter plot in 1993 produced only 280 kilograms of rice, far short of the amount needed to feed his wife, two grown sons, and their wives and three children. The family cannot plant a second crop on their fields because they lie at the far end of an irrigation system, meaning they rarely get water during the dry season. The village does not have electricity either, making it impossible to utilize a pumping station to increase the flow of water, even if they could afford to install one.

To boost their income, Tu's sons and daughters-in-law look for day-labor jobs with richer neighbors, earning 7 to 9 cents a day. Tu says the four of them average a total of about $4.50 a month, just enough to provide the extended family with one meal a day of rice and vegetables and a second one of thin rice soup. About once a week the family shares a few pieces of dried, salted pork ribs.

Vietnam's peasants spend 70 percent of their incomes just on feeding their families, and two-fifths of their children suffer from malnutrition.[13] Over half the people in central Vietnam consume less than 1,500 calories each day, substantially less than the minimum of 2,100 calories recommended by the United Nations' World Health Organization.

Tu spends most of his day in bed and can no longer contribute much to the family's income. The right side of his body has been partially paralyzed since he was injured in a fall several years ago. When he first got hurt, a local clinic gave him some free medicine, but he hasn't been back for treatment because he can't afford the fees recently introduced by the government.

Tu's two youngest grandchildren study in the first and second grades. The family pays monthly school fees of 45 cents for each of them. The oldest grandson, a thirteen-year-old, tries to supplement the family income by fishing in a nearby stream. "He dropped out of school after the third grade," says Tu. "He had nothing to eat. Even if school was free he wouldn't be able to study because his stomach would be empty."

Why does Tu think his village is so poor? "We have too little land, and in July and August, we suffer from floods and typhoons which seriously damage our crops," he says. "We have no capital to invest in our fields. The village has offered my family credit, but we don't dare accept it," he explains, adding: "We're afraid we won't be able to pay it back, and then they'll take away our house." Tu's family managed a few years ago to build a one-room brick house to protect them from northern Vietnam's harsh winters. They could not afford tiles, however, and the roof is made of thatch, which has to be replaced every year.

The nine-member family's furniture—all of it made from crudely sawn wood—consists of three single beds, a small, beat-up table, and four small, rickety chairs. Tu laments the fact that he can't afford to put up an altar to venerate his parents. The only real decoration in the house is a faded picture of Ho Chi Minh on the wall. One of Tu's daughters-in-law serves tea, which she pours into a couple of stained, cracked cups, while he talks about his life. Tu joined Ho's

Viet Minh army in 1945 to fight the French, and following independence nine years later was appointed to serve as a part-time village cadre. "I'd like to visit Uncle Ho's mausoleum, but I can't afford it," he says, referring to the imposing Soviet-built building in Hanoi, where hundreds of people line up each day to view the revolutionary's embalmed body.

The family cannot afford a bicycle for transport, so they would have trouble moving goods to the market even if they produced a surplus. The nearest road is two kilometers away. Tu does not have a radio to listen to the news and says he has no idea who was elected premier or who was chosen to head the Communist Party back in 1991. It has been five years since he saw his last movie and more than seven years since he visited the provincial capital only a dozen kilometers away. As miserable as it may seem, Tu insists his life is better than it was in the past. "Before, under the co-op system, our life was much harder because no one invested in their fields," he says. "Now it's our own land, and we invest more to get a bigger yield." Tu's life was even more wretched during the colonial period. "Life improved a lot under Uncle Ho," he says, referring to the Communists' land reform program that gave every farmer a plot of land. "Before that, we were literally just beggars."

Though Ho Chi Minh City, Hanoi, Vung Tau, and parts of the Mekong delta are booming, Tu and millions of other farmers are being left far behind. While the standard of living for most of Vietnam has improved under the reforms, the quality of life for others—minorities, those in backward regions such as Thanh Hoa, the unemployed, retirees, and many government employees—has remained the same or deteriorated. For them the flashy billboards, imported motorcycles, and construction boom of the cities seem a million miles away.

The World Bank–sponsored living standards survey completed in 1993 found that the consumption level of 51 percent of Vietnam's population falls below a widely used international poverty line. (The poverty line was set at roughly $97 per person per year, based upon a basket of goods that provides 2,100 calories of food per person per day, as well as some nonfood items, reflecting the cost of basic goods consumed by people who just reach the poverty line.) By comparison, this figure stands at only 9 percent in China and 16 percent in Thailand, two countries where the poverty rates two or three decades ago were similar to those in Vietnam today.[14]

Half of Vietnam's poor people—or a quarter of the population—are so impoverished that they cannot meet their daily basic calorie requirements even if they spend all of their income on food. At the same time there are wide regional income differences within the country. The incidence of poverty along the north-central coast, where Tu lives, stands at a whopping 71 percent, compared to only 33 percent in the southeast, where Ho Chi Minh City is located. Ethnic minorities face the highest incidence of poverty, with the figures near 100 percent among the Hmong of the northern mountain regions. Average per capita spending in the north-central region reaches only $89 a year, less than half the $182 average in the southeast. The national average is approximately $127.

Researchers also found sharp variations in the growth rates of different regions. The economy of the southeast—which includes Ho Chi Minh City, the industrial town of Bien Hoa, and Vung Tau, hub for most of the country's offshore oil exploration activities—is growing a spectacular 15 percent a year, nearly double the nationwide average of 8 percent. The north-central coast, meanwhile, is growing by only 2.5 percent, just a fraction higher than the population increase.[15]

The survey found that the rural areas with the highest incidence of poverty suffered most from shortages of land, jobs, and capital. They also had the fewest developed roads and irrigation systems. "Just because Vietnam has become a major rice exporter doesn't mean the life of peasants has improved much," a senior United Nations official in Hanoi observes. "The gap between the rich and the poor is getting wider." Overall, the household survey found, poverty reached 57 percent in rural areas, more than twice the rate of 26 percent in cities. Nine-tenths of Vietnam's poorest live in the countryside, while two-thirds of the wealthiest live in the cities. In addition, the study found that average per-capita spending in the cities each year is over $155, nearly 50 percent higher than in the country-side.[16]

"The growing gap is dangerous for Vietnam's political stability," warns a Vietnamese sociologist in Hanoi, who has researched the impact of the reforms. The country's history has been interrupted repeatedly by peasant uprisings, including the one that brought the Communists to power with the promise that they would create a more egalitarian society. So far, however, Vietnamese farmers have not staged demonstrations like peasants in China, who have protested increasing taxes, corruption, and wealth in the cities. Still, disap-pointment sometimes bubbles to the surface. "We're frustrated that so much investment goes to the cities," complains Bui Thai Buon, deputy director of the agricultural service department in Thanh Hoa province, where Tu's village is located. "We only ask the govern-ment to be fair," says Buon, a member of Vietnam's Muong minor-ity group.

Despite the high levels of poverty, the country's social indicators are surprisingly good. The literacy rate stands at 88 percent, which is better than many countries with five times Vietnam's income. Life expectancy is an impressive sixty-seven years, while mortality among children under five years is only one-third that of other low-income countries such as Indonesia, the Philippines, India, and Bangladesh. Much of this can be attributed to the Vietnamese Communists' em-phasis on health and education after they seized power.

If Vietnam continues to grow by approximately 8 percent a year until the end of the decade, the incidence of poverty will drop to 29 percent of the population by the year 2000, according to World Bank calculations. This means that nearly half of the poor in Viet-nam today will pull themselves out of poverty before the beginning of the next millennium—that is, if the country manages to maintain its remarkable growth rates. Unless there are changes in the regional disparities of growth, however, the incidence of poverty will fall insignificantly in the already poor rural north-central coast, while dropping to almost zero in the urban southeast.[17]

Parading for Work

Long before dawn breaks over Hanoi each morning, hundreds of young men from the countryside begin gathering along Lang Ha Street, a divided, tree-lined thoroughfare in the western suburbs of the capital. The street is best known for its dozens of shops selling wood, nails, plumbing pipes, roofing tiles, and other construction materials. The men arrive hoping that some of the buyers will come seeking construction workers as well.

The Lang Ha labor market, one of about half a dozen that gather each day at various places around Hanoi, marks another change since the Communist Party initiated its reforms. Until a few years ago city officials regularly rounded up migrants without residence papers and trundled them back to their farm cooperatives in the countryside. Today, however, migrant workers are not only tolerated but also have become a source of cheap labor for Hanoi's construction boom.

Vietnamese farmers, like those in many other developing countries, are attracted to cities owing to the increasing difficulties of making a living in the countryside. Although farmers have been given their own fields under the reforms, plots in the Red River delta surrounding Hanoi are so small that many peasants have to look for other jobs to support their families.

The World Bank report on poverty found that 26 percent of Vietnam's rural labor force is underemployed.[18] (Unemployment in Vietnam officially stands at 6 percent, but the jobless rate in urban areas is estimated by the U.N.'s International Labor Organization at 25 percent.)[19] With the cost of consumer goods and services rising much faster than the price of rice, farmers face increasing difficulties in making ends meet. Some, like farmer Tu's children, look for jobs with wealthier neighbors. Others go to the cities during the slow agricultural season to pedal *cyclos*, recycle waste bottles and newspapers, or to wash dishes in the hundreds of makeshift sidewalk restaurants that have sprung up in recent years. So far, migration in Vietnam is small compared to China, where nearly 100 million peo-

ple wander the country looking for work. Still, Hanoi in 1993 recorded an estimated 100,000 new migrants, two times the figure for
the previous year.[20] The flow into Ho Chi Minh City is thought to
be even higher, and neither city is equipped to accommodate so
many new arrivals.

"I don't earn enough from farming to feed my family," says Vu
Anh Xuong, a muscular, forty-year-old farmer from Ha Tay province, southwest of the capital, who is working on a new housing
compound for Hanoi's nouveaux riches. For seven months each year
Xuong works as a carpenter for a Hanoi-based construction company.

Even though his 2,880-square-meter plot is larger than that
farmed by many northern peasants, "the price of rice is so low that I
only earn enough from two crops to feed my family for four
months," he points out. As a construction worker Xuong earns
about $36 a month, of which he sends nearly a third home to his
wife and two children. "If construction salaries increased, I would
move my family to Hanoi," Xuong says.

Vietnamese officials fear that the hardship of making a living in
the crowded countryside coupled with rising urban wages could
induce a surge of workers into the cities, as has happened in Latin
America and Africa. Such a development would further exacerbate
urban unemployment. Despite the recent success of agriculture in
Vietnam, farmers face some intimidating obstacles. Much of the
rapid growth over the past few years was prompted by the Communist Party's decision to return land to the peasants, something that
could only happen once. Without sizable investments the rapid production increases since the late 1980s will soon peter out.

The country is one of the most densely populated nations on
earth, with just one-tenth of a hectare of farmland per person. Its
forests, already covering less than one-quarter of Vietnam's land area,
continue shrinking by approximately 200,000 hectares a year as the
rural poor seek new fields in the hills and mountains. Economists
warn that Vietnamese leaders can ill afford to ignore the countryside
and focus solely on rapid industrialization. Farmers are the backbone

of the nation, and the nation's success depends on their welfare. Agriculture will have to drive Vietnam's economy through the 1990s, for industry cannot successfully absorb the country's rural inhabitants all at once. The countryside is home to fully 78 percent of Vietnam's population—some fifty-seven million people.

Moreover, farmers provide 36 percent of the nation's total economic output and nearly one-tenth of its export earnings. The country will not get rich from agriculture, but this sector still has potential to expand. Only a third of Vietnam's rice fields are irrigated and only half are double-cropped. The country's average yield is just over three tons per hectare, only about half the level harvested by Chinese farmers.[21]

All of Asia's roaring economies (except for city-states Hong Kong and Singapore) invested heavily in their farmers. "No rapidly growing Asian economy . . . has managed to grow rapidly without first developing a solid rural base," argues Dapice, who advises the Vietnamese government on economic reform. "Ironically, the nations that looked after their rural sector not only did better in reducing poverty, but [they] also had faster non-farm growth than those that simply supported industry." Dapice points out that investing in agriculture will boost other sectors of the economy as well. "As large numbers of farmers buy local consumer goods and demand products and services to support their growing output, both urban and rural non-farm output grows," he states. "The rural non-farm growth provides jobs close to where people live and slows, without coercion, a too-rapid inflow into urban areas which might otherwise face crowding and expensive investments in infrastructure."[22]

Boosting Vietnam's agriculture, however, will require increased investment. Perhaps none will be more important than investing in rural roads, most of which are currently old and in poor shape. Of the country's roughly 100,000 kilometers of roads, less than 15 percent have a hard surface.

The World Bank–sponsored living standards survey found that people living in communities located near all-weather roads had annual per-capita expenditures of nearly $118, some 26 percent higher than those who did not have easy access to roads. "In the absence of good transportation, agricultural development is greatly hindered: prices for inputs are higher and output lower; marketing of high value perishable products is impossible; and access to new technology and information is more limited," the World Bank concludes. "The presence of all-weather roads improves the flow of goods, services, and information. This leads to greater economic diversification, labor mobility (in and out of the household's home village), more productive use of farm land, and higher living standards."[23]

Dapice argues that the rates of return following road repairs alone often reach as much as 50 percent a year. In addition to lowering marketing costs and increasing competition, improved roads make it easier for food-processing industries to develop. Roads create a more vibrant national economy by making it possible for different parts of the country to trade with each other as well.[24] Rehabilitating and expanding crumbling irrigation systems is another major priority. The World Bank claims that irrigation facilities would increase farm output by 645 kilograms per hectare per year.[25]

Vietnam must also expand credit to farm households. Even though the state-owned Agricultural Bank is rapidly expanding lending, it only has enough capital to provide short-term credits to about one-third of the country's farmers. In addition, Hanoi needs to breathe new life into its extension services that prior to the reforms introduced farmers to the latest innovations in farming techniques and helped them to overcome problems such as pest attacks on crops. Hanoi also needs to step up its research on new high-yield crop varieties. World Bank economists estimate that an effective extension service, coupled with good seeds and access to inputs, can ratchet up production by more than 50 percent.[26]

Vietnam must also explore ways to absorb more of its rural work force. Neighboring China soaked up more than one hundred million surplus rural workers by encouraging townships to set up myriads of local enterprises. These workshops, which produce everything from metal buckets to silk carpets, often employ less than one hundred workers each, but by the early 1990s they were contributing roughly one-third of China's gross national product.

Despite the advantages of investing in rural areas, it is very possible that Vietnamese officials as well as foreign aid donors and investors will be tempted to focus on more glamorous projects in the cities. At least some technocrats recognize this danger: An official report prepared for a donors' conference in Paris in late 1993 expressed "concern that the donor community may be attracted to supporting high profile programmes and projects, to the detriment of rural infrastructure investment and other forms of support for the agriculture sector."[27]

Gentleman Farmer

Not all Vietnamese farmers are poor. Le Ngoc Minh, fifty-nine, is not only one of the country's richest men but also is a card-carrying Communist in good standing. Even though the country's law limits one person's land holdings to no more than three hectares, Ngoc cultivates a whopping 640 hectares of land in southern Vietnam. Despite Communist Party rules forbidding its members from hiring employees other than family members, the amiable gentleman farmer employs 140 people full time, as well as hundreds of seasonal workers.

"The government limits the size of one person's farming fields, but there's no limit in terms of his land holdings," Ngoc says, pointing out the loophole that allowed him to gain control of land that had not been developed for agriculture. He doesn't take any chances, though. "I'm the real owner, but I register it in the name of my wife, mother, children, and other relatives." Among the handful of prominent new businessmen to emerge in Vietnam in the last ten years, Ngoc is the first to invest in agriculture. Most of his peers have focused on garments, textiles, and shoes for export. Ngoc says his income in 1992 topped $250,000, a hearty sum in a country where most peasants earn less than $100 a year. Farming is not even Ngoc's "real" job. Officially he is chairman of the Department of Economics and Sociology at Ho Chi Minh City's Social Sciences Institute. Like countless other state employees, he has found a way to supplement his woefully small government salary.

Despite his success, Ngoc still looks more like a self-effacing farmer than a prominent entrepreneur. The first time I met him at his institute he was wearing a stained, crumpled shirt, threadbare trousers, and an old pair of sandals. His wire-rimmed glasses were tilted at an angle on his head, and it had been months since he had his last haircut. Ngoc acquired his first forty hectares of land in 1990, in the central-highlands province of Lam Dong. Years earlier the government had designated this land for a "new economic zone," but had done nothing to develop it. No one from Vietnam's densely populated cities or the northern Red River delta had been willing to migrate to this remote, poorly developed region. Unable to fulfill their goals, local officials "sold" the land to Ngoc for a mere 45 cents a hectare. As part of the package, he agreed to build a health clinic and a kindergarten in the district and to construct a road linking his fields to the main highway.

Ngoc hired local peasants to clear the land and plant sugar cane and tea shrubs, along with banana, mango, durian, and avocado trees. Because he opened up new land for cultivation, the authorities granted him a three-year tax holiday on his earnings. What about the country's constitution, which holds fast to the Communist notion that land belongs to the public? "They avoided using the word *selling* land," Ngoc says of the officials. "Instead they said they were transferring the land-use rights to me." During the handover ceremony, he recalls, the local Communist Party boss asked him whether he feared that the government would take the land back, as had happened in the north in 1956 and in the south two decades later. "I told him if the policy changes, it will take at least one hundred years," Ngoc says. "And in the worst case, I'll accept it if they really give the land to the peasants. I'm a Communist and I fought for them for a long time."

Since this first land deal Ngoc has obtained another 360 hectares in Lam Dong. In addition, an unprofitable state farm in Dong Nai, a coastal province northeast of Ho Chi Minh City, "sold" him some 200 hectares on which he raises sugar cane. At the same time, he has purchased from private farmers the rights to another forty hectares near the southern beach resort of Vung Tau. Here, Ngoc grows cashew nuts, custard apples, and eucalyptus trees.

Soaring real estate prices in this popular coastal town have turned Ngoc into one of Vietnam's first new U.S.-dollar millionaires since the Communist victory two decades ago. The scholar-farmer reaped a windfall, at least on paper, when the government rezoned his Vung Tau land for housing. Instantly, the value of his forty hectares shot up to $780,000, ten times what he had paid for it.

Ngoc's foray into agribusiness was not hurt by his revolutionary credentials. His father was Le Viet Luong, one the first members of the Indochinese Communist Party, founded in 1930, and a long-time associate of General Vo Nguyen Giap, the legendary strategist best known for defeating the French colonial army at Dien Bien Phu in 1954. His mother participated in the 1930 Nghe Tinh peasant uprising against French rule in north-central Vietnam and was arrested by police loyal to her father, a provincial governor appointed by the French. Ngoc's grandfather even adopted a sister of Ho Chi Minh. In 1946, Ngoc, then age nine, went with his father to live in one of the revolutionary army's mountain bases near Vietnam's border with China. Six years later he was sent to study in China, along with many other children of Vietnam's future Communist leaders. Ngoc graduated in 1959 with a specialty in Chinese and Russian literature.

When he returned to Vietnam, he was appointed to the Philosophy Institute of Hanoi's Social and Natural Science Committee. After the conflict between China and the Soviet Union (both of whom supported Vietnam in its war with the United States) burst into the open in the early 1960s, his institute was given the job of deciding "which country was a real friend of Vietnam and which one was revisionist," Ngoc says. "Even though I had been influenced by

Chinese literature and philosophy, I was pro-Russian," he explains, reflecting a sentiment common among many Vietnamese at the time.

Following Vietnam's Communist victory in 1975, Ngoc moved to Ho Chi Minh City, where he researched labor issues for the Social Sciences Institute. Four years later, with the Communist Party reluctantly inching toward economic reform, he set up a family workshop that produced yeast from sugar cane scraps. Over the next decade he made enough money to invest in his agribusiness.

Ngoc also used some of his earnings to design a marvelous house for his family in the western suburbs of Ho Chi Minh City. "I tried to integrate Eastern and Western styles, the old and the modern," Ngoc says of his five-bedroom mansion, divided into two sections by a fish pond. The living area is Western; the arches and the curved, tiled roof are Asian. One of the rooms has an elaborate altar dedicated to the veneration of his ancestors. Much of the house's charming mother-of-pearl inlaid furniture was built by Ngoc's grandfather one hundred years ago, when he served as a scholar-official in the Nguyen dynasty. An immaculately manicured garden, sections of which depict the northern, central, and southern regions of Vietnam, surrounds the residence. "The house reflects my contradictions," Ngoc notes. "I come from a feudal Asian family, but I'm a Communist and I've been Westernized."

Ngoc's wife too has impeccable credentials. She is the daughter of a legendary hero of Vietnam's struggle against France, who was charged with masterminding the assassination of a French police chief in Saigon in the 1940s. She later studied in the Soviet Union and taught in Ho Chi Minh City's Economics University until retiring a few years ago. Both of their daughters and the oldest daughter's husband are graduates of the Economics University.

Ngoc is not bothered by the apparent contradiction of being a rich socialist. "When I bought the state farm in Dong Nai, I told the director that you're only a good Communist if you carry out your obligations to your workers," he says. "I'll set up a private farm to make profit, but the workers will earn more and will be happier to work for me," he says, alluding to the low salaries paid in state enterprises. "So which of us is a better Communist?" But why does this apparent capitalist bother maintaining his membership in the Communist Party? "In reality," Ngoc admits, "the old idea of establishing a socialist bloc died in 1986. But socialism is a dream that all people should enjoy social equality and happiness," he says. "If you think of socialism in that way, it's still valid."[28]

6

A Tale of Two Cities

◆ ◆ ◆

Good Morning Saigon

It's Saturday night in this city that used to be called Saigon, and one shiny new Honda Dream II motorbike after another pulls up to a discotheque on Dong Khoi Street. Young men in silk shirts and pleated pants drop off women dolled up in tight miniskirts, high heels, coiffured hair, and layers of makeup. Inside, under pulsating strobe lights, Vietnamese yuppies smoke imported cigarettes, drink beer from the city's newly opened Heineken joint-venture brewery, and dance to earsplitting American rock music.

A money-changer springs out of a dark doorway as two Westerners cross the street in front of the disco. "Do-la . . . do-la, okay?" the middle-aged man pleads in pigeon English. He skips backward down the block in front of the two foreigners, repeating his offer. When he finally turns to leave, he nearly trips over a beggar—a former soldier who lost both legs to a mine—shuttling himself along the sidewalk on a dirty piece of cardboard with his hands.

It is here on Dong Khoi Street, at the edge of the Saigon River, that Vietnam's past bumps into its present and its future. Under the French the street was known as Rue Catinat, after the French ship sent to Vietnam in the 1850s to demand the surrender of its emperor. After the country won its independence a century later the street's name was changed to Tu Do, meaning freedom. During the American war (as the Vietnam War is known in Vietnam) this thoroughfare was lined with shops and bars; it is famous as a place where U.S. soldiers came to drink and to meet prostitutes.

The Communists abruptly ended all of this in 1975, shutting down the private shops and renaming the street Dong Khoi, meaning uprising. This prompted some irreverent Saigonese to joke that they had "lost their freedom after staging an uprising." Not surprisingly, now that Vietnam's once-stalwart Marxists have taken the leap toward capitalism, Dong Khoi is once again sizzling with commercial activity. A quiet stroll along Dong Khoi these days is nearly impossible. A foreign visitor brave enough to leave his or her hotel on foot will quickly encounter a squadron of child pickpockets and street hustlers selling everything from pornographic playing cards to Wrigley's chewing gum and used postage stamps.

After suffering through decades of war, near economic collapse, and the flight of thousands of boat people, Ho Chi Minh City today has recaptured its title as Vietnam's most vibrant city. In the midst of all of this bustle it is sometimes easy to forget that two decades ago the city was so humiliated by its conquerors that it had to forfeit its name. "Ho Chi Minh City is starting to look a lot like the old Saigon," my boss, Peter Kann, observed during a visit to Vietnam in 1993. "It's a lot more like the Saigon of 1968 than like the Saigon of 1985." Kann, now president of Dow Jones & Company, was the *Wall Street Journal* correspondent in Vietnam during the war. He had returned for a visit on the tenth anniversary of the 1975 Communist victory, but this was still more than a year before the Communist Party would launch its "second revolution" in 1986.

The elegant French colonial buildings Kann encountered on Dong Khoi Street in 1985 were the same ones he had left a decade earlier but were badly run down, and the atmosphere on the street had changed completely. The old boutiques and bars were closed; a handful of them had been converted into gloomy state-run shops offering poor-quality lacquerware and bamboo wall hangings to foreign tourists, most of whom came from the former Soviet Union and Eastern Europe. Sullen clerks sat gossiping behind dusty counters trying to avoid interruptions from customers, who were viewed as nuisances. The most common outfit for both women and men at that time was blue or white shirts worn outside dark trousers. By seven in the evening most stores and restaurants had closed, and by nine most people in this once bustling "Pearl of the Orient" were in bed.

The Communist government nearly bankrupted Ho Chi Minh City with its imposition of central economic planning, ration cards, and campaigns to strip the city's capitalists of their wealth, but getting back down to business after the 1986 reforms was fairly easy for the old Saigon. The city of 4.5 million people that Kann revisited in 1993 was entirely different from the one he had encountered eight years earlier. The reincarnation had begun slowly in the early 1980s as private peddlers—mainly women with baskets hung from bamboo carrying poles balanced across their shoulders—began walking the streets, hawking fruit, coconut-milk desserts, and fresh baguettes. Others set out blue jeans, shampoo, medicines, and other consumer goods sent in by their refugee relatives abroad. As confidence in the reforms took hold in the late 1980s, shopkeepers on Dong Khoi and the nearby shopping streets of Nguyen Hue and Le Loi reopened their shutters. The city regained its flashing neon lights, display windows sported imported Citizen watches and mannequins decked out in the latest women's fashions, and clerks, now paid commissions for sales instead of being reimbursed for just showing up, cheerfully served their customers.

The streets became a constant hubbub of shoppers, blaring music, food smells, honking motorbikes, and hustlers. Each alley seemed to have its own specialty: for some it was spicy noodle soup or blended fruit drinks, while for others it was smuggled foreign cigarettes, imported alcohol, paper supplies, or "Good Morning, Vietnam" T-shirts. Almost every block seemed to have a stall selling glossy calendars featuring Western pinup girls, the Virgin Mary, or cuddly kittens.

In an apparent effort not to offend the United States, with which Vietnam has now normalized diplomatic relations, Ho Chi Minh City has dropped the word *American* from the name of its War

Crimes Museum. Few local residents (over half of whom were born after 1975) bother to visit the museum, with its rusty American howitzers and tanks or the model of the infamous "tiger cages," where many Communist prisoners once were detained. Grim, grainy pictures of the My Lai massacre and the South Vietnamese officer executing a Communist suspect are fading on the museum walls.

Tourists from Taiwan—which backed the U.S. war effort in Vietnam—make up the largest group of museum visitors. After decades of pain and hunger most Vietnamese seem to want to get on with their lives. They don't spend time pondering the meaning of war and the millions of deaths now that the victorious Communists emulate the regime they conquered. A visitor, however, cannot help reflecting on the fact that Hanoi now courts the same capitalists it once fought so terribly at so high a cost.

By the early 1990s overseas Vietnamese and European businessmen had opened a handful of high-class bars and restaurants on Dong Khoi and nearby streets. Firms from Hong Kong had remodeled a couple of run-down hotels for the growing horde of foreign entrepreneurs and tourists who were filling existing facilities weeks in advance. Over a dozen airlines now have regular flights into a city that only a decade ago had two Air France flights a week.

A Taiwanese company in 1993 finished refurbishing the burned-out shell of a building into the city's first modern, fifteen-story glass office tower. Half of the companies that moved into this deluxe building came from the United States and Japan, demonstrating their enthusiasm for what they believe to be Asia's next frontier. Ho Chi Minh City's skyline has begun to change, although it still has a long way to go before its buildings compete with the glittering glass-and-marble high-rises of Asia's boom towns. A visitor to the rooftop of the Caravelle Hotel, from which foreign journalists watched the Communists' final assault on Saigon in 1975, now sees construction cranes dotting the landscape of Vietnam's largest city.

Construction is the most rapidly growing sector in the country's economy, soaring some 18 percent in 1994, or double the overall growth rate; the figures for Ho Chi Minh City are believed to be even higher. The pounding of pile drivers interferes with the rock music, much of it produced by overseas Vietnamese, blaring out of many storefronts. Even at night, the glare of giant lamps at construction sites reveals workers scampering up the sides of new buildings on bamboo scaffolding. Perhaps the only dilapidated structure so far to escape the hammer and paintbrush is the fortresslike U.S. Embassy building, from which thousands of Americans and Vietnamese fled by helicopter on the final night of the war in April 1975. It housed the offices of Vietnam's state oil company until Washington and Hanoi in early 1995 signed an agreement settling claims to diplomatic property seized during the war. The rooftop helicopter pad is now covered with rust.

Just down the street from the former embassy, Mercedes-Benz has opened a showroom in the compound housing Premier Vo Van Kiet's southern office. Nearby, in the giant lobby of the Ho Chi Minh City branch of the State Bank (long a key player in the march toward dyed-in-the-wool socialism) carpenters have begun preparing that most capitalist of institutions: a stock exchange. Vietnamese officials say they hope to have enough regulations in place to open an experimental stock market by 1997, but observers guess a full-fledged exchange will not be up and running before 2000. So far, Vietnam has few companies large enough to list and lacks accounting skills to measure their performance.

All of the enthusiasm about Vietnam's economic future has fired up a real estate boom. In 1992 alone property prices jumped fivefold in parts of the city. Rents for prime office space now top an annual rate of $675 per square meter, more than any other city in Southeast Asia, except Hanoi. Despite all the spending on new buildings, little is being done to upgrade the city's infrastructure, particularly its streets. Planners say traffic congestion could become a major problem in the city before the end of the 1990s.

On the Saigon River, at the southern end of Dong Khoi Street, huge illuminated billboards trumpet Sony and Philips electronic products, Tiger beer, Fuji film, and DHL couriers. A jumbled clutter of signboards at major intersections near markets and around Tan Son Nhat Airport have replaced red banners that a decade ago exhorted the city's proletariat to fulfill the Communist Party's latest five-year plan on the road to a socialist paradise.

Ho Chi Minh City is once again the engine behind Vietnam's growth, serving as an entry point through which capital, technology, and ideas make their way into the country. It is the manufacturing and service center, a key financial center, and often plays the role of matchmaker between the rural areas of southern Vietnam and the outside world. At times, however, the city seems to be caught in a time warp between its sullen Communist past and its energetic, money-hungry, somewhat raunchy capitalist future. The state-run bookstore on Dong Khoi, across from the Continental Hotel, where Graham Greene wrote *The Quiet American*, displays dusty tomes of Marx, Lenin, and Truong Chinh (a Vietnamese ideologue) next to a stack of translations of American economist Paul Samuelson's *An Introduction to Economics*. The shoppers, however, seem most enthusiastic about books teaching English and offering prescriptions on how to get rich.

It is the energetic entrepreneurs of Ho Chi Minh City who, in their rush to embrace the free market, point the way to Vietnam's future. The Communist Party's reforms caught hold here first owing to the city's more recent capitalist experience and its more modern infrastructure. By the early 1990s the city, which had only 6 percent of Vietnam's population, had captured a hefty 40 percent of the country's foreign investment licenses. It also accounted for more than a third of the country's industrial output, and contributed more than one-fifth of its exports and 30 percent of national revenue. Ho Chi Minh City is growing much faster than any other region of the country. Its output in 1995 surged over 15 percent—compared with nearly 12 percent in Hanoi and a nationwide average of 9.5 percent—and contributed nearly one-fifth of the country's total gross domestic product. Its foreign trade grew an even more impressive 39 percent.[1]

Some say the city is more prosperous today than it was during the heyday of American foreign aid. The annual per-capita income of Ho Chi Minh City is estimated at over $900, compared to just over $650 in Hanoi and a national average of around $200. Relative to nearby Singapore or Kuala Lumpur it remains a poor city, but it is quickly getting richer. Actual per-capita purchasing power in the southern metropolis is believed to have reached at least $1,000.[2]

In the late 1980s city residents snatched up black-and-white television sets and tape recorders, and a few years ago they switched to color televisions, video cassette players, refrigerators, and rice cookers. Today the craze includes washing machines, air conditioners, and microwave ovens. Foreign companies, recognizing that growing numbers of city residents have money to spend on consumer goods, have launched a television advertising war. Only hours after Washington lifted the U.S. trade embargo in 1994, PepsiCo was airing slick ads of Miss Vietnam sipping the company's "choice of a new generation." Coca-Cola, San Miguel beer, Ching Fong's motorbikes, Lux soap, and Sony Walkman were not far behind in the international battle for the hearts and minds of the city's consumers.

People are beginning to fix up homes that had been allowed to deteriorate during the heyday of socialist fervor. Many are replacing their Asian commodes with Western-style toilets and installing hot water heaters and wall tiles in their bathrooms. Judging by the furniture making its way down streets on three-wheeled pedicabs, overstuffed, fake leather couches and formica dining room sets are all the rage.

Plastic surgeons are among the busiest people in the city. Growing numbers of young women are paying to have their eyes made rounder, their breasts enlarged, or to have extra eyebrows tattooed onto their faces. Even relatively poor maids are having "nose jobs" to raise the bridges of their noses to the height common among Westerners. Growing numbers of middle-aged women get facelifts or have their abdominal fat surgically removed so they can fit back into their brightly colored, imported spandex. Dozens of aerobics clubs have opened around the city for upwardly mobile women determined to watch their waistlines.

Young people have another preoccupation. Every Sunday night, hundreds of youths on motorcycles gravitate to the center of the city for what they dub the *chay long rong*, which translates roughly as "meandering race." They cruise down Dong Khoi Street, swing right at the Saigon River and come back around the block in a rite that goes on for hours, the main goal of which seems to be for young people to show off their $2,500 motorbikes and to flirt. Those taking part are the elite, children of the politically powerful, or the nouveaux riches. Others watch from striped beach chairs set up by vendors along the sidewalks, munching on roasted strips of dried squid and sipping draft beer. Some intellectuals complain that the city today has only one value: getting rich. "They've lost their moral values," Duong Quynh Hoa, a sixty-six-year-old French-trained pediatrician and former deputy minister of health, laments about the country's youth. "Their only objective now is money." Hoa quit her job and the Communist Party in the late 1970s to protest some of its policies, including the detention of tens of thousands of former Saigon officials and military personnel in reeducation camps.

As in other Asian countries, cellular phones have become the quintessential status symbol for Vietnamese sitting around newly refurbished hotel lobbies or restaurants, but the city's new bright yellow taxis, piles of video cassette players, and partially restored glitter cannot mask the fact that not all are sharing equally in Ho Chi Minh City's new wealth. In densely packed slums, behind the soaring shade trees and the refurbished, cream-colored French villas of the city's main boulevards, thousands of the city's unemployed and permanently poor live in shacks of rusty tin and old boards. Beggars, often wounded veterans or landless peasants in tattered clothes carrying small, malnourished children, shuffle along the main thoroughfares near the city's major hotels. They have fallen through the gaps in the country's once socialist safety net.

Youthful pickpockets have become a menace. Late one night while walking down Dong Khoi to the Majestic Hotel after dinner I was approached by three intent-looking, young teenage boys carrying folded city maps. "Look out," I warned my companion, "they're after us." I clasped my left hand over my shirt pocket that contained a plane ticket and some dollars and stuck my right arm out to ward off the boys, who were poking maps into our faces insisting that we needed their merchandise to help us navigate the city. Less than ten seconds later they had passed, and I assumed we had escaped unscathed. When I got to my room, however, I noticed my watch was gone from my wrist. While two of the boys distracted us with their map-in-the-face routine, the third had slit my watch band. Over the years I have lost count of how many pens the young pickpockets on Dong Khoi Street have relieved me of.

On a nearby sidestreet a refugee family repatriated from a camp in Malaysia opened the Apocalypse Now bar in 1992. With the strains of old Doors hits and the haze of marijuana smoke, a visitor could be forgiven for thinking that he or she had set foot on the set of the Francis Ford Coppola movie. The clients were not American GIs but European and Australian tourists and businessmen, most of whom were barely out of the crib when the last desperate Americans in 1975 scrambled onto helicopters on the U.S. Embassy roof a few blocks away. Only a few months passed before police shut down Apocalypse Now and its neighbor, B 475 (as in "before 1975"). The authorities never explained exactly why—sex had been available for sale, although never openly, as in the unmarked, dimly lit *bia om* (literally, "hugging beer") cafés nearby. In the *bia om* bars young women called "flower sellers" are dressed in satiny miniskirts, hot pants, or skintight blue jeans and sit behind curtains with groups of men, necking, fondling, and offering other à la carte services. Short-term rooms are available in the cafés or nearby.

Unaccompanied males walking the streets around Dong Khoi after dark can expect to be approached by prostitutes or transvestites on motorbikes offering a "massage." Off Dong Khoi, on Nguyen Thi Minh Khai Boulevard, an army of prostitutes line up each night and openly solicit sex under a health ministry billboard that declares: ONE WIFE AND ONE HUSBAND, AVOID FEAR OF AIDS. Police estimate that the city today has some 50,000 prostitutes, about 10,000 more than were operating when the Communists took over. Many of them are unemployed women from the Mekong delta or the children of poor urban families hoping to cash in on what has become the country's most lucrative service industry. Anywhere from one-fifth to one-third of the city's prostitutes are believed to be under age eighteen.

Ho Chi Minh City police regularly shut down enterprising entrepreneurs running sex tours for tourists (mainly from Taiwan and Hong Kong) who are afraid that AIDS has reached epidemic levels in other Asian cities renowned for their sex industry. Two coffee shop rings closed in 1992—Anh Dung and Bambi—had hired surgeons to restore the hymens of prostitutes for clients willing to pay $500 or more for "virgins." Several young women told journalists that they had sold their virginity more than twenty times. Police investigating Anh Dung found that its owner, Nguyen Thi Kim Suong, employed forty full-time women in her "coffee shop" and had a network of hundreds of others who worked part-time on an on-call basis. Suong solicited clients by hiring pimps to work in more than fifteen hotels (including some operated by the country's security apparatus) around the city. According to police records, Suong, now fifty-two, has been arrested eight times since she was sixteen for engaging in prostitution, and twice more for running brothels.

Officials often blame the sudden influx of foreigners for the country's exploding sex industry, but researchers have found that nine out of ten clients are Vietnamese. Sexual permissiveness, prominent in many Asian cultures but long repressed by Vietnam's Communist leaders, has soared under the reforms. Some 54 percent of the Vietnamese men interviewed in a 1993 survey conducted by the private relief agency Care International, said they had had sex with two or more partners in the preceding two weeks.[3] "Sex with prostitutes seems to be a way for men to enjoy each other's company," says Barbara Franklin, who headed up Care's research team. "It is part of a night out with friends who share food, drink, and sometimes even sexual partners." Care's survey found that over 30 percent of the prostitutes interviewed never use condoms.

By the end of 1995 Vietnam had recorded 3,375 cases of HIV, the virus that leads to acquired immune deficiency syndrome, or AIDS. Four-fifths of the cases detected so far have been found among intravenous drug users in Ho Chi Minh City and the coastal city of Nhatrang; 293 people had full-blown AIDS, and 135 had died of the disease. Vietnamese health officials readily admit that these figures represent only the tip of the iceberg because only a small sample of the population has been tested, but an epidemic is expected. The United Nations World Health Organization estimates the number of HIV cases to be 570,000 by 1998.[4]

In early 1996, as the Communist Party prepared for its Eighth Congress scheduled for the middle of the year, the government launched a nationwide campaign against "social evils"—prostitution, pornography, gambling, and superstitions. Hundreds of videos portraying sex and violence were destroyed and pornographic posters were burned in public ceremonies. "Protection against poisonous cultural items is the duty of all society," declared billboards announcing the new morality war.

This campaign was accompanied by an offensive against foreign influences as Vietnamese officials ordered the downgrading of English-language advertisements. In a move to enforce regulations that had long been ignored, Coca-Cola and Kodak signs were painted over and newspapers were plastered over billboards advertising Sony television sets. Newspapers carried articles condemning "poisonous cultural products."

Still, most Vietnamese expect it won't be long until Ho Chi Minh City is back to the wheeling and dealing that has prompted some visitors to ask what the founder of modern Vietnam would have said if he could revisit the city that bears his name. "I can't predict what Uncle Ho would say if he were still alive," says Deputy Mayor Pham Chanh Truc, who had been imprisoned in the 1960s for opposing the U.S. military intervention in Vietnam. Truc, who holds the city's economics portfolio, blames the growing social problems on uneven development, the flood of unemployed migrants from the countryside, and the downside of the country suddenly opening itself to the outside world. Although the physical wounds of the

American war have begun to heal, psychological scars still divide Vietnam and thwart its economic take-off. In many cases it has been easier for northern victors to forgive Americans for damage they inflicted on the country than to reconcile with the war's losers in the south.

In early 1995, as Vietnam prepared for the twentieth anniversary of the Communist victory, Hanoi released its estimates of the suffering caused by two decades of conflict with the United States. More than a million northern and southern Communist soldiers had died and another two million civilians had been killed in the hostilities. Hanoi never mentioned the deaths of 200,000 southern soldiers (most of whom had been drafted) or the 360,000 others who had been crippled—most of them by mines. Many Southerners who consider themselves every bit as patriotic as their northern victors are rankled by the fact that those who opposed the Communists are still regularly referred to as "American puppets." "Our press is still celebrating victory over the Saigon army," a northern official told my deputy editor Nayan Chanda, one of the few foreign journalists who had covered the Communist victory in 1975. "Mothers of northern heroes have been decorated and given rewards, but mothers of Saigon troops have only humiliation."[5]

Many of the roughly 200,000 southern civilian and military officials sent to so-called reeducation camps after 1975—some for more than a decade—have had to survive on menial jobs since their release. Some educated, fluent English-speakers support their families today by pedaling tourists around the city on their *cyclos*. Each day dozens of alienated Southerners gather in a park across from the city's foreign affairs department, where they wait to meet officials from the Orderly Departure Program set up by the United States to provide asylum to soldiers and supporters of the former Saigon government who were persecuted after the war. "I must go to the U.S. to live because I have difficulty in my life in Vietnam," Le Duc Thanh told a foreign journalist. Thanh, now age fifty-five, had worked as a translator for the American Embassy from 1967 to 1975 but missed the evacuation because a thief had stolen the bag containing his personal documents. "Because I worked for the Americans, my children couldn't go to university and they cannot find decent jobs now," he explained. "That is why I want to go to America."[6]

Soaring Dragon

The metamorphosis of Hanoi, commonly viewed as quieter and more reserved and refined than its brasher, busier southern sibling, has been slower. Although visible scars of the wartime bombing for the most part have disappeared, years of neglect and overcrowding have given this city, long populated primarily by Communist bureaucrats and state workers, a decidedly run-down look.

When I arrived to work in the Vietnamese capital in 1990, Hanoi had few modern amenities and was a quiet backwater of Asia. Within four years, however, the city became transformed by meter taxis, mobile phones, satellite television, pizza parlors, karaoke bars, and private hotels; streets are now crowded with cafés, beauty parlors, and tailor shops.

Perhaps nothing in Hanoi has changed more dramatically than traffic. Any trip around the capital has become a hazardous venture. Although still years away from the gridlock and smog of Jakarta or Bangkok, the explosion of private motorcycles and cars in the wake of Communist reforms has created near-total anarchy on the city's streets. Until a few years ago Hanoi's traffic consisted of thousands of bicycles moving quietly at near-uniform speed down the city's tree-lined boulevards. A few trucks, buses, and diplomatic cars—mostly Russian-made Volgas and Ladas belonging to embassies from the former Soviet empire—edged their way around this procession by honking for space.

As soon as the Communist Party removed the shackles on private enterprise this subdued life ended abruptly. Hordes of farmers descend on the city each morning with fresh cabbages or squealing pigs loaded in wire-mesh baskets suspended from the backs of their bicycles, while chickens or ducks hang upside-down from their handlebars. Young Honda riders, beeping frantically, weave through traffic with as many as half a dozen Panasonic video cassette players or up to ten cases of Halida beer tied precariously to their seats. Whole families—often four or five people—squeeze onto a motorbike for a trip across town, while *cyclos* clump down the street hauling anything from passengers to newly built beds or two-meter stacks of foam rubber.

This motley jumble of vehicles fights for every available space until the horn of a Russian-made army jeep, decrepit bus, or shiny new Toyota Land Cruiser sounds threatening enough to convince drivers to move over. Somehow traffic flows along unimpeded until it reaches an intersection, where a new battle of wits and nerves unfolds. In 1993 Hanoi had less than twenty traffic lights for nearly six hundred intersections, and the aim of every driver is to find a gap and slip through without stopping. One foreign businessman calls navigating Vietnam's city streets "the ultimate video game." It isn't easy, nor is it for the faint of heart. Minor collisions are common and often attract crowds of spectators as the drivers shout insults at one another. Occasionally a fistfight erupts, attracting even bigger crowds. There is a justice system of sorts: usually the driver of the bigger, more expensive vehicle has to pay off the other party.

Nationwide the number of serious accidents is increasing. According to estimates by the ministries of health and transport, in 1994 traffic deaths reached 4,800, more than double the 1990 figure, roughly one-third of which were caused by motorcycles. Another third were attributed to archaic trucks and buses that often have poor brakes, worn-out windshield wipers, and no lights. When I first arrived in Hanoi I bought a Honda motorbike, but it was not long before I decided to switch to a car to protect myself from traffic hazards. "A car won't be enough," joked a Hungarian diplomat friend, who had lived in Vietnam for more than a decade. "You need an armored personnel carrier." This anarchy and congestion is likely to get worse. By 1995 Vietnam had some 330,000 cars, double the number it had five years earlier, and the number of motorcycles had reached four million, a fourfold increase since 1990.[7]

Traffic problems are exacerbated by the almost total lack of public transportation. Like Ho Chi Minh City, Hanoi has no subway system and only limited bus service. The number of passengers in Hanoi using buses each year is only about twelve to fifteen million—roughly a quarter of the number who used public transport in the 1970s, before trolleys dating back to the French colonial era were taken out of service. Hanoi officials have installed a handful of new traffic lights and introduced some roundabouts and one-way traffic on some of the city's busier streets in an attempt to create a modicum of order, but many residents appear to get a kick out of violating traffic regulations. It is not uncommon to see two teenagers on a bicycle run a red light and laugh hysterically while a policeman on foot chases after them. Judging by traffic, it would often seem that the Communist Party has created a free-for-all rather than a free market.

Small "people's" restaurants serve so-called *com bui*, or "dusty rice" meals and draft beer on tiny tables set up along the sidewalks. Some offer such exotic dishes as eel soup, sweet and sour dog liver, fried snake, or stewed pigeon. Their kitchens consist of little more than a chopping board, a kerosene burner and a small bucket for washing dishes. Tea stalls offer puffs of *thuoc lao*, a powerful tobacco, from long bamboo water pipes to passersby. Old women in traditional conical hats sit on sidewalks with bathroom scales, offering "health checks" for less than 5 cents a throw; others refill old pens or cigarette lighters.

Some people with more capital have turned their front rooms into video game parlors, where children play the latest Nintendo games by the hour. The ubiquity of video cassette recorders has made videotape rental a lucrative business. A dog craze has also hit the city. Like Beijing, Hanoi had banned dogs during the war because they were considered bourgeois and unsanitary. But as a dog-raising fad swept Hanoi in the early 1990s, some entrepreneurs found they could make a living transporting dogs from Moscow or smuggling dogs to the booming market in southern China. Others began raising exotic dogs in their houses, having moved their families into tiny makeshift rooms out back.

Everyone seems to have a scheme for making money. Hawkers openly peddle World Bank studies and confidential government reports. In 1993 the *Far Eastern Economic Review* reprinted about three dozen of my feature articles on Vietnam in a small paperback that soon was banned locally owing to some comments about Ho Chi Minh and a chapter on the future of the Communist Party. It was not long, however, before entrepreneurs put out a photocopied, hardback version of the book. Even the state-owned distributor Xunhasaba joined the fray, selling the pirated version for $4 less than the $18 charged for the original.

Vietnamese are prohibited from entering the country's only casino—operated by Macau casino king Stanley Ho near the port city of Haiphong—but this has not stopped Hanoians from satisfying their urge to gamble. In recent years city residents have taken to betting on the government-sponsored lottery, in which daily winners take home up to $5,000. Under an illegal racket devised by cunning ticket sellers, buyers are given the option to take out an additional bet that in most cases involves predicting the last two numbers of the ten-digit winning lottery number. The seller records the name of the person betting and collects the cash. Those who guess the correct numbers win seventy times the amount they bet. Most bets range from $1 to $10, but some go as high as $100.

Perhaps the only street that has not been turned into a giant outdoor bazaar is the two-hundred-meter stretch in front of Ho Chi Minh's mausoleum, still one of the most popular tourist attractions in the city, although the number of visitors has declined in recent years. Each day hundreds of people line up outside the Soviet-built, marble mausoleum waiting to briefly glimpse the embalmed body of the founding father of independent, Communist Vietnam. The building is guarded by goose-stepping soldiers in white uniforms. A quarter century after his death, despite the repudiation that most of his Communist contemporaries have suffered, Ho's image as the venerated leader survives unscathed. White ceramic busts of the wispy-bearded president are displayed in most government buildings; his portrait gazes down from the walls of most schools, homes, and shops around the capital.

Ho is not the only one who has survived. So has Lenin. He may be discredited in his Russian homeland, but in the capital of Communist Vietnam the founder of the former Soviet Union lives on. A giant stone statue of him—perhaps the only one of its kind left anywhere on the planet—still towers over a park not far from the Ho Chi Minh mausoleum. Early each November Hanoi's old Communist stalwarts still commemorate Lenin's October Revolution. Even before the collapse of the Soviet empire, Vietnamese often joked that the statue—depicting Lenin holding a hand over his pocket—showed that the Russians, long Vietnam's largest aid donors, were tight-fisted. Pranksters put a conical peasant hat on Lenin's head during the night of Vietnam's September 2 National Day in 1991, giving fits to the city's security police.

Another remnant of the past is the tinny-sounding outdoor loudspeakers that the Communists use each morning to broadcast their version of the news and to rouse any late sleepers. Even this service has been commercialized: One of my Hanoi friends arranged a reprieve from this acoustic pollution by bribing local officials to move the noisy contraption to the end of the street.

A construction boom is transforming the skyline of this nine hundred-year-old city. Carpenters are slowly renovating the architectural heritage of one of the most splendid cities in Asia. Foreign embassies and multinationals are refurbishing the exquisite French colonial villas on the boulevards south of Hoan Kiem Lake. Expatriates, once restricted to living in decrepit, Soviet-style apartment buildings in one of the city's three foreigner compounds, are now free to live wherever they can find or afford housing. Hanoi's security apparatus no longer deems it necessary to keep foreigners segregated from ordinary Vietnamese.

A French joint venture battled an army of cat-sized rats to turn the decaying Sofitel Metropole Hotel into the capital's first modern hotel. The "Hanoi Hilton"—the grungy, French-built prison where many captured Americans were held during the war—has been razed and a glitzy, twenty-two-story hotel called the Hanoi Towers will be built in its place by a company from Singapore. This $60 million project ran into a buzzsaw of protest from former Communist inmates from the 1940s and 1950s, who believed that the prison (whose real name is Hoa Lo, which means "oven") should have been kept as a monument to their struggle. The first wife of General Vo Nguyen Giap died there before her husband orchestrated France's defeat at Dien Bien Phu in 1954. In the end the builders conceded to set aside a small portion of the old prison for a museum.

As developers look to turn a quick profit, environmentalists and architects, fearing that development will doom the ancient charm of the Vietnamese capital, are even more vocal in their protests against the city's unregulated construction boom, in which minihotels, office buildings, and houses are sprouting willy-nilly. One of their first targets was a planned sixteen-story office complex on the site of a run-down, state-owned department store at the southern edge of Hoan Kiem Lake. The protesters argue that the high-rise would overshadow this enchanted lake in the center of the city. (According to Vietnamese legend, a huge turtle emerged from Hoan Kiem lake in the fifteenth century bearing a magic sword with which Le Loi drove out Chinese invaders.) Environmentalists are deeply concerned that many of the city's lakes and ponds are being filled in to make way for the chaotic construction boom. They blame the serious flooding in the city during recent summer monsoon rains on the shrinking number of reservoirs to hold excess water.

Yet nothing has prompted as much alarm as the threat to the ancient commercial quarter of Hanoi, located north of the lake. This area—with its confusing warren of small streets and low, narrow shop-houses topped with curved, red-tiled roofs—has long captured the hearts of Vietnamese artists and foreign visitors. This part of Hanoi, known as the "thirty-six streets," has suffered for many years from neglect and overcrowding; now it is threatened by the city's newfound prosperity. Merchants are rapidly replacing quaint, old structures with tall, flat-roofed shop-houses with grate-metal doors, much like those that dominate other Asian cities. Some even have satellite dishes on their rooftops.

The old quarter traces its origins back to the eleventh century, when King Ly Thai To moved the Vietnamese capital to Hanoi.

Over the next few centuries silversmiths, cloth dyers, and other craftsmen migrated from the countryside and set up guilds to supply handicrafts and consumer goods to the royal family and its employees. The streets are still named after craftsmen who first settled there in groups according to their trades. As the population increased on the "thirty-six streets," residents were forced to develop a unique architectural style: long, narrow structures known as tube houses. They were designed to provide each family with a room looking onto the street from which it could do business. Many of the surviving "tube houses," some of which are only two meters wide but up to one hundred meters long, were built in the late nineteenth century.

Behind the front room, which served as a shop for selling the family's products, is an open-air courtyard that provides light, ventilation, and a place to raise plants or relax. Beyond this is the family's living quarters, with the kitchen and bathroom located in another courtyard at the back of the house. The most distinctive feature of the tube houses is the low, upturned roofs made of red tiles. Because cement had not yet been introduced in Vietnam when these houses were built, the bricks in the walls are held together with a mixture of sand, lime, and sugar cane juice. Not many of the houses were damaged during the American bombing, but most of them deteriorated rapidly during the war due to lack of maintenance, and this decay continued after peace returned. Tenants were reluctant to fix up the houses because they were uncertain whether the Communist authorities would force them to move.

The city's soaring population added to the pressure for greater development. Hanoi's population has jumped from only 500,000 people in 1954 to over three million today. Five or more families now live in houses intended for only one family. City officials say the average resident of the "thirty-six streets" has only 1.5 square meters of living space, less than half the already Spartan 3.6-square-meter average in other parts of Hanoi. Some tiny bedrooms have a mezzanine floor dividing the room in half, thereby providing living space for two families.

As merchants started making money since the economic reforms, many have begun to expand and remodel their homes, constructing three- and four-story structures, that have totally altered the skyline of the "thirty-six streets." Hanoi has regulations—at least on paper—prohibiting residents from modifying the roofs and façades of the tube houses, but fines for violating these ordinances are too low—less than $10—to serve as much of a deterrent. Some officials have suggested relocating some of the tenants to the suburbs to reduce the pressure on the old houses, but the idea has not caught on. "People don't want to move," explains architect Nguyen Truc Luyen, a tireless champion for protecting the old quarter. "They are used to life here and they use their houses not only for living but for making their livelihood."

Hanoi officials are considering introducing clearer regulations for residents and stiffer penalties for violators, but these proposals have been tied up in bureaucratic wrangling for several years. Some architects suggest that the city should introduce incentives such as reduced business taxes for families maintaining the traditional houses. As the debate drags on, more of the tube houses are being destroyed. Luyen says half of them have already been lost, but others think the actual number is much higher. "If they don't do something fast, they'll spoil the town," a European diplomat warns. "If they turn Hanoi into a new Bangkok, no one will come," he adds, alluding to Vietnam's plan to attract foreign tourists.[8]

More than buildings are at risk. A proliferation of new, still largely unregulated factories and workshops threatens the environment of cities such as Hanoi and Ho Chi Minh City. Pollution is increasing rapidly, although Vietnam's urban environment remains in much better condition than that of most neighboring countries. In Hanoi some 250 factories dump untreated waste, including chemicals, dyes, and heavy metals, directly into the city's canals, rivers, and lakes. Hanoi has no plant to treat waste water, and its aging sewage network built by the French more than five decades ago serves only part of the city. This creates a critical environmental threat, particularly during the rainy season, when streets are flooded with a mixture of domestic waste water, industrial discharges and rain water. In addition, Hanoi's factories belch clouds of coal particles, sulfur dioxide, and carbon monoxide into the air. According to a study conducted in 1993 by the city's Commission for Science, Technology and Environment, the heavily industrialized southern suburbs suffer sulfur dioxide and carbon monoxide levels two to five times higher than permitted levels.[9]

In 1993 the National Assembly, Vietnam's parliament, passed an environmental protection law that requires among other things that factories undergo environmental impact studies. The government also has set up the National Environmental Agency to draft guidelines to regulate such problems as industrial discharge and air standards. Environmentalists worry, however, that most monitoring will remain ineffective so long as people find that they can profit, at least in the short term, from allowing the ecological degeneration to continue.

Hanoi remains the subdued political and cultural capital of Vietnam, while Ho Chi Minh City is the country's bustling commercial and industrial center. Yet Hanoi's share of the economy has risen in recent years as more domestic and foreign companies launch business ventures in what had been the hotbed of orthodox Vietnamese socialism. By the end of 1995 the capital had captured foreign investment projects worth some $3.7 billion, or one-fifth of the total pledged for the country.[10] Firms such as Daewoo of South Korea (which recently signed its fourth investment contract in Hanoi) are attracted to the city by its more reliable electricity supply, simpler approval procedures, and less free-wheeling atmosphere.

7

Reality Check

◆ ◆ ◆

When Vietnam's Communist leaders launched their economic reforms and began wooing foreign investors, Arve Varleite met Vietnam's best expectations. The sturdy, energetic Norwegian brought his checkbook, expertise, and foreign connections to help jump-start an economy struggling to overcome years of stagnation brought on by socialist mismanagement and international isolation.

Varleite—who controls half the shares in Scansia, a Scandinavian, Scottish, and Malaysian furniture-building venture—first visited Ho Chi Minh City in the early 1990s. He was looking for a new production base to supplement his firm's two workshops in Malaysia, where labor costs are soaring. Varleite liked what he found. "Labor here is very motivated and hard working," he enthuses. "The skill level is the main reason we're here. . . . A Vietnamese worker getting $50 is more motivated than a Malaysian getting $250."

Within two years Varleite had invested $1.8 million to equip three workshops producing wooden barstools, folding chairs, and cane furniture. Two of the plants belong to Scansia outright, while the third is a joint venture with the quasi-governmental Union of Wood Workers. All of the company's products are sold abroad, primarily to northern Europe, bolstering Vietnam's exports. Varleite employs approximately 1,600 workers, which makes him one of the largest employers in Vietnam today.

Observers are hopeful that foreign investors such as Scansia will help pull Vietnam out of the ranks of the world's poorest nations,

particularly if the government continues to pursue its economic reforms. Just how long it will take for the country to join Asia's other
tigers will depend on how competitive Vietnam becomes in the tug-
of-war for investment dollars. Foreign interest in Vietnam has soared
since it adopted a liberal investment law in the late 1980s. Some
capitalists, such as Varleite, have been attracted by the country's diligent, low-cost labor force. Others have come hoping to discover oil
or to tap its potentially hefty domestic market of seventy-four million consumers. Most are impressed by Vietnam's relatively stable
political environment.

Foreign businessmen received an added boost in 1994 when the
United States dropped its trade embargo and the following year normalized diplomatic relations with Hanoi. Total project approvals
surged 30 percent in 1994, topping $10.9 billion by the end of the
year. Investment fever continued in 1995, with approvals hitting
$18.2 billion by the end of the year.[1] Actual foreign spending con-
tinues to be sluggish. It was expected to reach $6 billion by the end
of 1995, or one-third of the total pledged since the country opened
up to foreign investors seven years earlier, but this is still small change
compared to what is being spent in neighboring countries. In 1995
alone Malaysia approved foreign investment projects in manufacturing worth $8.2 billion. Foreign investment in China totaled $33.1
billion, up 11 percent over 1994.[2]

Roughly one-third of actual spending in Vietnam has been dis-
bursed by foreign oil companies that have secured more than two
dozen contracts to look for offshore oil. Much of the rest has been
spent on ventures that generate hard currency such as hotels, office
buildings, and services targeted toward tourists and foreign businessmen. Recently, however, a growing share of the licenses has been
granted for industrial ventures, and more approvals are being issued
for the north. Earlier, two out of three projects were licensed for Ho
Chi Minh City and its surrounding provinces, even though the government tried to promote investment in the north. Foreign investors
seemed to prefer the south because it had a better developed infrastructure and more experience with capitalist-style business practices.

Now, firms such as Daewoo Corporation of South Korea—which has contracts worth over $500 million to produce television tubes, build a luxury hotel, assemble cars, and construct an industrial complex in the vicinity of Hanoi—are discovering that it is easier to get projects approved for the north. The Korean giant decided to invest in the north because it was offered cheaper land prices, lower taxes, and a more reliable supply of electricity than it would have received in the south, according to Joo Sung Kim, Daewoo's Hanoi manager.

It is true that the country still lags far behind such regional rivals as Thailand, Malaysia, and China in the tussle to woo investors, partly because of the obstacles foreign firms face in trying to penetrate the Vietnamese market. "There's a long gestation period in any dealings with Vietnam," observes Richard Martin, who set up the Australian & New Zealand Bank's branch in Hanoi. "Yet the name plates are an indicator of the level of interest—Motorola, IBM, Caterpillar, General Motors, Westinghouse," he says of multinationals that have established representative offices in Vietnam or regularly send senior executives to visit. "The level of interest is there." Martin is convinced that all of this interest will result in future spending.

Nonetheless, major hurdles continue to hold back many Western firms. Even some of the early arrivals who are starting to see their efforts pay off worry that the country's attractions are being overshadowed by the costs of doing business. For example, Varleite points out that Scansia pays twice as much for housing foreign staff in Vietnam as it does in more developed Malaysia. Richard Ellis, the international property firm, figures that one square meter of prime office space in Ho Chi Minh City costs $675 a year, one of the highest rates in Southeast Asia. Rents in an export-processing zone under construction near the central Vietnamese city of Danang are expected to cost 50 percent more than plots in the more advanced industrial estates along Thailand's eastern seaboard.[3]

Telecommunications services are equally exorbitant. A fax from Ho Chi Minh City to Kuala Lumpur costs Varleite more than twice as much as he pays to send the same message in the opposite direction. Many businessmen get their offices overseas to call them back

A teller rings up dong at the *Viet-Hoa* (Vietnamese–Chinese) Bank in Ho Chi Minh City. The opening of this bank by ethnic Chinese shareholders represents the reemergence of this minority as an important force in Vietnam's economy. Ethnic Chinese entrepreneurs had been devastated by a crackdown on capitalists in 1978.

Ho Chi Minh City's Mr. Gold, Nguyen Huu Dinh, head of the state-owned Saigon Jewelry Company. "He's a one-man band," says a competitor who admires the extensive empire Dinh has built in finance, banking, distribution, hotels, and soft-drink production. The gold bars popularized by Dinh's company have become the currency with which houses, motorcycles, and most other big-ticket items are purchased in the south.

Today, in what was once a Communist Party training school in the suburbs of Ho Chi Minh City, workers at Vuu Khai Thanh's Biti factory churn out more shoes than any competitor. Thanh is firing up Vietnam with an entrepreneurial flair reminiscent of the ethnic Chinese, who have helped jump-start many of Asia's economies.

The life of Dao Tam Tu, a seventy-one-year-old peasant from the north-central coast, hasn't improved much under Vietnam's economic reforms. For him, the flashy billboards, imported motorcycles, and construction boom of the cities seem a million miles away. Tu's village doesn't have enough land to feed its inhabitants, and almost every year its crops are ravaged by typhoons.

Ethnic minorities such as this Hmong woman in Sapa, near the Chinese border, have benefited least from the reforms. Only one in ten can read and write, and many suffer from malaria. Their persistent search for food has also led to the rapid destruction of Vietnam's forests and a sharp decline in soil fertility.

Farmers in the fertile Mekong delta harvest another bumper crop. Nothing exemplifies Vietnam's economic turnaround better than agriculture. Only one year after the Communist Party decided to abandon farm collectives and return land to its tillers Vietnam graduated from the ranks of grain importers to the world's third-largest rice exporter, behind Thailand and the United States.

As the population in Hanoi's ancient quarter increased over the centuries, residents were forced to develop a unique architectural style: long, narrow structures known as "tube houses," designed to provide each family with a room looking onto the street from which it could do business. Today five or more families live in houses intended for only one, giving the average resident in this quarter only 1.5 square meters of living space.

Many Vietnamese and Chinese, such as this porter in Mong Cai, seem to be seizing all opportunities—including some that aren't legal—to better their lives. Much of the commerce along Vietnam's northern border with China is in fact smuggling. Some importers avoid passing through customs; others pay bribes to get crooked officials to lower tariffs on their goods.

The 1986 *doi moi* reforms have brought an explosion of motorcycles to Ho Chi Minh City. On Sunday nights hundreds of youths on motorcycles gravitate to the center of the city for a "meandering race." They cruise down Dong Khoi Street, swing right at the Saigon River, and come back around the block in a rite that goes on for hours.

An advertising war has erupted in Ho Chi Minh City as multinationals compete for the "hearts and minds" of Asia's newest market. A jumble of signboards at major intersections has replaced the red banners that until recently exhorted the city's proletariat to fulfill the Communist Party's dream of a socialist paradise.

The three million followers of the indigenous Cao Dai religion in southern Vietnam have not been authorized to reopen their religious training schools since the end of the war. Founded in 1919 by a mystic, Cao Dai is a syncretistic blend of Buddhism, Confucianism, Taoism, and a handful of local cults. Its pantheon of saints includes Buddha, Jesus Christ, Joan of Arc, and French writer Victor Hugo.

Vietnam's greatest hope for prosperity and success lies in its youth, such as this class at the Tri Duc secondary school in Ho Chi Minh City. More than a third of the country's population of seventy-four million is under fifteen years old and has not experienced the horrors that rocked the country during its long, painful civil war. To date the Communists get high marks for expanding and improving Vietnam's education system, bolstering the country's chances for developing an educated work force.

to save money. "If prices keep going up, Vietnam will not get the best investors," the businessman warns. "People coming in are killed with overheads before they even get started." Hanoi admits that it faces a risk of pricing itself out of the market and has pledged to bring its international communications rates in line with those of its neighbors over the next few years.

Property prices will be a harder nut to crack, even though the country is witnessing a construction boom. Hanoi's extravagant rates are due to a combination of factors: a desperate shortage of housing and office space resulting from an exploding population, destruction of parts of the city by U.S. bombing during the war, and the Communist Party's earlier prohibitions on private construction. Ho Chi Minh City witnessed very little construction in the first fifteen years following the Communist victory in 1975.

Another obstacle hobbling investors—the country's decrepit infrastructure—is now finally being tackled. No longer shackled by an American embargo, the World Bank and the Asian Development Bank have approved soft loans to upgrade Highway One, the country's main north-south road. In addition, they are lending money to refurbish Saigon port, rehabilitate Ho Chi Minh City's water supply system, modernize Hanoi's electricity grid, and repair the dike protecting the capital from flooding. Japan is providing aid as well. As reconstruction continues, Hanoi has offered tax holidays to manufacturers wanting to set up factories in export-processing zones, but actual spending remains slow. Estimates of foreign aid expenditures in 1995 run as low as $500 million, out of a total of $2 billion pledged.

Varleite is troubled by the growing number of hands seeking kickbacks. For example, Vietnam has banned timber exports to protect the country's degraded forests and fledgling local industry, yet a lot of unprocessed logs are being exported by corrupt officials, making it difficult for Vietnam's local wood industry to obtain raw materials. "Corruption is becoming worse and worse," he complains. "It's like a cancer in society." Varleite is not the only one who feels he is being bilked. An American Fortune 500 firm wanting to set up a plant producing consumer goods in Ho Chi Minh City was told by its Vietnamese consultant that it would need $15,000 just to bring together the officials that would consider the application. Hanoi's first luxury hotel, the Sofitel Metropole, had to pay $70,000 to get approval to expand its facilities, according to one technocrat frustrated with the growing level of graft among government officials.

Although Hanoi has mounted several campaigns to combat corruption, the problem has worsened in recent years. Low salaries, which make it impossible for an official to survive on government wages, are one obvious cause. Another is the country's collegial decision-making style that requires investors to get approval from both central and local officials and gives many bureaucrats an opportunity to demand kickbacks in exchange for not blocking projects. The Communist Party's reluctance to punish officials exacerbates this problem. Due to relationships built up during years of revolutionary struggle, the party remains an elite "old boys" network.

Another difficulty holding back foreign companies as well as domestic investors is Vietnam's lack of an institutional framework, legal infrastructure, and financial system under which a free market economy can flourish. The National Assembly has passed scores of new laws since the late 1980s, and the government is constantly revising its regulations to accommodate complaints of foreign businessmen. Yet investors often crash headlong through the remaining gaps in the legal system. Others find that the interpretation of laws or regulations changes from one locality to another or from one month to the next.

For example, in early 1993 the Hong Kong–based Sundance Duty Free Sales Limited was told that the commerce ministry had issued a license for a second company to operate the duty-free shop in Hanoi's Noi Bai airport less than three years into its own five-year contract. Vietnam still had no contract law or economic court to which Sundance could appeal, so the firm complained directly to Premier Vo Van Kiet. His office ruled in favor of Sundance, prompting the commerce ministry to cancel the contract with the second company. Several months later nothing had changed. Noi Bai's director (who supported the second company) physically blocked Sundance's manager from entering the airport and running his shop, despite direct orders from the commerce ministry and the premier. Sundance's case highlights the legal problems often faced by foreign investors—and Vietnamese citizens—as Hanoi seeks to build a smooth-functioning legal system.

Many sensitive questions remain. The most important is that of land-use rights, which need to be clearly defined so that businessmen can put up security for loans. This, coupled with the fact that Vietnamese banks have limited capital, means that investors must finance themselves. Varleite, for example, borrows money abroad by putting up his workshops in Malaysia for collateral.

One of the most common gripes of foreign businessmen is the country's bureaucratic tangles that delay investment approvals. The State Committee for Cooperation and Investment (SCCI) that approved foreign investment projects until the end of 1995, when it was incorporated into the newly formed ministry of planning and investment, long pledged to decide on licenses within ninety days. Yet investors find that their approvals are delayed by eight central government ministries or agencies—in addition to local administrations—that play key roles in vetting projects. Owing to this overlapping authority, officials admit that many approvals take as long as three years.

In a 1994 review of Vietnam's economy the World Bank warns that the government's "highly centralized decision-making will inevitably become a severe bottleneck for development. Thus, the most important strategic choice that the government faces is whether to give up some control and to decentralize decision-making in return for a faster pace of development."[4] Senior Vietnamese officials recognize the problem. So far attempts at overhauling the Vietnamese bureaucracy have bumped into stubborn resistance, particularly from local bureaucrats unwilling to give up their fiefdoms. In an attempt to streamline the system, Premier Vo Van Kiet decreed in late 1994 that he was taking personal charge of approvals for major investment projects. Bureaucratic hassles are nothing new in Asia. In neighboring China, where economic reform is often said to be about a decade ahead of Vietnam, this problem was resolved by allowing provincial or local officials to approve all except the biggest investment projects. Thailand and Malaysia have gone even further in streamlining their approval procedures.

In Vietnam, foreign companies often find themselves trapped in bureaucratic tussles between Hanoi and local officials. The Norfolk Group of Australia, for example, was told by the People's Committee of Ho Chi Minh City that it had to knock down the top five floors of its office building, even though the construction ministry in Hanoi had approved its blueprint. Frustrated by this seemingly arbitrary ruling, the Australian company argued its point to the committee. After several months, a compromise was reached under which Norfolk was allowed to retain the top floors of its building but had to add on a tripod-shaped structure and paint the original gray marble light blue so that the building would blend better with its environment.

Foreign banks setting up branches in Vietnam also were squeezed by the government's decision to increase taxes and change other regulations after they had been licensed to begin operating. Other companies get into conflicts with their local partners. Most investors form joint ventures with domestic outfits to help them battle their way through the Vietnamese bureaucracy and attain easier access to land-use rights, but sometimes these parties have a falling out, usually owing to Hanoi's ruling that corporate decisions must be approved unanimously by all parties in the venture, regardless of the size of their holdings.

For example, Westralian Sands of Australia formed a joint venture to mine and process ilmenite, a mineral sand used to produce plastics, paints, and cosmetics, in the north-central province of Ha Tinh. The project was stopped in June 1995 after a dispute with local government officials, who confiscated $2.5 million worth of equipment intended to boost ilmenite output. Two senior project managers were put under house arrest by the Vietnamese government after being questioned about problems at the project. Operations resumed again in November following months of negotiations, but relations once again soured, prompting Westralian to pull its last expatriate workers out of Vietnam in May 1996.[5]

In other cases, investors find they cannot accept Hanoi's conditions. The French oil firm Total SA pulled out of Vietnam's first oil refinery project in 1995 in response to Hanoi's decision to locate the $1.2 billion refinery in the remote central province of Quang Ngai, far from Vietnam's offshore oil fields and the main markets around Ho Chi Minh City and Hanoi. The government chose this site in an effort to create jobs and raise incomes in impoverished central Vietnam. Officials refused to back down, confident that other companies would soon offer to take over the project, as indeed they did. South Korea's LG Group, Malaysia's Petroliam Nasional, the United States' DuPont Company, and Taiwan's Chinese Petroleum Corporation and Chinese Investment and Development Corporation have already said they are interested.

A few weeks later, P & O Australia Limited announced that it was pulling out of a project to build a $19 million container port in southern Vietnam. "Despite many attempts at meaningful negotiations, no serious progress has been made for eight months," the company said in announcing its withdrawal. P & O had planned to boost the Ben Nghe port's container-handling capacity from 20,000 to 500,000 units a year by the end of the decade. The experiences of P & O and Total offer a sobering counterpoint to the government's glowing reports about soaring levels of foreign investment pledges.[6]

Foreign businessmen are not the only ones frustrated. The Vietnamese government finds that a sizable number of investors refuse to pay the minimum monthly wage of $35, while others set up offices without bothering to apply for approval. In addition, many early investors did not have money to finance their projects, yet hoped to sell their licenses for a profit. By the end of 1995 Hanoi had revoked some $983 million worth of projects that had never gotten off the ground.

The first labor conflicts are also erupting in a country where until a few years ago everyone worked for the state or in a cooperative. In

February 1993 more than six hundred workers staged a wildcat strike at the Reeyoung Company, a South Korean-Vietnamese joint venture, to protest against long working hours, poor pay, and mistreatment by their foreign bosses. The walkout marked the largest labor strike in Ho Chi Minh City since the Communist victory nearly eighteen years earlier.[7]

In contrast to labor disputes in other countries, the strike at Reeyoung was a subdued affair. "The workers gathered in front of our gate, standing around in small groups and talking quietly," said Ok Man Park, the Korean director of the company, which produces luggage for export. "No one was wearing headbands, shouting, or waving their fists in the air," he added, alluding to the more militant style of strikers in South Korea.

The walkout at Reeyoung is one of a growing number of labor conflicts that have erupted in Vietnam since authorities opened the door to foreign investors. Hoang Thi Khanh, head of the city's Labor Confederation, warns that the number of strikes will increase unless foreign companies begin implementing Vietnam's labor regulations. Most of the conflicts have occurred at textile, garment, and shoe-making enterprises set up with investment capital from South Korea, Taiwan, and Hong Kong, but most have been settled quickly with the owners giving in to the main demands of the workers. The walkout at Reeyoung ended after two days, when the company agreed to increase salaries to the minimum set by the government and allow workers to form a labor union. In addition, Reeyoung pledged to discuss in advance with the head of the new union any requests for overtime, for which workers would be paid 50 percent more than their normal salaries.

Most strikes are generated spontaneously by the workers themselves. Workers complain that they get little support from the country's only legal union, the 4.2-million-member Labor Confederation, which is under the control of the Communist Party. Disgruntled workers say that the confederation—originally established to defend their rights under a socialist system—usually presses them to find a quick resolution to labor disputes. The growing number of strikes creates a dilemma for the Communist Party and the confederation: On one hand, they have billed themselves as the champions of the working class, while on the other they are worried that a more powerful labor movement could challenge their authority and scare off foreign companies.

One gripe of workers is that only one in five firms have unions even though Hanoi's labor code mandates that all companies have them. Even fewer firms have signed collective-bargaining agreements with their workers. These problems are beginning to attract growing attention overseas. "Workers in Vietnam have no freedom of association, no right to collective bargaining, and no effective right to strike," an official of the AFL-CIO labor organization told the U.S. Overseas Private Investment Corporation in December 1995 when it was holding hearing on whether to provide risk insurance to American investors. The official complained that Hanoi maintained "an outmoded labor policy systematically contaminated by violations of workers' rights."[8]

Although Hanoi has put out a welcome mat, not all Vietnamese are as enthusiastic about the foreign invasion of capitalists trying to make money in their country. Nationalism helped Vietnam defeat the French and the Americans and can create difficulties for foreign businessmen as well. Domestic producers of soap, shampoo, and cosmetics actively lobbied the government to block such multinationals as Procter & Gamble and Lever Brothers from setting up plants in Vietnam.

Some foreign businessmen would undoubtedly agree with Henry Kissinger, the former U.S. secretary of state, who dubbed the Vietnamese the world's toughest negotiators. "I'm often scolded by officials who fear foreigners are trying to take over Vietnam's industry," said one European businessman in the midst of negotiating an agreement to set up a brewery. "The guys in power smile, but they're fighters and they bring that mentality to business. They approach business like war," he says, adding: "They don't understand cooperation, only power. Everyone seems to be trying to outdo the other in being tough on foreigners."

Many businessmen working in Vietnam would find that charac-
terization a bit harsh, but foreign bankers still warn investors to be
careful. "While looking at Nirvana, you need to be sure not to miss
the ten-foot pothole right in front of you," Frank Hawke, who
established Citibank's representative office in Hanoi, cautioned
shortly after Washington lifted its trade sanctions against Hanoi.
"Doing business here is very complex," continued the veteran
American banker, who had earlier worked in China. "You need a
solid grounding in facts and need to look for a Vietnamese partner
very carefully. Don't leave your common sense at customs."

Open for Business

Although Vietnam at least on paper remains one of the last bastions
of socialism, one of its single largest foreign investors is Chiang Kai-
shek's old anti-Communist bulwark, Taiwan. Central Trading & Development, a venture-capital company belonging to Taiwan's ruling
Kuomintang party, has licenses for four long-term projects in Vietnam worth a hefty $600 million.

The cash-flush Taiwanese political party surveyed numerous
countries including Russia, Hungary, South Africa, and Myanmar
before making its decision. The company's findings about the work
force in these countries tilted the balance in favor of Vietnam. "Vietnam has the last intelligent, cost-effective labor in Asia," enthuses
Lawrence Ting, the company's suave, American-educated chairman.[9] Central Trading's decision to focus on Vietnam was bolstered
further by the fact that he believes Vietnam to have one of the most
stable economies among the world's competing emerging markets.

Central Trading's most visible Vietnam venture is the eighty-nine-
hectare Tan Thuan Export Processing Zone on the Saigon River
near the port of Ho Chi Minh City. Tan Thuan, a 70-30 joint
venture with the city government, was the first of six zones licensed
to begin operating in Vietnam. About a dozen factories, including

several Taiwanese firms producing textiles and garments, were up and running by the end of 1994. More than thirty others had rented sites. The company's biggest project, another joint venture with Ho Chi Minh City, is called the Saigon South Development Project. It is expected to cost over $240 million and will include an eighteen-kilometer highway to serve the export-processing zone and a 2,600-hectare expansion of the city, complete with a commercial district, residential areas, two universities, hotels, and parks.

By late 1995 businessmen from Taiwan had secured investment contracts worth $3.3 billion, making the small island republic Vietnam's leading source of foreign capital; Hong Kong ranked second, Singapore fourth. Together these three overseas Chinese enclaves—which have provided much of the investment, technology, and marketing know-how stoking southern China's astonishing growth—account for nearly two-fifths of the total foreign investment in Vietnam. Some observers believe that actual overseas Chinese investment figures may be considerably higher. For every dollar brought in through official channels, another is invested informally through ethnic Chinese relatives and friends in Ho Chi Minh City, says John Brinsden, who heads up Britain's Standard Chartered Bank in Vietnam and previously served in Taiwan. This money is underwriting the growing number of small workshops in the city that turn out textiles, garments, foodstuffs, shoes, and other consumer goods. Some companies, such as Ching Shing Textile, a garment venture, produce for export; others, such as Ve Wong Company, which operates a factory producing instant noodles and monosodium glutamate (MSG), compete for the sizable domestic market.

Most of the ethnic Chinese companies operating in Vietnam are small or medium-sized, allowing them to make decisions more quickly than their large competitors. "When the Taiwanese move, they're up and running in six months," observes Brinsden, contrasting their style with that of most Western conglomerates. "They don't bother with paperwork and the foreign investment law." Most Asian investors seem less bothered by neatly packaged legal systems than their Western rivals. But in Vietnam, even bullish Taiwanese capitalists sometimes get unnerved by having to work everything out as they go along. "The difficulties can be overwhelming," Ting, the optimistic head of Central Trading, admits about Vietnam's maddening red tape and frequent regulation changes. "They change the laws very often, so the situation is very confused," says Lee Chi Kuang, manager of Ching Shing's $1 million garment factory in Ho Chi Minh City. "Today you can do something, tomorrow you can't. Nobody tells you about the change."

Investment from Japan, Vietnam's largest trading partner and most important aid donor, surged in 1995, making that country the third leading source of foreign capital. Japanese businessmen say they were slow out of the starting gate because they felt uncertain about Vietnam's investment climate. A 1995 survey by the Export-Import Bank of Japan found that 28 percent of the 336 Japanese companies surveyed ranked Vietnam among the most promising countries for investment over the next three years. But if the time frame is extended to ten years, the survey indicated that 41 percent of 274 firms ranked Vietnam among the most promising investment targets. This is second only to China, which three-quarters of the firms in the survey ranked most promising.[10]

American companies also started out slowly but nevertheless pledged $1.1 billion worth of projects in the first twenty-two months after Washington lifted its embargo in early 1994, making the United States the sixth largest investor. (By comparison, U.S. companies signed $6 billion worth of contracts in China in 1994.) Although U.S. corporations are unlikely to displace Taiwanese or Japanese investors any time soon, they do have strong prospects in several key sectors, including energy, infrastructure, and aviation, but they have some catching up to do first. "American companies first have to come to learn how to do business here," Huynh Buu Son, deputy managing director of Saigon Bank for Industry and Trade in Ho Chi Minh City, points out. "The Japanese, Koreans and Taiwanese are dynamic and aggressive here now. They know how to take risks. But the Americans may be too prudent," he says. "They're not one step, but many kilometers, behind."[11]

Oil exploration is one area in which Americans are expected to do well. Because their competitors already have grabbed Vietnam's most promising exploration blocks, U.S. oil firms will have to "farm in" with other companies. Mobil has joined three Japanese companies in exploring for oil in the Thang Long (Blue Dragon) offshore field, and now that the embargo has been lifted American companies (which control over half of the world's oil-service market) will be able to compete for these contracts.

U.S. construction and equipment firms can bid on Vietnamese infrastructure projects funded by the World Bank and the Asian Development Bank. Caterpillar says it expects that over the next few years Vietnam will provide "a $350 to $700 million sales opportunity" for its heavy equipment. American airlines and aircraft suppliers could also do well. Vietnam Airlines officials say they plan to lease or buy thirty to forty aircraft by the year 2000 to upgrade their aging fleet of Russian-built planes. The Vietnamese flag-carrier is talking with Boeing and McDonnell Douglas, as well as Europe's Airbus Industrie. At least four major American airlines—Continental, Delta, Northwest, and United—are jostling to begin service for the nearly one million ethnic Vietnamese living in the United States and the growing number of tourists queuing up to visit Vietnam. The rival airlines, however, will have to wait for Hanoi and Washington to negotiate an air-services agreement.

Some American consumer goods will excel as well. Anxious to capture the loyalty of Vietnam's still largely untapped market, Coca-Cola and PepsiCo launched an advertising war only one day after the U.S. embargo was lifted. Coke spent $250,000 over the next ten days on a "Glad to see you again" campaign, featuring concerts, billboards, and TV commercials that ran alongside Pepsi's "Choice of a new generation" ads featuring Miss Vietnam. The two soft-drink giants also were among the first three American firms to submit applications to invest in local production facilities in Vietnam.

But Vietnamese officials say they will be forced to limit big-ticket purchases in the United States until they get most-favored-nation trading status, which would lower barriers on Vietnam's exports.

Without reduced tariffs Vietnam cannot compete with suppliers from neighboring countries such as Thailand or China. For example, a Vietnamese-made cotton T-shirt bears a 90 percent tariff, compared to only 21 percent charged to the same product produced by one of Vietnam's neighbors. "Now Vietnam can buy Boeings, but it can't sell textiles in the United States," says Le Dang Doanh, director of an economic think tank in Hanoi. "A one-way street can't be maintained forever."

Washington and Hanoi began talks on normalizing trade relations a few months after they exchanged embassies, but the U.S. Congress must approve any moves to grant Hanoi most-favored-nation status. Some observers believe congressional critics may try to delay lowering tariffs on Vietnam's exports to press Hanoi to be more forthcoming in its accounting of missing American servicemen. In addition, the Vietnamese must agree to conform to certain U.S. conditions on labor laws and respect for intellectual property rights.

Wooing Them Home

For several weeks in 1990, Nguyen Trung Truc was beginning to wonder whether he might have been had. He had imported a $300,000 shipment of medicines for a Vietnamese company that refused to pay him back. Vietnam still had no contract law or economic courts to which he could turn for help. Just when it was beginning to look as if his first business venture in Vietnam would be his last, Truc's sister came to the rescue. She managed to use some old political connections to get the government to force the company to pay up.

The soft-spoken forty-four-year-old had not been ready to give in, and his stubbornness paid off. Practicing survival tactics he had learned growing up in a once heavily fought-over region of the Mekong delta, Truc has emerged as one of the most prominent businessmen in Vietnam today. Truc left Vietnam in 1972 to study economics in Australia, where he ended up involved in merchant banking, car distribution, and a Papua New Guinea plantation. In 1989 he revisited Vietnam, then three years into its reforms. Intrigued by what he found, Truc returned to try his hand at doing business in his native land. "It was a big gamble to drop everything we'd done overseas," he says. After his first medicine shipment had threatened to bankrupt him Truc shifted to running tours for Asian visitors but soon abandoned that after finding out many of his clients were interested only in sex tours.

By 1991, Truc says, he knew what he wanted: a diversified business network modeled on the great Chinese-family conglomerates, which started out in trading and expanded into property development, manufacturing, and other areas. Lacking capital, Truc and his Malaysian-Chinese wife, Diedre Low, formed a joint venture with Peregrine Capital International, a Hong Kong–based merchant banking group.

Today he is managing director of Peregrine Capital Vietnam, 60 percent of which is owned by Peregrine and the balance by Truc and his wife. In recent years Peregrine Vietnam has established a wide-ranging business network involved in distribution and marketing, manufacturing, property development, and banking. Truc's company has secured distribution rights for Johnson & Johnson pharmaceuticals and baby-care products, Kenwood electronic equipment, and Mercedes Benz cars. It also has applied for a license to produce pharmaceuticals in a venture with Ciba-Geigy of Switzerland. In addition, Peregrine Vietnam has acquired one-fifth of the shares in a $30 million office building to be constructed next to the former American Embassy by a Singaporean property developer.

Through family and business associates Truc controls 30 percent of the local Dai Nam Bank. He hopes the bank will serve as a steppingstone into broader financial operations and provide a seat in Vietnam's first experimental stock exchange, which is expected to open in 1997.

Truc has not always found a capitalist-friendly environment in the new Vietnam. "There are no fixed rules," he says, adding that his hair has started turning gray since he returned to work in Vietnam. "It's a moving target. You have to be very adaptable, which makes it hard for big corporations. That's why Asian companies led by one person do better." Truc agrees with his foreign rivals that the country's bureaucracy is a nightmare. "There's never an end to an application" process, he says. "There are so many requirements to meet nonexisting guidelines. We submitted an application recently which had to be changed six times. This leaves the system open to abuse and corruption." Nonetheless, Truc is convinced that Vietnam's business climate has improved since he first arrived. "People understand better how the capitalist system works, and we understand better how the Vietnamese system works," he observes. "We've come halfway to meet each other."[12]

Overseas Vietnamese businessmen such as Truc are still rare, an important difference between Vietnam and the successful southern provinces of China. Quangdong's booming exports and phenomenal growth have been fired up by investment and know-how from overseas Chinese. Vietnam, in contrast, has relatively few compatriots overseas and even fewer with vast amounts of capital abroad. Vietnamese traditionally have been less interested in business than in such fields as computer science, medicine, teaching, and scientific research. In addition, many overseas Vietnamese are still reluctant to deal with their native land. The number returning is growing but is still only a tiny fraction of the roughly two million Vietnamese living abroad (nearly half of whom live in the United States; France, Canada, and Australia also have large Vietnamese communities).

"Vietnam can only become a tiger if overseas Vietnamese contribute to the motherland," argues journalist Ly Quy Chung. "To succeed, the party must attract Vietnamese abroad and convince them to invest. No one else will bring the technological revolution," says Chung, whose mother and ten siblings migrated to Canada and the United States after the Communist victory. The majority of Vietnamese who return come to visit their families, although some come to share technical skills learned abroad. Only a handful return to do business or to invest. By early 1996 overseas Vietnamese had snared investment licenses for projects worth $128 million (less than 1 percent of the total foreign investment in the country).

Much of the reluctance of the overseas Vietnamese in dealing with Vietnam is caused by the circumstances under which they fled the country. Many left from the south as boat people to escape repressive policies or the country's crushing poverty following the Communist victory in 1975. Some of them—particularly those in the United States—still have hopes of ousting the country's Communist rulers.

In September 1992, for example, a Vietnamese-American, Ly Van Tong, hijacked a commercial airplane over Ho Chi Minh City and began throwing leaflets out the window, calling for the toppling of the government. Tong parachuted to safety but was arrested and sentenced to twenty years in prison. In early 1993 more than a dozen overseas Vietnamese were arrested for allegedly planning to plant bombs at several key Ho Chi Minh City installations during the visit of French president François Mitterrand. Official newspapers regularly publish reports charging that "exiled reactionaries" are working with "imperialists" to overthrow Vietnam's "socialist regime."

Many overseas Vietnamese do not believe that the country's former hard-liners truly have mellowed under the Communist Party's reforms. "When I first came back, I was afraid I was risking my life," a man in his early thirties told me not long after he had returned to visit Ho Chi Minh City for the first time. He had fled in 1980 and was working in a restaurant in Houston. "But I was surprised how much the city has changed," he said of his old home. "People are now left alone to make money. Sometimes I think I'd like to come back here to live, but I don't know what will happen in the future," he said, implying that he still did not completely trust the country's leaders.

Politics is not the only barrier separating overseas Vietnamese from their homeland. Some returnees create resentment by flaunting money earned abroad or by cheating Vietnamese who have only limited experience in international commerce. In late 1994 a Ho Chi Minh City court sentenced an overseas Vietnamese from the

United States to twelve years in jail for defrauding a furniture company. According to press accounts, Khuu Thang Vi had cheated the firm out of $32,000 by delivering goods worth only $13,000 after signing a contract for $45,000. Sometimes overseas Vietnamese are blamed for contributing to the country's social ills. When the first case of AIDS was reported in Ho Chi Minh City in 1990, state-run newspapers blamed it on the woman's sexual relations with some overseas Vietnamese men.

It cannot be denied, however, that overseas Vietnamese companies from France and Canada played a crucial role in opening up Vietnam's economy in the early 1980s. These companies began trading with their native land when it was still largely closed and dependent on its then Communist allies in the Soviet Union. Overseas Vietnamese companies also were among the first foreign firms to begin investing after the Communist Party opened the country's doors. Most of the investment was small and appears to be slowing down rather than picking up. What does not appear to be slowing down, however, is the amount of money overseas Vietnamese send to relatives back home. Exact figures are not available, but economists estimate that they reach $500–700 million a year.

Perhaps most important is the technical know-how overseas Vietnamese bring back to their native land. Owing to decades of war and international isolation, Vietnam long had been isolated from technological and scientific advances in the Western world. Many returning Vietnamese professionals visiting their families have helped Vietnam's modernization by holding seminars or giving lectures on economics, law, medicine, business management, and computer science.

Overseas Vietnamese also play an important role as brokers between Vietnam and foreign corporations. Bank of America appointed Luu Le, one of its vice presidents, to reopen its branch in Vietnam after Washington eased its trade sanctions. The urbane, smart-dressing Luu, who reverses the traditional Vietnamese order of his name to follow American convention, had helped open Bank of America's first branch in Saigon in 1966. He also closed the bank's operations in 1975 as Communist tanks approached the gates of the city. Luu thinks overseas Vietnamese businessmen have an advantage in understanding how things work. "Nonverbal language has its place in every country, but it's even more so in a country which is turning from one system to another," he says about Vietnam's transition from socialist economics to the free market. "Understanding a culture helps to build bridges. In negotiations, it can make a lot of difference."

Nguyen Mai, the tall, balding deputy chairman of the State Committee for Cooperation and Investment, the government's foreign investment watchdog that was incorporated into the newly formed ministry of planning and investment at the end of 1995, agrees. "Generally speaking, companies bringing back overseas Vietnamese enjoy an edge. These people understand the Vietnamese culture and the foreign culture of the company they're working for." Mai also hopes that the growing number of foreign companies investing in Vietnam will give overseas Vietnamese more confidence to come back and invest in their former homeland.

8

Dancing for Buddha

◆ ◆ ◆

Truong Thi Phuong sits on the floor swaying back and forth in front of a golden Buddha. The Buddha stands with a dozen smaller statues of guardian deities on a wooden altar laden with burning incense, brightly colored flowers, and plates of oranges, lychees, and apples. An old woman chants a prayer to the beat of her small stringed instrument, while two dozen of Phuong's friends and neighbors sit around the room with their hands clasped in prayer.

Without warning, Phuong, heavily made up and dressed in a bright red and gold *ao dai* (a traditional Vietnamese tunic), jumps up and begins to dance in front of the altar's deities. She has a sword tied behind her back and is swinging burning incense sticks back and forth over her shoulders. She stops abruptly, kneels down, covers her head with an embroidered red cloth, and begins to pray. Someone hands her a glass of fiery rice liquor, which she gulps down in a single swallow. She jumps back up as two assistants help her change into a green *ao dai*.

The *hau bong* ceremony goes on for nearly three hours. Over and over again Phuong changes her clothes as she prays first to Buddha and then to one of a variety of local guardian deities, including the Trung sisters, who fought against Chinese invaders nearly two thousand years ago. The *Far Eastern Economic Review*'s news assistant, Tran Le Thuy, aptly referred to the ceremony in English as "dancing for Buddha." Though anthropologists might term it something like a spirit medium ceremony with Buddhist trappings, I have never figured out a better name.

152

Phuong, a sturdy, jovial woman of forty-eight and mother of four, dances four times a year. "The first ceremony of the new year is to pray for luck and good fortune," says Phuong, a part-time spirit medium who makes a living selling lottery tickets and running a coffee shop. Her husband, a retired civil servant, works for a shipping company. He and Phuong have prospered under the reforms. Their newly completed four-story house in the eastern Hanoi suburb of Gia Long is big enough to include a special room for Phuong's altar and another for her new exercise bike. She bought it in an effort to hold down her weight, which has blossomed since the family started making money.

Phuong began dancing almost ten years ago during a visit to a local temple. "I felt very strange, like I was in a forest, not in a temple," she says about the visit. "I acted like someone else had entered my body and started dancing merrily. The police then were still very strict about such activities and told the people around me that I could worship, but not dance," she recalls. "People in the temple called another spirit to enter me, and I became normal again." Not long after the incident Phuong went to talk to a local spirit priest. He checked his centuries-old, Chinese zodiac calendar and found that Phuong had been predetermined to be a dancer. "If I don't do this job, I'll go crazy and have to live on the street," she says. "I feel very fortunate that I found this way to avoid going mad."

How has dancing changed Phuong's life? "After I finish a ceremony I feel very relaxed and contented," she says. Some of Phuong's neighbors think it has done much more. They attribute her recent prosperity to her dancing, believing that pleased deities helped her get rich, but Phuong insists that she and her husband acquired their wealth by working hard. Regardless, she is lucky to be doing well because many of the thirty-odd costumes she wears for her ceremonies cost over $30 apiece.

Phuong's dancing may not boost her income, but there are temples in Vietnam believed to have the power to make worshippers rich. One of these is the Ba Chua Kho Shrine, often dubbed the "businessman's pagoda" or the "free market shrine," located thirty kilometers east of Hanoi. Each day thousands of people descend on this temple, built in the eleventh century in honor of Chua Kho, a heroine who helped fend off Chinese invaders. She allegedly provides capital and advice to people wanting to start businesses or buy property. Many of those blessed by the goddess come back to repay their loans by burning stacks of fake gold bars and $100 bills that she supposedly recycles as startup capital for the next generation of entrepreneurs. Dozens of villagers make their living working as "interpreters" for Chua Kho—the goddess cannot read the romanized Vietnamese alphabet—or selling fake money and gold to the worshippers.

Not everyone is convinced by this new mix of religion and capitalism. "It's a type of bribery to the gods," declares a cynical young businesswoman in Hanoi. "Now many Vietnamese feel they have to do good, or the gods will take their things away from them." Many popular folk religions and so-called superstitious practices such as astrology, divination, faith healing and communicating with the dead were banned in Vietnam after the Communist Party ousted the French in 1954. Now, since the party has begun loosening its once draconian social controls, many of these long-repressed practices have returned.

Traditional Vietnamese cosmology is a world intertwined with a pantheon of gods, spiritual beings, historical personages, and ancestors intimately involved in the daily affairs of people. Some spirits are thought to be benevolent, providing protection from misfortune and bringing good fortune, while others are malicious. All must be propitiated through ritual offerings and correct behavior. According to this tradition people's lives were divided into auspicious and inauspicious days, and daily existence was governed by a host of practices and taboos. Parents, for example, would give their babies distasteful names to ensure that they weren't snatched by evil spirits. A pregnant woman and her husband would not be allowed to pound nails into their house because it was believed that this would delay the birth of their child indefinitely.

Ancestor veneration and filial piety have long played key roles in the lives of most Vietnamese. It is believed that when someone dies he or she doesn't truly leave this world. Instead, that person's spirit remains close to the living and can be called back by mediums to give advice to those left behind. If the spirits of the dead are properly cared for, they will help their descendants. Similarly, the country and each of its villages are believed to have guardian deities responsible for taking care of their inhabitants.

Traditional Vietnamese religious belief is an amalgamation of these indigenous animist beliefs intertwined with Taoist and Buddhist philosophies and Confucian ethics, all of which arrived in Vietnam during China's thousand-year occupation beginning in 111 B.C. Many of these traditional religious beliefs are being resurrected today. Throughout the year Vietnamese organize feasts for the dead and religious ceremonies to propitiate guardian spirits to ensure good fortune, success in business, luck on an examination, or help in conceiving a child. Farmers believe that they need to appease spirits who help protect them from floods, drought, pests, or other vagaries of nature that might ravage their rice crops.

Folk Revival

It is the sixth day of Tet, the lunar New Year, and thousands of villagers are converging on Co Loa (about twenty kilometers east of Hanoi) for a ceremony commemorating An Duong Vuong, the emperor who in the third century B.C. founded Co Loa as one of Vietnam's first capitals. Emperor Vuong is now considered the village's guardian spirit.

Accompanied by drums, gongs, and flutes, processions of men, elegantly robed in the traditional blue, black, red, and yellow tunics of the mandarin era, bear gifts of incense, candles, flowers, fruit, and rice cakes to pay tribute to the former emperor's spirit. This is followed by an elaborate religious ceremony in which people from Co Loa and six neighboring villages give thanks to the emperor and appeal to his spirit to protect them from calamity and shower them with prosperity, longevity, happiness, and fertility.

According to Vietnamese legend, Emperor Vuong built Co Loa and its two protecting earthen walls with the help of a giant golden turtle sent as an emissary of the sea god. During a series of attacks Chinese rulers failed to penetrate the citadel, so one of them sent his son to marry Vuong's daughter. After living in Co Loa for three years, the son returned to China and told his father how to conquer Co Loa. Realizing that his empire had been betrayed, Vuong ordered his daughter killed and built a temple in her honor.

The Co Loa festival is one of hundreds of centuries-old folk festivals celebrated by villagers in northern Vietnam. Most are simplified versions of traditional Confucian ceremonies borrowed by Vietnamese emperors from China hundreds of years ago. All of these festivals were banned as wasteful and feudal after the Communists seized power in 1954. The new rulers sought to rid Vietnam of outdated notions and superstitious practices that they believed kept people from becoming masters of their own fate. Most Vietnamese became reluctant to openly practice traditional rituals out of fear that the Communist Party would interpret their behavior as political dissent, but many families continued performing these rituals in their homes at night.

Finally, in the late 1980s Co Loa and many other villages once again began to organize large public festivals. Under the Communist Party's reforms Hanoi no longer frowned on such pomp and ceremony and no longer had much energy to squelch "superstitious" rituals. With their new freedom peasants were producing more and had cash to spend on festivals. The villagers found, however, that freedom and money were not the only ingredients they needed. Most of the costumes, musical instruments, and other paraphernalia required to perform the ceremonies had been damaged or lost during the four-decade interval. As a result, older villagers, who had witnessed the festivals in their youth, assumed the painstaking task of trying to recreate the ceremonial regalia from memory.[1]

Women played a leading role in resurrecting these ancient folk festivals and other religious rituals. According to one male villager in Co Loa, women are "less afraid to challenge the government." American anthropologist Shaun Malarney attributes this to the fact that "women were marginalized in the local power structure" and that they had "always engaged the supernatural in order to assist them in the fulfillment of their responsibilities on this earth." Malarney continues, "When the wars were over, and the economic situation in Viet Nam [sic] began to improve, women began to more openly and actively engage the spirit world, seeking not only prosperity for themselves and their families, but simply to give thanks for having survived."[2]

The Communists originally sought to ban many ancient rituals because they thought they were based on superstitious beliefs, perpetuated an inegalitarian social order and wasted the villagers' limited resources. In the days before the revolution families would have to spend a large part of their annual income to organize a wedding or funeral ceremony.

Today most villages have rebuilt their *dinh*, the open-sided, red-roofed communal houses that until the defeat of the French had served as the political, social, and religious centers of each community. The communal house held the altar of the village guardian spirit, and the council of village notables met here to resolve local disputes and redistribute the community's land from time to time. After the Communists seized power they moved quickly to shut down the *dinh*, converting many of them to rice warehouses.

Today the *dinh* are being reactivated, but their roles are largely social and religious, that is, conspicuously apolitical. For example, villages again worship their guardian spirits in the old communal halls, but the ceremonies are much simpler than they once were. Women are no longer banned from the communal houses as they had been earlier, and the village social hierarchy has been broken so men no longer spend hours haggling over their rank in the local pecking order.

Sometimes the blend of old and new creates interesting problems. In Giap Tu village, south of Hanoi, where anthropologist Malarney was doing research in the early 1990s, a conflict erupted over who should be the village guardian. Many villagers wanted to retain a traditional medicine doctor who had saved lives in the past. But others, mostly men with revolutionary backgrounds, wanted to have Ho Chi Minh adopted as guardian owing to his heroic feats in saving the nation from foreign invaders. Some villagers became upset when Ho's supporters put a huge, white plaster bust of the former president on the *dinh's* main altar. But in the end, the village found a compromise: The bust was removed and replaced with a cabinet that, when its doors are open, reveals a lacquered portrait of Ho.[3]

One of the biggest social changes, particularly in the countryside, is the resurgence of wedding and funeral feasts that the Communists had long tried to ban. During the socialist heyday, the Ho Chi Minh Communist Youth Union organized wedding receptions, often serving guests little more than tea. Today, families are once again putting on elaborate wedding feasts for their children, sometimes feeding as many as five hundred to one thousand guests. "The size of feasts is a common topic of conversation and people are constantly comparing and criticizing," observes Malarney. Ironically, after the Communists tried for three decades to change their function, ritual feasts are once again playing an important role in projecting "social difference and inequality in the Vietnamese village" as families try to outdo each other.[4]

Weddings, which have long been treated largely as civil ceremonies, are again being performed in front of traditional ancestral altars. The size of gifts given by parents also is increasing, with richer families sometimes including gold and motorcycles. One traditional practice outlawed by the Communists that has not made a comeback is arranged marriages. Couples are now free to choose their own partners, and families no longer engage in years of negotiations before a wedding.

Funeral ceremonies that, like those in neighboring China, are designed to help the soul of the deceased make the journey to the other world, have become more elaborate. Sad funeral music played on a long bamboo wind instrument known as a *ken* and once frowned on by the Communists has reappeared. Children of the deceased have resumed wearing traditional funeral garb: straw hats for sons and peaked hats made of cheesecloth for daughters. Small gold bars fashioned out of paper once again are dropped along the route to the cemetery so that the deceased can find his or her way home after burial. Families have again put up wooden altars in their houses to venerate their ancestors, whose spirits are believed to have a powerful influence over the world of the living. Ancestral spirits bring good health and fortune to descendants who care for them and misfortune to those who neglect them.

Households have resumed organizing elaborate gatherings on the death anniversary of their deceased parents and grandparents, and grandmothers are again "adopting" their grandchildren to child-guardian deities to fend off evil spirits. Some people also have resumed holding superstitious rites to determine the cause of a person's illness, particularly if it can't be cured. Yet most Vietnamese now use the health services introduced by the Communist government, believing that they are more effective in treating most diseases than their ancient practices.

Fortune-telling and geomancy have returned with a vengeance to help Vietnamese, who, like the Chinese, believe they must prepare for auspicious and inauspicious days. To minimize the chances of misfortune many people consult horoscope experts, who analyze the lunar calendar to find the most propitious time for certain activities. Few people in Vietnam make important decisions without first consulting fortune-tellers, many of whom camouflage their activities behind "real" jobs such as selling newspapers. Businessmen check which day to reopen their shops after Tet, when to take a trip, or pay for a new piece of land. Young people check whether their sign is compatible with that of a proposed marriage partner, on which day to hold the wedding, and at what hour to consummate their marriage. Computer buffs install astrology software in their computers to explore their fortunes each morning.

Others use mediums to "talk" to departed relatives. I once attended an elaborate ceremony in which Nguyen Thi Sen—a Haiphong medium who is so popular that she runs a guest house to serve people waiting to see her—helped members of a Gia Long family talk to the husband and father, who had died thirty years earlier. (Sen says that government officials no longer harass her, although she recalls that police destroyed the first temple she had built, in 1981.) After more than an hour of praying and chanting the spirit of Nguyen Van Tuc arrived and, through Sen, began chatting and joking with the living members of his family. He told one of his daughters to stop working with a "deceitful partner" in her transport business and advised another daughter how to cure her breast cancer, saying she should burn a votive paper image of herself and put an amulet under her pillow for nine nights. She should also drink a glass of rice liquor and a cup of water from the ancestral altar every day. (A year later, after three medical checkups, the daughter claimed she had no remaining signs of the cancer.) "Sometimes I come back to visit and play tricks on you by hiding some of your things," Tuc said to his wife, who is now in her mid-eighties. He also told her that he needed more money and new clothes for his life in the "other world." "It is no longer common to use small currency, so please send me bigger bills," he said, adding that he also needed a new hat, shoes, and a suit.[5]

Many Vietnamese believe that when they burn paper replicas of clothes, money, houses, and motorbikes, their deceased relatives get to use them in the hereafter. The Communists launched repeated campaigns to stamp out the use of *hang ma*, or votive paper objects, but they never quite succeeded. Today a hefty cottage industry producing paper hats, shoes, bicycles, and even refrigerators has sprung up as the living are once again allowed to serve the dead.

Buddha and Jesus

Vietnam's more formal religions are also experiencing a revival. Hanoi's imposing graystone Roman Catholic cathedral, where men and women still sit on opposite sides, is packed for four masses each Sunday, with the first service starting at 4:30 A.M. Over half of the participants are young people, even though the liturgy has not been modernized since the cathedral was built by French missionaries at the turn of the century.

Protestant house churches, informal meetings for Bible study, and prayer in people's homes and shop-houses are the fastest-growing religious phenomenon in Vietnam today. In remote northern mountain regions thousands of Hmong are converting to Christianity in response to foreign radio broadcasts.

On the first day of each lunar month Buddhist pagodas around the country are crowded with believers coming to pray and study Buddhist scriptures. "I pray for health and good fortune," an employee of a state-owned factory in Hanoi told me. "After that my heart and mind are more content." Some believers undoubtedly display their religion publicly because it is no longer frowned on by the country's allegedly atheist rulers. "As the religious policy of the government has slowly opened up, people are no longer afraid to go to pagodas," observes Thich Minh Chau, director of the Buddhist Research Institute in Ho Chi Minh City and a member of the National Assembly. Many turn to religion to find new meaning in the wake of the collapse of the Communist system. "The massive changes which the reform policy has engendered in Vietnamese life have created a great deal of chaos and uncertainty in people's lives," observes Malarney. "Buddhism, for many, is a way to invest one's life with a bit more peace and security."[6]

Relations between Vietnam's government and its religious communities have improved a great deal under the reforms. These institutions had frequently crossed swords in the years following the Communist victory in 1975. Remembering the role that Buddhist dissidents had played in toppling the southern government of Ngo Dinh Diem in 1963 and how the Catholics and indigenous Hoa Hao and Cao Dai groups had supported Hanoi's enemies during the war, the Communist Party moved decisively to preempt any challenge from religious groups. Hundreds of clergy were trundled off to reeducation camps and prisons, all theological training schools were shut down, and the network of schools and hospitals run by religious communities were taken over by the new regime. The party insisted on having a veto in the selection, ordination, and transfer of religious leaders in an attempt to promote malleable clergy.

In the past decade, most clergy have been released from detention while Buddhists and Christians have been allowed to reopen small seminaries. Religious groups now find it easier to refurbish pagodas and churches ravaged by years of war and neglect, and to get permission to publish or import religious materials. Catholic priests can again visit the Vatican. The cash-strapped government has allowed religious groups to resume social work activities as well. Catholic nuns in Ho Chi Minh City run schools providing free tuition, lunch, and clothing to poor children. The Linh Quang Tinh Xa Pagoda has taken over a school formerly run by the state for eighty handicapped children in the suburbs. It also operates a home for the elderly poor in the beach town of Vung Tau.

Still, tensions remain. One problem revolves around the Communist Party's rigorous controls over the training and ordination of new clergy to replace those who died or fled the county as refugees. The number of Buddhist monks—who serve roughly two-thirds of the country's population—has fallen to about 20,000, down from approximately 30,000 in 1975. Many Catholic priests, particularly in the north, are forced to serve half a dozen or more scattered parishes. Catholics—who number about six million—complain that the government allows only half of their seminary graduates to be ordained, even though all have been screened by the government before admission to the seminary. Protestants—whose numbers have doubled to approximately 400,000 in the past twenty years—say they have less than half of the five hundred pastors they had in 1975.

Unlike the Buddhist and Christian groups, the indigenous Cao Dai religion has not been authorized to reopen its religious schools. The Cao Dai religion, founded in 1919 by mystic Ngo Van Chieu, is a syncretistic blend of Confucianism, Taoism, Buddhism, and popular local cults whose pantheon of saints includes Buddha, Jesus

Christ, Joan of Arc, Chinese leader Sun Yat-sen, and nineteenth-century French writer Victor Hugo. The religion believes in a Supreme Being, or Cao Dai, that makes its wishes known through mediums. The movement's most important symbol is the Heavenly Eye, represented by the huge painting of a human eye on the ornate cathedral in Tay Ninh, near the border with Cambodia in the southern Mekong delta. The eye symbolizes the omniscience and omnipresence of Cao Dai. The religion has elaborate religious ceremonies and a highly developed hierarchy, and it pledges to maintain harmony in the universe and restore morality on earth. Most of the group's three million believers are farmers from the Mekong delta.

The roughly two million followers of the Hoa Hao religion still are not allowed to make their annual pilgrimage to the birthplace of their founder, Huynh Phu So. So, a frail faith healer with prophetic talents, established this reformed Buddhist religion in 1939. In contrast to the Cao Dai movement, the Hoa Hao reject elaborate temples and complex hierarchies in favor of individual spiritual enlightenment and family-based worship. The simplicity of the movement attracted hundreds of thousands of poor Mekong delta peasants after World War II.

Cao Dai and Hoa Hao followers clashed repeatedly with the Communists during the wars against France and the United States. Both groups continued to resist the Communists after their victory, which resulted in many of their leaders being sent to reeducation camps.

Religious freedoms have increased most in urban areas that are easily monitored by foreign observers and government officials, but abuses continue in remote rural areas. Ethnic minority Christians from the northern mountains sent a delegation to Hanoi in early 1993 to complain about being harassed, beaten, and fined by local officials for their religious beliefs. Protestant farmers living near Pleiku in the central highlands told me a few years ago that officials prevented them from sending their children to secondary school.

Unlike China, Vietnam has never severed ties between its Catholics and the Vatican. In fact, in an effort to improve relations with the

Holy See Hanoi has welcomed several visits by Vatican representatives to discuss differences, one of which centers around the appointment of new archbishops and bishops. "Religious freedom of the people of Vietnam is like a bird trapped in a cage," Monsignor Claudio Celli, the Vatican's deputy foreign minister, observed following a 1994 visit. Celli recognized that religious freedom had improved in recent years but added that "the road ahead is still long and complicated before the Vietnamese Catholic Church reaches true religious freedom."[7]

Undoubtedly Hanoi's most dramatic clash in recent years has been with Buddhist dissidents opposed to the Communist Party's formation of the Vietnam Buddhist Church in 1981. The new group was intended to replace the Unified Buddhist Church that had been active during the war in calling for peace and criticizing the abuses of the American-backed regime in the south. In an effort to silence the dissident Buddhists, who unlike the Christians have few ties abroad, Hanoi exiled Executive Vice President Thich Huyen Quang to the central Vietnamese city of Quang Ngai and General Secretary Thich Quang Do to Thai Binh in the north.

Tensions erupted in May 1992 during the funeral of Thich Don Hau, the eighty-eight-year-old acting supreme patriarch of the outlawed movement, in the central city of Hue. Quang, age seventy-nine, staged a hunger strike to force officials to free him from "pagoda arrest" and allow him to attend the funeral. The fiercely independent-minded monk turned his eulogy for Hau into a blistering attack against the regime. Quang followed this with a string of letters to Hanoi in which he demanded that the outlawed group be allowed to resume its activities and charged that the rival group established by the government was "a political and temporary tool of the current regime which has lost its links to Vietnamese Buddhism." He called the Communist Party's reforms "half-way measures" and said it was impossible for Buddhists to cooperate with a regime "which is inimical to religion" and seeks to "intervene all the time in the internal affairs" of religious groups.

The conflict escalated on the first anniversary of Hau's death, after a man immolated himself at the Linh Mu pagoda in Hue where Hau had worked. Buddhists said he was a Buddhist believer, while government officials insisted he had been depressed about family problems. When officials called in Thich Tri Tuu, the pagoda's superior monk, for questioning about the incident, protesters—in a stunning display of defiance—blocked traffic along Highway One for six hours and burned a government jeep. Four monks and five other persons were arrested and later sentenced to prison terms of six months to four years for "creating a serious disorder."

Another incident erupted more recently when the dissident Buddhist group, flying its flag on a convoy of trucks, tried to distribute blankets and medical supplies to flood victims in the Mekong delta in November 1994. The trucks were stopped and five monks were arrested. Quang mounted a hunger strike to protest their detention, which prompted officials in late 1994 to move him to a remote pagoda located about twenty kilometers from Quang Ngai. His deputy, Thich Quang Do, a prominent Buddhist scholar who had returned to Ho Chi Minh City in 1992, was arrested a few days later. A month after the United States established diplomatic relations with Vietnam in July 1995 a court sentenced Do and five of his followers to jail terms of up to five years. A foreign ministry official said they had been found guilty of "taking advantage of the rights of liberty and democracy to try to attack the interests of the state." With the imprisonment of Quang and Do virtually all of the renegade Buddhist church's senior leaders are in detention.[8]

Modern Women, Modern Teenagers

One of the Communist Party's most impressive accomplishments has been the promotion of the position of Vietnamese women. Although such heroines as the Trung sisters had been glorified throughout history, women in feudal Vietnamese society had been viewed as second-class citizens with a status lower than that of their husbands and sons. "One hundred girls aren't worth one boy," an ancient Vietnamese saying declared. Under the Confucian system a Vietnamese woman was taught that she had three obligations: to obey her father, her husband, and her oldest son.

Following the Communist victory, however, peasant girls were sent to school for the first time. Women were encouraged to work in factories, to join the Communist Party, even to become government officials. New legislation granted many of them the same privileges as men, including the right to own land, which gave them some degree of economic independence. The revolutionaries banned polygamy, prostitution, child marriages, and the sale of brides. Neighborhood committees harangued abusive husbands to stop beating their wives. Yet major gaps exist between the Communist Party's theory and practice. For example, women hold only 5 percent of the country's cabinet-level posts and make up just 18 percent of the National Assembly. Not a single woman has ever made it into the ruling Politburo. In 1991 Truong My Hoa became the first woman appointed to the Secretariat, which runs party affairs on a daily basis; around the same time another woman, Nguyen Thi Binh, was named vice president, a largely ceremonial post.

Nonetheless, women have played an important role in overhauling Vietnam's political environment. After the war it was women who first looked for ways to circumvent the Communist Party's hard-line principles. Not only were they the first to return to the country's temples, but also the first to find ways to sell or barter their surplus. "Renovation in Vietnam came first from women," Hanoi sociologist Pham Bich San points out. "They were the first to go to the market. Men had to keep their prestige, but women had to keep their children."

Although it is true that the market economy has raised living standards for both women and men, it also has increased the pressures on women. One problem is that the reforms have expanded the workload of women, argues Le Thi Quy of the Center for Women's Studies at Hanoi's National Center for Social Sciences and Humanities. During the period of farm cooperatives, men and women were roughly equal members, with men assigned to do heavier jobs, such as plowing. Now, a decade after the reforms, researchers say women perform an increasing share of the farm work, including such heavy tasks as tilling the soil. In many cases, men have migrated to cities to look for better-paying jobs in construction or to pedal *cyclos*, leaving their wives at home to cultivate the family plot and raise the children.

In a survey conducted at Hanoi's Dong Xuan Textile Mill Quy found that women spend an average of twelve to fourteen hours a day—almost twice as long as men—working at their jobs and doing housework for the family. Women are responsible for cooking in over 79 percent of the households represented in the factory; men cook in only 16 percent of the families.[9]

"The negative side of a woman's emancipation is that she has been burdened with another job," Quy says about women working outside of their homes. "If a woman wants the same status as a man, she has to put in double effort. When staff in an office are chosen for promotion or further training, bosses choose men because they're afraid of the family burdens of women." Women, the Russian-trained historian says, make up half of the country's labor force, but roughly 70 percent work in low-paying, menial jobs in agriculture, forestry, and construction. As in many countries, men are promoted faster and given more opportunities to upgrade their skills because they are assumed to have fewer demands on their time after normal working hours, Quy adds. Roughly 60 percent of the country's unemployed are women, who have been hardest hit by layoffs from troubled state enterprises.

Since the Communist Party's reforms, men again occupy the best-paying jobs and positions of greatest authority, and there is little talk of equality. "Power now belongs to the people who have money," argues one young woman who works for a foreign company in Hanoi. "It's an old boy club, and it's harder for a woman to get into that club than it is to get into the central committee," she jokes, referring to the Communist Party's 161-member elite group.

Sexism has also reemerged. Companies compete with each other in publishing calendars of scantily clad women at Tet, and bosses have begun hiring attractive young women as secretaries, many of whom complain of regular sexual advances by employers or their clients. "Before it was politically incorrect to say something bad about a woman," says one businesswoman who has studied abroad. "Now men can make sexist jokes about women. They'll say such things like 'a woman's brains are less expensive than a man's.' " Women complain that many Vietnamese men view them as little more than playthings. One of my friends, a married woman in her late twenties who worked for a foreign outfit in Hanoi, complained that men would make passes or try to fondle or kiss her in the elevator when she would accompany her boss's visitors to the front door. When she traveled to Ho Chi Minh City on business, men she had met during the day would call her repeatedly or stop by the hotel to ask her out, even after she had told them she wasn't interested.

Sexual harassment in Vietnam has not become the issue it has in many Western countries, yet I know of at least one case in Hanoi where a female worker blocked the promotion of a middle-aged technocrat. Frustrated by his repeated sexual advances, the woman began tape-recording her boss's brazen overtures. Later when he was trying for a promotion to a more senior post, the woman threatened to turn the tapes over to the ministry's personnel department. To avoid public embarrassment, her boss at least temporarily abandoned his pursuit of the position. But this case is the exception. Many young women complain that they simply have to put up with sexual harassment if they want to keep their jobs.

"The life of women improved after 1954," says Quy, the researcher. "Many women are now directors of companies, and the number of women with doctorates has increased. In the cities, women work as civil servants and as sellers in the market. These women have made it and this has changed the role of women in the family. . . . But there are also negative aspects and social problems," Quy continues, suggesting that in real terms women have gained less than men. "Prostitution and domestic violence are becoming out of control. In the countryside the spirit of honoring men, looking down on women, early marriages, and polygamy are increasing." Illiteracy among women, which had been almost eradicated two decades ago, is on the rise again. "In poor families, when parents can't afford school fees, they pay only for their sons," Quy says.

Vietnam's social upheaval is putting severe strains on families as people try to keep up with rapidly shifting values and a quickening pace of life. One sign of this strain is divorce. The incidence of family breakup, frowned on in traditional society and during socialism, is rising. In 1993 roughly 30,000 couples—three times the 1975 level—applied for divorce, according to Vu Khac Xuong, chief administrator of the People's Supreme Court in Hanoi. Although these figures are small compared to those in many other countries, the lanky judge says the number of applications for divorce is increasing 5 percent to 7 percent a year. Most of the applications come from urban couples, at least one member of which has a university degree or has spent time studying or working abroad. Women initiate 55 percent to 60 percent of divorce proceedings, according to Xuong.

Many urban middle- and upper-class parents are worried about another social phenomenon: the rebellion of their children. In recent years this has been expressed in the form of high-speed, nocturnal motorcycle races. In the wee hours of many a weekend morning, groups of twenty or more bikers turn the narrow, tree-lined streets of Hanoi into a race track. They roar around Hoan Kiem Lake, hurtle down Ba Trieu Street, and back up Hue Street at speeds topping 120 kilometers an hour. Around festive occasions they organize special races such as 100-kilometer night-time sprints from Hanoi to Haiphong. "I only find excitement when I'm driving at high speeds," confesses Tran Ngoc Tu, a twenty-two-year-old racer. "Racers want people to admire them. We want to be known as the best racers in Hanoi." Tu, whose parents run a motorcycle shop, dropped out of school in the eleventh grade. He is now taking a six-month car-driving course.

The racers are primarily young men age seventeen to twenty-two. Some wear white headbands—associated with death and mourning in Vietnam—to show that they are not afraid to take risks. Indeed, many of the races turn out to be deadly. Racers told me in mid-1994 that between fifteen and twenty bikers had died and dozens more had been critically injured in the previous year. Melees erupted on several occasions when police tried to break up the races. Some attribute the phenomenon to the shortage of jobs and the city's lack of recreational facilities. Like teenagers the world over, they have to find something to do. "The young people are bored," sociologist Pham Bich San argues. "They have to do something." Others believe racing is a by-product of sudden wealth after decades of war and socialism. "Many families today are too busy making money and have no time to take care of their children," says Le Thi Nham Tuyet, another Hanoi sociologist.[10]

Increasing crime is another result of the breakneck pace of social change. The most popular publication in Vietnam today is *Ho Chi Minh City Police*, which has a circulation of 400,000. Week after week it chronicles the costs of new freedom and growing prosperity—surging vice, rampant drug addiction, prostitution, and epidemic levels of smuggling and corruption. Many Vietnamese are worried that the country has been threatened by a general breakdown in social order since the Communist Party first slackened its controls. "The crime rate tends to increase in terms of severity, extent and organization," Bui Thien Ngo, the minister of interior, wrote in *Communist Review*. Ngo, a member of the ruling Communist Party Politburo, said there are 122 criminals out of 100,000 people and an average of 178 cases of crime reported each day.[11] These figures are still low compared to countries in the West but are much higher than Vietnam's crime rates before the reforms.

The surge in vice is not unlike what happened in Eastern Europe and the Soviet Union when communism collapsed. Ngo attributes Vietnam's problem to the "side effects of the market-driven economy," loopholes in the legal system, the growing disparity between the rich and the poor and the "negative influence imported from the outside."[12] Sociologists add that the rise in crime is due to the fact that millions who once were cared for under the Communists' cradle-to-grave social contract now find themselves marginalized. Urban unemployment is estimated by the International Labor Organization to have reached 25 percent since the government stopped guaranteeing jobs for everyone.[13] Young people are the hardest hit. Those without jobs hustle on the fringes of society, turning to crime, prostitution, and drug addiction. Fully 40 percent of crime takes place in Vietnam's four biggest cities—Ho Chi Minh City, Hanoi, Danang, and Haiphong—which account for only one-eighth of the country's population, Ngo says. More than 70 percent of the criminals are between the ages of eighteen and thirty, and juveniles under age eighteen account for roughly one in ten crimes.[14]

Ordinary Vietnamese complain most about the sharp increase in corruption and smuggling. According to the country's press, the number of officials involved in bribery and embezzlement is rising each year. Realizing that white-collar crime is in danger of veering out of control, the National Assembly in late 1992 stiffened the country's criminal code to allow capital punishment for officials found guilty of defrauding the state.

Some see the growing incidence of crime as part of the general breakdown of Vietnam's social system, which began with the defeat of the French and the Communists' attempt to wipe out the old feudal order. "The material life of the population was better, but there were no determined moral norms capable of replacing the traditional values," says Huu Ngoc, a Hanoi writer and social commentator. An abnormal social life continued throughout years of war. "During the war, individualism was repressed to serve the common cause," he explains. "All other developments of the heart or for individual happiness were silenced."

The Vietnamese social system began to change with the advent of peace. "Solidarity in society has been losing ground since the end of the war," says Ngoc. "Today we're facing an invasion of the Western way of life and the rise of individualism." In present-day Vietnam, Ngoc believes motorcycle racing and soaring rates of crime and malfeasance are signs of the "revenge of the individual." This moral breakdown has prompted Ngoc and other intellectuals to call for a revival of some aspects of Confucianism that stress social harmony and the importance of the family. They believe that a revival of a "reformed" Confucianism, overhauled to fit the modern world and its scientific advances, could form a counterbalance to the rapid economic and social changes sweeping the country.

Le Thi Quy, the women's researcher, agrees. "We don't have a suitable model for the family today. We fought against the old model, but we didn't build a new one. We're now looking for a new model that will enable us to emancipate women and at the same time maintain our Eastern traditions. There's a tendency now to develop the traditions of Confucianism," Quy adds. "But we need to abolish the negative aspects in order for Confucianism to have a positive role in Vietnam."

The Impact of the Arts

A visitor wandering through the maze of tiny footpaths in the southern suburbs of Hanoi could be forgiven for having trouble finding Nguyen Huy Thiep. His two-room, dried-earth house surrounded by a large flower garden is much like that of his neighbors. What sets his house apart is the four-meter cement Buddha statue that towers over his house and the rest of the neighborhood.

"I built it to make my house less sad," Thiep says. "If my house didn't have this statue, it would be very boring. Since I built it, my sons like to stay home more," Thiep says about his nineteen- and thirteen-year-old children. "They love each other more." Thiep is not even a Buddhist, so the unusual statue adds to his image. The man, whose face is as tan as a farmer's, is every bit as unconventional and original as his writing. Thiep created an uproar in Vietnamese literary circles when his short stories appeared in 1987, a few months after the Communist Party launched its retreat from old-fashioned socialism and granted greater freedom to artists.

Thiep first captured the attention of Vietnamese readers with

"The General Retires," a provocative short story about a military officer who is shocked by the society to which he returns after years of serving his country. He is particularly dismayed to discover that his daughter-in-law is feeding aborted fetuses obtained from a maternity clinic to a pack of guard dogs she is raising to supplement the family's income. Thiep caused another storm in 1988 when he published three historical stories, including "Chastity," which depicts Nguyen Hue, the eighteenth-century hero who defeated invaders from China, as speaking crudely and lusting after beautiful women. "If we denigrate Nguyen Hue today, tomorrow we will denigrate Uncle Ho," one critic warned.[15]

Thiep was born in Hanoi in 1950, at the height of Vietnam's struggle against French colonial rule. He spent most of his childhood in a remote northwestern province, where his mother worked as a farm laborer, before he came to Hanoi to study in a teacher training college. After graduating in 1970 Thiep went to teach in an ethnic minority area west of the capital. He stayed for a decade before returning to Hanoi to work for a string of publishing houses.

Thiep and other new writers who began publishing in the late 1980s prompted a more dramatic shift in Vietnamese literature than anything witnessed since the 1930s. "Revolutionary romanticism," which had dominated party-controlled literature since the 1940s, was "displaced rapidly by the individual in whose suffering person history was now concentrated and absorbed," notes Greg Lockhart, an Australian academic who has translated some of Thiep's stories into English.

Vietnamese literature had languished during the wars against France and the United States. Much of it was little more than "socialist realism," in which one-dimensional characters behaved according to norms of revolutionary heroism. Thiep and his peers started to challenge this heroic illusion in the late 1980s. This new generation of writers created multifaceted characters driven by ulterior motives. They depicted a society torn apart by greed and corruption and raised questions about the nature of heroism, the meaning of life, and the cost of war.

Duong Thu Huong's *Paradise of the Blind*, first published in 1988, exposed the brutality and incompetence of the land reform program launched by the Communists in the mid-1950s; many of the novel's characters are hypocritical bureaucrats. For Huong, the biggest threat to Vietnam does not come from the West but from party *apparatchiks* who have betrayed the revolution. Huong may not be Vietnam's most talented writer, but her books generate excitement because they explore the fate of ordinary people and the impact of the party's intervention in their daily lives.

It also helps that Huong, age forty-nine, has impeccable party credentials. In 1967, at the age of twenty, she volunteered to entertain soldiers fighting at the front during the American War, and in 1979 she was on the northern border when Chinese troops attacked. Somewhere along the way, Huong became disillusioned. In 1990 she severed her links with the Communist Party. Officials insist she quit; Huong claims she was expelled. In early 1991 she was arrested and detained for seven months for allegedly trying to smuggle "reactionary" documents out of the country. She says these materials were her own writings, which she was trying to send out of the country because local publishing houses refused to print them.

Another writer who captured the attention of Vietnamese readers was Bao Ninh, a veteran of the North Vietnamese army. Hanoi's writers have published dozens of books romanticizing Vietnam's war with the United States and lauding the bravery of its soldiers; Ninh's novel, *The Sorrow of War*, was the first to shatter these myths and depict a war full of anguish and suffering. For Ninh, the war produced no winners. "The ones who loved war were not the young men, but the others like the politicians, middle-aged men with fat bellies and short legs," says Kien, the novel's main character. "Not the ordinary people. The recent years of war had brought enough suffering and pain to last them a thousand years." Ninh's scouting unit forms the backdrop of the novel. Of the five hundred soldiers who went south in 1969, Ninh was one of only ten to return. He was critically wounded twice and participated in the final assault on Saigon in April 1975.

The novel begins with Kien, Ninh's alter ego, traveling to central Vietnam after the war to look for the remains of his fallen comrades. Kien is haunted by nightmares about gruesome battles in the Jungle of the Screaming Souls, where so many of his unit died. Following his release from the army, Kien returns home to an indifferent society and is overwhelmed by depression, alcoholism, and alienation. "After this hard-won victory, fighters like you, Kien, will never be normal again," an army driver tells him. "You won't even speak with your normal voice, in a normal way again." Ninh describes a disappointing peace and questions whether the struggle to reunify the country was worth all of the sacrifices. "Justice may have won," Kien writes about Hanoi's victory over the Americans, "but cruelty, death and inhuman violence had also won. . . . The psychological scars of the war will remain forever."[16] The Vietnam Writers Association voted Ninh's work one of the three best novels of the year in 1991, when it was first published. The award prompted a flurry of protest from army veterans and literary critics, who charged that Ninh had exaggerated the horrors of the battlefield.

These recent literary developments remind observers of the 1930s, when the publication of vernacular newspapers, magazines, and books exploded. Like today, most writers that emerged in the earlier period were seeking to address the social, cultural, and political dilemmas facing the country, then still a colony of France. The new generation was seeking to vent the powerful emotions of a colonized nation struggling to become a modern society.

With the sudden arrival of writings by Thiep and his peers, literature has become the country's most lively forum for the discussion of new ideas. As historian Keith Taylor points out, writers suddenly found themselves at the forefront of the "ferment in Vietnamese intellectual life that tested the limits of the forbidden and opened up mental space for the process of reform that gathered momentum in the mid- and late 1980s."[17]

The party made sure, however, that the process of reform did not spin out of control. At the end of 1988 it orchestrated the ouster of Nguyen Ngoc, editor of a literary magazine that enthusiastically promoted Thiep's writings. "There are those who sing his praises until they run out of words," observed one editor of Thiep's anthologies, while others "call for him to be brought to court and imprisoned."[18] A reviewer of one of his early stories added: "While I would not go as far as to consider this writer sick, his are not the ideas of a healthy and wholesome mind."[19] Vietnamese literary critics say the Communist Party, fearing the turmoil that engulfed its former socialist allies in Eastern Europe and the Soviet Union, in 1990 began restricting the literary freedom that had given artists a new lease on life. Hanoi's leaders insist that Vietnam will "adopt the free market, but keep the old political system," one literary critic observes. "This means they'll allow almost no change in the policy of literature and art."

"Current literature doesn't reflect real life like it did in the late 1980s," adds Le Minh Khue, author of *Little Tragedies*, a compilation of short stories that ran into a buzz saw of protest from pro-government critics in late 1993. "People haven't stopped writing. They just write less deeply," she says. "This is a delicate time." None of Thiep's recent writings have evoked the excitement and controversy of his early works, but he insists that "people can still breathe easier" than they could before the reforms began. The "phenomenon" still writes, but he spends more of his time running a restaurant, raising flowers, and maintaining the Buddha statue in his garden.

Resuscitating Health Care

Along Hanoi's bustling Hue Street, known for its restaurants and shops, one door remains locked until four each afternoon. Crowded inside a tiny, freshly painted room is some of the most sophisticated dental equipment in the Vietnamese capital. This is a *ngoai gio*, or after hours, dental clinic run by Pham Duong Chau. Chau, a suave, forty-four-year-old dentist trained in the former Czechoslovakia, opens the clinic each day after putting in eight hours at a government hospital. He treats five to seven patients each evening and fifteen to twenty more on Sundays. "Some are foreigners," he says of his patients. "Others are people who are too busy to go to a clinic during the day time."

Thousands of similar "after hours" health clinics have opened throughout Vietnam in recent years. The government began allowing these private clinics to operate in a move intended to help medical workers boost their meager salaries. Doctors working in a government hospital typically earn only $20 a month; an entrepreneurial health worker such as Chau earns another $135 on the side. Sanctioning private clinics was one of several reforms instituted by the Communist government since 1989 in an effort to resuscitate the country's health care system. For years Vietnam's Communist rulers had promised their population free medical care, but the system went into a tailspin in the late 1970s. The cash-strapped government lacked the funds to buy medical supplies, and poor salaries caused morale problems among doctors and nurses.

Vietnam had approximately fifty doctors to serve some twenty million people in 1954 when the French colonial rulers left. The Communists, who gained control of the north, moved quickly to mount a mass vaccination campaign against typhoid, cholera, and other diseases. They also urged people to boil their drinking water and to dig latrines and wells. The new government expanded the country's primary health network, and within ten years two out of three villages in the north had a trained assistant doctor.

The country's health conditions have witnessed a remarkable turnaround. Vietnam began recording better vital statistics than many countries with higher per-capita incomes. Infant mortality fell from 156 per 1,000 live births in 1960 to 53 three decades later. Life expectancy jumped from fifty years in 1970 to sixty-five by 1990. Still, Vietnam's health picture was mixed. "Health care coverage was extensive and mostly equitable," two Harvard researchers point out, but the system suffered from "inefficiency, lack of effectiveness, and poor quality."[20] By the mid-1980s the country's mounting economic crisis had caused improvements in health care to stall. Cases of malaria and dengue fever began rising in the highlands because the government lacked funds to continue spraying mosquitoes.

Malnutrition rates among children remain high. UNICEF estimates that 45 percent of Vietnam's children under age four are moderately to severely underweight, compared to 26 percent in nearby Thailand.[21] Despite Vietnam's surge in food production, 11 percent to 35 percent of the population (the exact number varies from one region to another) consumes less than 1,800 calories a day per capita, or 300 calories less than the minimum recommended by the United Nations. Only one in three rural families has access to safe drinking water. Many health care facilities, particularly in the countryside, are dilapidated and lack medicines. Visitors to remote rural areas find that the doors of village clinics are closed during normal working hours because health care workers are out planting rice or raising chickens. "You have to make an appointment in advance," jokes Nguyen Thi Ngoc Phuong, director of the Tu Du Women's Hospital in Ho Chi Minh City.

Vietnam has one of the highest densities of hospital beds in Asia, but its expenditures on health are among the lowest. In 1990 Hanoi spent less than $1 per capita, compared to almost $3 in China.[22] Inflation has caused the real salaries of health care workers to decline, resulting in low morale and poor productivity. The average rural health care center has five health care workers but can see only six patients a day. In an effort to inject new life into the health care system, the government has introduced user fees to supplement income from the state budget, privatized the sale of pharmaceuticals, and allowed health care workers such as Chau to set up private practices. The results so far have been less than spectacular. "The changes have been made very quickly and without adequate planning," a group of World Bank economists observed. "Paying more for less naturally led to decreased utilization" of the government's health facilities.[23]

Vietnam needs to pull health care out of its nosedive if it hopes to catch up with its neighbors, whose stunning economic growth was aided greatly by a healthy population. Economists say Vietnam must reduce the size of the public health care workforce and find ways to boost salaries of the remaining health care workers by increasing user fees. The popular 750-bed Tu Du Women's Hospital in Ho Chi Minh City has found several novel ways to bolster its income and the salaries of its staff. For example, doctors are allowed to run "after hours" clinics inside the hospital. Patients pay fifty cents for a consultation with a doctor, three times the amount paid by patients who come before 4 P.M. Health care workers also run the hospital's parking lot, which charges ten cents for each of the thousands of motorbikes that come there every day. Tu Du also has set up a ward with private rooms, complete with telephones and air conditioners, for which it charges wealthier patients $13 per day. The income from these rooms is used to subsidize the hospital's other wards, where beds cost only twenty-five cents per day. Several categories of people, including civil servants, family members of war veterans, and the very poor, are exempted from paying any fees at all.

Vietnam needs to find ways to slow its population growth if it hopes to achieve its goal of doubling the country's living standards by the year 2000. Its growth rate of 2.2 percent per year (China's rate, by comparison, is only 1.3 percent) makes Vietnam the world's seventh-fastest growing country. Its population, estimated at seventy-four million today, is expected to exceed eighty million by the year 2000. Vietnam has already made impressive strides in restraining population growth. The fertility rate for women age fifteen to forty-nine fell to 3.8 births per woman in the 1985–88 period, down from 4.7 births during the early 1980s.[24] More can be done. A survey conducted in the late 1980s found that fully 41 percent of women who want to regulate their fertility do not have access to contraceptives.[25] The lack of family planning services is only one cause for Vietnam's exploding population. The biggest families usually are found in rural areas, where peasants want large numbers of children to help work the fields.

Another problem is the strong Confucian preference for sons, to carry on the family name, meaning that many parents continue to have children if they have only daughters. One day I hailed a *cyclo* in Ho Chi Minh City, and discovered after a few hundred meters that the driver was drunk. I started to talk with him and learned that his wife had given birth to a daughter that afternoon. "Congratulations," I said, "you must be very happy." "No, I'm very sad," he responded. "This is my sixth daughter. I have no sons." What did he plan to do now? "I'll continue trying," he pledged as he dropped me off, suggesting that his seventh child would soon be on the way. As yet the government has not put any limits on the number of children a family may have, meaning that unlike China (where families are permitted only one child and the same Confucian preference for sons predominates), Vietnam has seen almost no female infanticide.

One challenge facing Vietnam's planners is the country's unusually youthful populace. The 1989 census revealed that 39 percent of the country's population was under age fourteen, which means that over one million new workers each year enter a labor force already suffering from severe unemployment.

The Learning Curve

Richard Martin did not bother trying to recruit local Vietnamese bankers when he arrived in Hanoi in 1992 to open the Australia & New Zealand Bank branch in a magnificent, refurbished French villa at the edge of enchanting Hoan Kiem Lake. Before arriving, the enthusiastic banker had read a World Bank report indicating that much of what is taught in Vietnam's socialist banking schools is of little use. He decided instead to put advertisements in local newspapers and on Hanoi television. Within three days he had received 750 applications. He culled out the thirty with the best combination of "youth and intellectual horsepower" and brought in bank trainers from Australia and India to give his new staff fourteen weeks of intensive training. Today Martin is very enthusiastic about his employees: "We have a nuclear physicist and quite a few engineers. Engineers know how to solve problems."

Martin is not alone in trying out unconventional recruitment tactics in Vietnam. Many businessmen complain that they are held back by a lack of capable personnel. Besides managers, people with skills in accounting, marketing, administration, law, and banking are in particularly high demand. Today Vietnam's education system "must react and adapt to support the rapid pace of development," warned the United Nations Educational, Scientific, and Cultural Organization (UNESCO) in a recent study. "If it does not, it risks becoming irrelevant, inefficient and a brake on development."[26]

Vietnam's business colleges have tried since the late 1980s to tackle this shortfall by revising their curricula and retraining their teachers. The National Economics University in Hanoi has added 40 new courses and is revising 110 others. The school's biggest problem is the shortage of qualified professors—most of the current staff studied in the former Soviet Union before its Communist Party disintegrated. As a result, it will take the university until the end of the century to finish overhauling its course materials, says Le Manh Luong, who heads the school's training department.

Nearly 10,000 students applied to get into the university for the 1994–95 school year, but it could accept only 900 owing to the dearth of teachers. Moreover, only about 1,000 Vietnamese students go abroad to study each year, compared to over 50,000 from nearby Malaysia, which has less than one-third of Vietnam's population. Only about half of the 1000 Vietnamese go to Western or neighboring Asian countries to learn skills needed to bolster Vietnam's economy. The rest still go to the former Soviet Union, where they study the hard sciences and foreign languages.

Despite the shortage of capable workers, a third of Vietnam's college graduates have to look at least half a year before finding jobs, says Le Thac Can, an adviser to the ministry of education. Most lack the skills employers are seeking. Can's daughter, for example, graduated from the Foreign Trade College a few years ago. Even so, she had to take private night classes in English and accounting, and scrape together enough money to buy her own means of transport, a motorbike, before she managed to get a job with Saigon Tourist's Hanoi office. Despite these problems, most observers give the Com-

munists high marks for their efforts to expand the country's education system following the ouster of the French colonial rulers in
1954. At that time Vietnam had only sixteen junior high schools and
three upper-secondary schools. Nine out of ten Vietnamese were
illiterate.

The Communists launched popular literacy campaigns that enabled millions to learn to read and write and established a wide-
ranging network of primary and secondary schools throughout the
north. With the defeat of the Americans in 1975 a flood of returning
soldiers went back to school, overtaxing a system that lacked materials, adequate classrooms, and qualified teachers. The south con-
fronted additional problems as Hanoi shut down over two thousand
private schools and alienated tens of thousands of former teachers by
sending Northerners to reeducate their southern counterparts. A
general decline in education continued in the 1980s as raging inflation caused the government's real spending on education to drop.
The country still boasts 88 percent adult literacy, but school enrollment rates are falling and many teachers are abandoning their jobs in
this Confucian society where education has long been treasured.

According to the World Bank, only half the students entering
primary school complete five years of education. Even though the
population continues to grow 2.2 percent a year, enrollment in the
last three years of high school plummeted from 710,000 in 1982 to
520,000 in 1991 before slowly rising again in recent years. Only 4.5
percent of the country's twenty- to twenty-four-year-olds were attending schools of higher education in 1991, compared to 16 percent in nearby Thailand.[27] In some cases, students drop out of school
owing to economic hardships brought on by government cuts in
spending on social services. Some parents cannot afford the school
fees that have been introduced in the wake of the reforms. In other
cases, children quit school because the market reforms have given
people greater freedom to make money, which has prompted some
parents to pull their children out of school to help on the farm or in
the family's tea stand or workshop.

At the same time, the quality of education in Vietnam has

slumped, threatening the gains of earlier decades. Many school buildings are overcrowded and dilapidated, especially in rural areas. Most schools serve two—and some even three—shifts of students each day. In the capital, where conditions are among the best, only 40 percent of student desks are considered "acceptable," and many of the schools do not have fans to fend off the summer's blistering heat.[28]

Textbooks and teaching materials are in short supply and the curriculum is often irrelevant to the needs of a rapidly changing Vietnam. Due to an emphasis on learning by rote, students learn few of the analytical skills needed in the country's new environment. Students who can afford it find their own solutions to these problems: They attend evening classes where they study English, computers, and other technical skills at the thousands of small private schools that have sprouted up in the major cities, costing about $10 to $15 a month.

Moreover, many teachers are underqualified and poorly paid. Of over 250,000 teachers who taught in primary schools in the 1990–91 school year only one-third had the proper credentials. Nationwide, Vietnam faced a shortage of some 70,000 teachers at the start of the 1994–95 school year. Low salaries (primary school teachers earn approximately $15 a month) force many teachers to find second and third jobs, causing absenteeism and low morale. Some 6,000 teachers quit their jobs in a recent three-year period in Ho Chi Minh City alone.[29] In addition, many parents complain that they have to pay teachers additional fees for organizing after-hours sessions, known as *hoc them* classes. Teachers often reserve their most important lessons for these sessions, which they use to boost their incomes.

Due to these problems, teachers no longer have the prestige they once did in Vietnam. Even Hanoi Teacher Training College, the country's premier training ground for new teachers, has had trouble recruiting. In the 1993–94 school year only 2,000 students applied, according to Vu Van Thanh of the college's international relations department. The following year the number of applicants quadrupled, but Thanh says many of these plan to use the college to get skills in foreign languages and computer science that they then will use to get jobs in business, not teaching.

Vietnam has boosted government spending on education in recent years (it reached $447 million in 1994), but much of this money is spent on teachers' salaries. Little is left to fund new textbooks or teacher training courses. As a result, Vietnam's rulers, who shut down private social welfare programs after seizing power, are slowly turning to the private sector for help. Alarmed by the degenerating quality of public education, groups of teachers in urban areas have established several private and semi-private schools and colleges. Some target the country's poorest; others seek out the country's brightest.

One of these new semi-private schools, prosaically named the Group Secondary School for Good Student Training, was set up in Ho Chi Minh City in 1992 by Do Duc Huyen and some colleagues. It had some 640 students in the 1993–94 school year, studying from grades six through twelve. The school admits an elite cadre of students who must pass a rigorous entrance exam. Of the 600 students who applied to enter the school's sixth grade in the 1993–94 school year only the top 150 were admitted. The school is funded entirely from student fees, which are approximately $15 a month, a whopping fifteen times higher than the amount charged by state secondary schools. But Huyen, the principal, insists that his school is a bargain: Students study all day and do not have to pay *hoc them* fees, which can run as high as $9 a month per subject. "We set up this school because of concern about the future of Vietnam's education," Huyen explains. "State schools have many problems. First there was the war, and then there were economic difficulties. This caused teachers to not put all of their heart into teaching," he said of poorly paid instructors in government schools. "As a result, students don't do well."

The school follows the general curriculum developed by the ministry of education, but teachers have adapted the courses to provide extra training in certain technical fields. For example, its students study English seven or eight periods a week, twice as often as their counterparts in state schools. In addition, pupils are required to take computer classes, which are optional in government institutions. All of the school's teachers have full-time jobs in state schools around the city. The principal, for example, teaches Vietnamese literature in Ho Chi Minh City's teacher training college. Most teachers teach about eighteen periods a month, for which they earn $90 to $180, more than four times what teachers in state-run secondary schools earn.

Foreign aid donors are helping as well. The World Bank provides advice and offers financial credits. France has established a management training center on the National Economics University campus in Hanoi. The Bangkok-based Asian Institute of Technology has set up a project to train economics professors in Ho Chi Minh City. Similar projects are being funded by Sweden, Canada, and the Ford Foundation. Yet these projects and schools such as Huyen's still provide only a fraction of the skilled personnel needed to jump-start Vietnam's economy.

9

When Will the Party End?

◆ ◆ ◆

Like other foreign journalists and diplomats working in Vietnam, I constantly struggled with how to portray this rapidly changing country. Is it one of the last outposts of communism, brutally repressing its citizens in order to cling to power? Or is it shedding totalitarianism and allowing its citizens to rapidly boost their living standards? In the midst of all the bustle and confusion, who best represents Vietnam today, political detainee Doan Viet Hoat, or businessman Dang Viet Hung?

Hoat, age fifty-four, decided to stay in Vietnam in April 1975 as Communist tanks rolled into Saigon. The American-trained English professor and deputy rector of the city's Buddhist university rejected offers to flee abroad. He told his friends that he wanted to stay to help rebuild his country after the war. The city's new Communist rulers promptly closed the university, and it was not long before Hoat—along with several hundred thousand former South Vietnamese soldiers, politicians, religious leaders, writers, and artists—was trundled off to a reeducation camp. He was held twelve years without formal charges or a trial.

After his release in 1988 Hoat and several other intellectuals began producing *Freedom Forum*, a mimeographed newsletter that urged the Communist Party to introduce democratic reforms and allow freedom of speech. After publishing their fourth issue Hoat and eight of his colleagues were arrested. The official *Saigon Giai Phong* newspaper declared the group's guilt in an article entitled "Smash the Dark

Schemes of the Reactionaries at Their Sources." On March 29, 1993, Hoat was sentenced to twenty years in prison for "attempting to overthrow the government." A few months later, following international protests, the court of appeals reduced Hoat's term to fifteen years. Since his sentencing, Hoat has been moved to at least five different prisons and labor camps. For several months his wife lost track of where he was but she finally found him in K-4, an infamous prison camp for common criminals near Vietnam's border with Laos. In July 1994 she was allowed to visit Hoat for fifteen minutes. She found that her husband was suffering from a kidney ailment and that he was not receiving any medicine to relieve the pain or cure his condition.

Hoat still manages to express his views from detention. "Our fatherland is undergoing a very important transition period," he said in a letter smuggled out of the prison camp in late 1993. "Communism is dying but the future of our country is still obscure," he continues, adding that "democracy is the sole surviving road for the country. Up to this point, warning voices have not only been ignored but crushed. . . . This government has only one single concern, which is to maintain a monopoly in politics." Hoat nonetheless rejects the use of violence to overthrow the Communist regime. "Even though we have suffered cruelty, we must not abandon the spirit of reconciliation, tolerance, and the way of nonviolence. . . . In all compassion, we should never forget that our struggle is the struggle for righteousness, for love, and for peace."[1]

For every Doan Viet Hoat there are scores of apolitical Vietnamese such as Dang Viet Hung. Hung sells used air conditioners, washing machines, and refrigerators to foreigners and Hanoi's nouveaux riches from a thriving little shop along Ly Nam De Street (often dubbed Army Street by locals because many of the country's military offices are located here). The affable, twenty-eight-year-old entrepreneur does not understand why intellectuals like Hoat and Western governments are so worked up about Vietnam's human rights situation. "The question of human rights in Vietnam isn't very serious," Hung told me in early 1994, shortly after Washington had lifted its trade embargo against Vietnam. He had heard a report on the BBC saying that the United States wanted to talk to Hanoi about human rights. "I think someone has built human rights up into a big problem." Sipping lemonade and smoking powerful Vinataba cigarettes in a coffee shop just down the street from his store, Hung sounds upbeat about life in Vietnam these days. "I think the reforms are quite good," he says. "They've had a very positive impact on life. What I like best is that I'm allowed to do business." Many Vietnamese today echo Hung's feelings: Vietnam may not be paradise, but at least the government is off the backs of the people.

Hung grew up on Ly Nam De Street. His father is a doctor in the army and his mother is a schoolteacher. After graduating from high school Hung was drafted into the army and posted to the Mekong delta in the south. Four years later he was discharged and assigned to work in a local office of the Ho Chi Minh Communist Youth Association, at one time an important training ground for new party members. While working there, Hung and a colleague took advantage of the Communist Party's economic liberalization to set up a shop selling secondhand appliances. Hung gradually saved enough to open his own store with two of his brothers. Today they sell about $10,000 worth of appliances each month.

What does Hung think about the call by Vietnamese intellectuals for a multiparty system? "I think one party is much better," the businessman argues. "I don't think many political parties necessarily bring stability. When Vietnamese see the situation in the former Soviet Union, they consider it very carefully," he says, alluding to the chaos that followed the collapse of the Soviet Communist Party. Similar turmoil in Vietnam, he says, would derail Vietnam's fragile economic progress. Of course, not everything is perfect in Hung's Vietnam, and he would have plenty of advice for Premier Vo Van Kiet if he had an opportunity to meet him. "I'd tell the premier to think carefully before introducing new regulations and rules," Hung said, echoing a common complaint of Vietnamese businessmen. "I don't like a legal system which is constantly being changed. A lot of officials use gaps in the law to profit themselves."

Who best represents Vietnam today, Hung the entrepreneur, or Hoat the detainee? Human rights activists and Western governments focus on the abuse of political prisoners, while fund managers and conference organizers highlight the triumphs of Vietnam's new millionaires. The two faces exist side by side, and those who see only one are missing a major piece of the story.

A New Sense of Space

"Vietnam's political system hasn't changed much," says Ngoc, a bright young woman who won a scholarship to study in the United States in the early 1990s before signing up with a foreign firm in Hanoi. "But the country's political psychology has changed dramatically." Ngoc is referring to the fact that even though the Communist Party retains a monopoly over the country's politics, the economic reforms have reduced its meddling in the private lives of people.

For many Vietnamese who lived through years of war followed by hunger and political repression during Vietnam's hard-line socialist years, life has improved immensely under the reforms. A new sense of space and individualism has emerged now that people are encouraged to make money. The family, rather than the work collective, once again has become the foundation of society and the economy.

Vietnam's increasing contact with the outside world, as Hanoi courts foreign investors, aid donors, and new markets, has reduced people's fear of the country's once-dreaded security police. Vietnamese are now free to do and say almost anything as long as they do not challenge the supremacy of the ruling party. The de-Stalinization of Vietnam has transformed not only the world of business but the political landscape as well. Yet the increasing freedom has sharply defined limits: As Hoat and other dissidents have discovered, people who organize dissent against the government still end up in jail.

People are free to find jobs on their own outside of government controls. With the end of state shops the *ho khau*, or residency booklets, have become almost irrelevant and people are much freer to travel and live wherever they please. Private employers do not care much about one's political dossier (which in the Vietnamese political system includes data not only on the applicant's political past but also on that of his father and grandfather).

Western-style political democracy in Vietnam is not likely in the cards, but a sort of liberalization is clearly under way. Even though Vietnam is unlikely to adopt a multiparty system any time soon, the country's politics are evolving. Vietnamese leaders warn that rapid political change could cause instability that would be disastrous for the country's fledgling economic gains. Businessmen such as Hung agree.

"We conduct our political changes step by step," explains Huu Tho, the chain-smoking, sixty-four-year-old editor of the Communist Party daily, *Nhan Dan*. "You need to be sympathetic with us. On one hand, we need to develop the economy, and on the other, we need to maintain stability. . . . If we didn't maintain strong leadership, the minority people in Bac Thai would expel 120,000 people from the delta," the white-haired, bespectacled Tho says about the ethnic Vietnamese who have moved into the midlands north of Hanoi. "The Tai people would kick out 150,000 Hmong. An ethnic war would start for sure," he says, alluding to the ethnic hostilities that erupted out of the ashes of the former Soviet empire following the collapse of communism.

Vietnamese officials are convinced that Western governments and human rights activists that criticize Hanoi are not truly concerned about the welfare of the Vietnamese but rather in finding ways to overthrow the Communist Party. "We've been divided a long time," continues Tho, who is also deputy director of the party's ideology and culture department. "When the French dominated our country, we were split into three regimes. In the U.S. period, we were divided again. If we don't take care, chaos is inevitable."

Vietnam is run by a Leninist party that adheres to the principles of centralized decision making but is no longer Marxist now that it has dropped central economic planning. Hanoi says the country is still in "transition to socialism," though most of its leaders seem more preoccupied with trying to catch up with its high-performing neighbors. "Vietnam applied a policy resembling that of Deng Xiao-ping [*sic*] in China: the dismantling in practice of socialism, retention of the [one-party] state and a somewhat revised and diluted communist rhetoric with nationalistic and Confucian overtones," argues Stein Tonnesson, a Scandinavian researcher. "So far, however, the reforms have aimed at preserving a softened version of authoritarian rule rather than allowing any opposition to the leadership of the party."[2]

A cultural and intellectual renaissance of sorts is under way, as writers and artists have begun to expose abuses of the past. The country's press has become more daring, although its role is still limited to exposing corruption and government mismanagement; it does not dare to publish blatantly dissenting political views.

Foreign television is becoming more widely available, thanks to cheap satellite dishes smuggled in from China. Pirated videos and cassette tapes from abroad can be found even in remote villages, although the government started reining in foreign news and entertainment as part of the "social evils" campaign launched in early 1996. The proliferation of photocopiers and fax machines makes it easy for dissidents to circulate their views, even if they are ignored by the country's newspapers.

But the government seems determined to limit access to opposing views, even as computer buffs link the country electronically to the rest of the world. In mid-1996, the country's telecommunications authority introduced strict rules to control the use of the internet, including a provision that allows the interior ministry to monitor traffic, and another that prohibits the distribution of information considered damaging to the interests of the country. The ruling was in response to a growing concern about what officials see as negative foreign influences and attempts to destabilize the government. Hanoi is concerned that the information superhighway will not only link one of the world's poorest nations to the economic data it needs, but also give internet surfers access to human rights reports, pornography, and the many World Wide Web sites created by overseas Vietnamese groups hostile to the government.[3]

The Communist Party today no longer expends much energy trying to control ideology, explains Son, a party member who works for the foreign ministry in Hanoi. "In the past, when we met in party cells, we'd talk a lot about ideology and we didn't deal with daily issues like how to find an answer to a foreign policy problem," the Vietnamese diplomat says. "Today, party members think we shouldn't talk as much about ideological things." Nonetheless, Son adds, "some decision makers are still confused about ideology." For example, "some honest communists" believe that for the government to abandon state-owned enterprises or to allow the private ownership of land "means to deviate from communism." But in other cases, officials such as managers of state enterprises "use ideology to protect their own interests." At the same time, "all leaders try to prove that they aren't conservatives. . . . Even in the ministry of interior, leaders always want to prove that they're reformers," the official says about the ministry responsible for monitoring dissent and running the country's prisons. Presumably ministry officials feel that they will be politically sidelined if they do not champion reform.

All of this has created "a more liberal atmosphere when we discuss politics," Son continues. For example, professors in the Ho Chi Minh National School of Politics, where the country's top officials are trained, are now freer to discuss the party's mistakes. According to Son, they no longer conceal the fact that Ho Chi Minh lost his position as head of the Communist Party in the 1930s to Tran Phu, who supported the Comintern's call for an international socialist revolution. The lecturers also don't hide the fact that General Vo Nguyen Giap opposed the Communists' 1968 Tet offensive against the American military because he thought it would result in the deaths of too many of his guerrillas. Son adds, however, that this more open debate does not extend to events following the defeat of the United States in 1975. Dissenting opinions over Vietnam's occupation of Cambodia after the 1978 invasion, Hanoi's ensuing conflict with Beijing and Vietnam's alliance with Moscow are not openly discussed. "They're related to people still in power," Son says of these events. If the Politburo—the elite seventeen-man group that makes Vietnam's most important decisions—"reviewed these decisions, it would create disunity."

The upheaval in the Communist world in recent years has created ideological confusion in the Vietnamese party. "Since the crisis of ideology in 1989 and 1990, people have seen old-style socialism collapse," another official explains. "They see Marx isn't real to life, so what do they believe in? Many have found the answer in Ho Chi Minh Thought," he continues. "Ho said: 'I want every Vietnamese to have enough food to eat, a shirt to wear, and his children to have an education.' Most intellectuals now believe that and don't think much about other ideology."

Few of the country's political institutions have been transformed as much as the 395-delegate National Assembly, which long had been little more than an echo chamber for the Communist Party. Under the reforms parliamentarians have become more independent-minded, sometimes almost totally rewriting draft legislation, as happened with the laws on land and farm taxes passed in 1993. As early as 1988, during a vote for a new premier, observers were surprised to see more than a third of the assembly's members—90 percent of whom were party members—vote for Kiet when the Politburo had endorsed Do Muoi. Kiet was finally elected in 1991, after Muoi had been chosen party chief.

In recent years government ministers have been grilled openly from the National Assembly floor about their performance. "If on Monday a minister has to answer questions from the National Assembly, I'm sure he won't have much of an appetite on Sunday," says Huu Tho, who is also a member of parliament. The National Assembly plays an increasingly important role as a check on the government and on the Communist Party, but it is only a check and not a true policy-making body. "No minister wants to get criticized by the National Assembly, but his position is determined first of all by his relationship with the Politburo," one official explains.

Parliamentary candidates are still carefully screened before elections. In 1992 forty-four independents applied to run, but in the end only two were approved under a rigorous screening process established by the party-controlled Fatherland Front, a mass organization that includes labor, youth, religious, and women's groups. Neither candidate won, but some other interesting things happened. In Ho Chi Minh City four of six candidates endorsed by the local Fatherland Front committee lost. In his constituency in Hanoi, Communist Party boss Do Muoi received only 80 percent of the vote, meaning that one in five voters crossed his name off the ballot. Nationwide almost 1 percent of the ballots cast were spoiled, mostly by intellectuals disgruntled that they were not offered a broader choice of candidates.[4]

During the closely monitored election campaign many voters were surprisingly blunt in their criticisms of the government. "Corruption has become universal and it's so serious it could cause political instability," an angry retired army officer who clearly has not benefited much from the reforms declared in a meeting with five candidates in the Dong Da suburb of Hanoi. The audience was made up of invited "voter representatives," for the most part retired civil servants and soldiers who had been vetted by local officials prior to the meeting. "We're losing confidence in the government because of growing social inequality and corruption," declared the veteran, who has spent most of his life fighting for Vietnam's independence from France and the United States. "Our Communist Party should draw lessons from the mistakes made by the Soviet party."

For nearly four hours the "voter representatives"—who were provided free cigarettes and tea by the organizers—pummeled the candidates with demands for more jobs for the district's unemployed young people, a cut in the price of electricity (which had been doubled shortly before the meeting), and better benefits for retired soldiers and civil servants. "In the past, when you left your house you met a hero," another voter declared, repeating one of Ho Chi Minh's famous wartime sayings. "Now when you leave home you meet social inequality," he declared, referring to the yawning gap that has emerged between rich and poor in the wake of the party's reforms.[5]

The voters' comments reflect an overall loosening of Vietnamese society that is causing the Communist Party's once tight grip on society to slip. Much of the change in Vietnam today happens from the bottom up. A growing number of businesspeople, intellectuals, and even officials are busy building a new society without bothering to seek the blessing of the ruling party. The chamber of commerce champions the concerns of businessmen, the private Open University in Ho Chi Minh City trains new managers, and groups of intellectuals meet informally to discuss their vision for Vietnam's future. "The past seven or eight years have seen an explosion in the number of informal organizations concerned with welfare, education, professional advancement, revival of traditions, arts and culture, science and technology," observes historian David Marr. "The decline of [government-sponsored] mass organizations and proliferation of informal organizations have put the Party in a difficult position, since no one is naive enough to believe the latter will remain apolitical forever."[6]

Disgruntled Revolutionaries

Not everyone is benefiting from the reforms, and some are angry that they are being left behind. My wife Linda bumped into this problem a few years ago while visiting Thanh Hoa, one of the country's poorest provinces along the north-central coast. Linda headed up the Vietnam office of Save the Children Fund (a private British child welfare agency) and was in the province talking to villagers about setting up a rice bank to provide food loans to needy farmers between rice harvests. As she walked through one village with a district chief, they came across a rail-thin man in his early thirties lying on a rough wooden bed in a thatch hut with only three walls in the middle of a parched rice field. When the official explained the purpose of her visit the man became highly agitated. "Why isn't the government helping us?" he angrily demanded of the embarrassed official. "We have no food to eat," he shouted, adding that he wanted to know why the district chief brought foreigners in fancy cars to the village to ask questions but poor farmers never ended up getting any help. After Linda and the official moved on, he explained that the frustrated man had been recently demobilized from the army. He had returned to his native village, which had given him a small plot of land, but it was not very fertile. According to the district chief, the village had no funds to help the veteran—who had spent his youth serving the country—to build a house and buy farm tools to start a new life with his wife and five-year-old son.

As the country's leaders discovered while preparing for the Communist Party's Seventh Congress in mid-1991, this soldier-turned-farmer is not the only one who is upset. In the midst of trying to hammer out the final wording of the documents for the meeting, news arrived in Hanoi that thousands of disgruntled veterans of Vietnam's wars against France and the United States were planning to march on the capital during the congress. The veterans wanted to protest the fact that they were not sharing in the country's newfound prosperity. General Le Duc Anh, former defense minister and one-time military commander in the Mekong delta and neighboring Cambodia, was appointed to meet the protesters' representatives. In the end Anh managed to defuse the demonstration. "He told them that the congress was for the survival of the party," an official later told me. He said Anh had explained to the veterans that the party had been forced to abandon socialism and adopt market reforms to maintain its grip on power. As the reforms took hold, the general argued, everyone—including the veterans—would benefit. The congress rewarded Anh for his effort by electing him Number Two in the ruling Politburo.

International affairs specialist Gabriel Kolko explains the veterans' feelings: "Many thoughtful revolutionaries, men and women who made immense sacrifices, have very justifiably asked themselves privately, and increasingly publicly, whether it was worth fighting a war that cost millions of lives and caused immeasurable suffering to drive out a foreign-imposed society, only to reproduce it in a superficially different form and even appeal for aid from those Americans, French, and Japanese who once tormented them. For them," says Kolko, who actively opposed the American intervention in Vietnam, "the war was won, but the peace is quickly being lost."[7]

Many observers believe that Vietnam's government will face its greatest challenge from the south owing to that region's more vibrant economy and its recent experience under the Americans. The Vietnamese security apparatus, however, is more anxious about an uprising in the north. "If chaos comes, it will come from the north," a Vietnamese official said. "The Politburo pays a lot of attention to the south to avoid demonstrations and sabotage, but the force they're most afraid of is in the north. The salaries of people in the military and in the interior ministry were recently increased to allay that concern," he said, referring to the institutions charged with keeping the Communists in power. "One lesson the Vietnamese party drew from the former Soviet Union is that its greatest challenge will come from within the party." It isn't about to take any chances. In November 1995, as the Communist Party was preparing for its Eighth Congress, scheduled to take place in mid-1996, it sentenced two long-serving Communist officials for "abusing the rights of freedom and democracy to damage national security." Independent sources believe they were punished for calling for a more open political system and as a warning to other potential dissidents prior to the party conclave.

Do Trung Hieu, age fifty-eight, had been a ranking party cadre in the south during the war and later was put in charge of religious affairs in Ho Chi Minh City. Hieu, who had written frequent tracts demanding greater political pluralism, was sentenced to fifteen months in prison. He had previously been arrested in 1990 and was ousted from the party two years later. Hoang Minh Chinh, age seventy-seven, was a decorated hero of the independence struggle against France and later head of the influential Institute of Marxist-Leninist Philosophy in Hanoi. Chinh was sentenced to a year in jail for criticizing the party's monopoly grip on power and calling for the rehabilitation of members purged in the 1960s. Chinh had spent twenty years in detention and under house arrest between 1967 and 1991 for criticizing Maoist tendencies in the Vietnamese party after it turned to China for support in the war against the United States.

One of the Vietnamese party's most serious challenges had already come from disgruntled revolutionaries in the south in the late 1980s. They had formed a group called the Club of Former Resistance Fighters and distributed a mimeographed newsletter called *Resistance Tradition*. Its articles criticized the party for the hasty reunification of the country and for the poorly conceived collectivization of agriculture in the late 1970s. These southern revolutionaries also railed against corruption, called for greater political openness, and championed the problems of the country's war veterans. In 1990, as Vietnam was preparing to celebrate the one hundredth anniversary of Ho Chi Minh's birth, the party moved to ban the group. Two top leaders were put under house arrest and several others—including General Tran Van Tra, who had led the Communists' final offensive against the U.S.-backed Saigon government in 1975—were appointed to work for a new government-sponsored veterans organization.[8]

The move, however, did not silence Hanoi's critics. Whenever the party prepares for important meetings, urban intellectuals crank out clandestine tracts lambasting the Communists. One of the most stinging diatribes was written by Lu Phuong, a southern intellectual who challenged the party to give up its Marxist-Leninist ideology, just prior to the party's midterm conference in January 1994. Phuong, a former culture ministry official and long-time party activist, argued that Ho had simply "borrowed Leninism as a tool" to fight the French colonialists and the Americans. Ho never imagined he had adopted an ideology that would "turn intelligent people into foolish ones" and "bog down the nation in stagnation," Phuong wrote in his sixteen-page tract. "The incompetence in economic development and brutal suppression of politics and culture brought by the socialist model on behalf of Marx and proletarian revolution resulted in Vietnam for many years having independence, but not liberty and happiness. . . . Economic development can only accompany political liberalization," he continued. "We have to give up the idealism that Uncle Ho chose in a very simple manner . . . but the question is by what means: Will change come through collapse or will it come through peaceful means?" Interestingly, Phuong's views got him expelled from the party but not thrown in jail.[9]

Similar critiques were launched by a handful of prominent intellectuals prior to the party congress in 1991. Nguyen Khac Vien, seventy-eight years old at the time and a long-time propagandist for the party, sent a petition to the country's leaders calling for them to resign and introduce more political reforms. The French-trained pediatrician warned Vietnam's leadership that it was "plunging the country into disorder and preventing all development." Many of the country's leaders are "too old, physically inept, and incapable of following the changing times," Vien charged. "Unless a set of broad-based rules for democracy are drawn up and implemented, the country will never be able to . . . compete with its neighboring countries."[10]

Most of Hanoi's critics want nonviolent change. They call for evolution toward a more open political system rather than an upheaval. "We non-Communists accept the peaceful way," insists Russian-trained mathematician Phan Dinh Dieu, one of the first Northerners to openly criticize the party. "The old Soviet Union has given us a lot of experience," he says. "Change is necessary, but it's best to be peaceful." So far Hanoi has not faced open confrontation with its intellectuals as Beijing encountered at Tiananmen Square. Critics such as Lu Phuong, Nguyen Khac Vien, and Phan Dinh Dieu excite urban intellectuals but do not threaten the regime. In truth, most people seem to be too busy pursuing the opportunities of the free market to pay much attention to the beliefs of a handful of dissidents. Even though the Communist Party does not face the threat of being overthrown by angry peasants or disgruntled workers, a legion of challenges undermines its rule.

One of these challenges is the declining moral standards among its members. A study conducted by the Communist Party several years ago found that less than one-third of its members have maintained their "revolutionary" qualities.[11] Probably no issue has stoked as much public anger as corruption, which people say has soared under the reforms. Communist Party leaders recognize that malfeasance causes popular resentment and could cause the organization to collapse from internal rot and decay. In a 1993 article in the party daily, *Nhan Dan*, former party chief Nguyen Van Linh warned that "the evils of bureaucratism, corruption, and bribery . . . have reached a serious level without any sign of abating." The architect of the 1986 reforms said that these "filthy deeds . . . cause the people to doubt the party's leadership, breed internal disunity and erode the masses' confidence in the party. . . . It is true that acts of sabotage from within are always more dangerous than those from without," the retired party leader warned his successors.[12]

The Communist Party has launched several campaigns against corruption by quoting the ethical sayings of Ho Chi Minh and disciplining thousands of low-level officials, but the problem only seems to be getting worse. One cause is that officials expected to implement party reforms have lost much of their earlier revolutionary zeal and desire for Spartan frugality. Many simply refuse to struggle to feed their families on an income of less than $20 a month while people all around them get rich.

No charges have ever surfaced about corruption in the highest echelons of the Communist Party, but the "bamboo telephone" is abuzz with reports of patronage and sweetheart deals for "princelings." The son of one senior official runs a trading company in Hanoi appropriately named *Doi Moi*, or renovation, after the party's reforms. "The children and in-laws of the leaders are suspiciously oversuccessful in business," one Hanoi economist joked. "In the 1970s they followed careers in science," he said, alluding to the fact that they got the lion's share of scholarships to study in the former Soviet bloc. "Now they're successful in business. God blesses them more than others."

Occasionally when I was living in Hanoi I would hear of cases in

which villagers in the countryside decided to dispense justice themselves. A group of peasants in Thanh Hoa province's Quang Loc
village were angered in 1992 by the fact that officials were saving the
best communal land for their relatives and overcharging households
for electricity. The villagers devised a plan to arrest the local Communist Party boss, the village head man, his assistant, the police
chief, and the leader of the local agriculture department. The
scheme worked, at least in part. Three officials were captured, but
the two others got wind of the plot and managed to escape. Several
months later, despite attempts by provincial authorities to obtain
their release, the three were still being held in a crude bamboo
enclosure.[13] The central government hears of forty to sixty such
cases a year, one official told me.

Most Vietnamese insist that corruption was rampant long before
the market reforms. When the state owned everything and employed
everyone, officials would frequently pilfer cement, gasoline, or office
supplies to sell on the black market. "Everything in society belonged
to the people," Hanoi historian Vu Minh Giang observes about the
hard-line socialist years. "If you could get a lot and no one detected
you, you were considered very talented." Giang thinks that corruption in fact was worse under socialism than under the earlier feudal
regime. "Moral values were no longer important," he says. "Only
politics was important, so people were no longer afraid of anything."
Today, under the reforms opportunities for corruption have increased even more because the country has become more prosperous.

Not only is the Communist Party having trouble controlling the
behavior of its own members but it also faces difficulties finding
recruits. According to official estimates, the number of people joining the party fell from roughly 100,000 in 1987 to 36,000 in 1991,
the year the Soviet Communist Party collapsed. It jumped back to
60,000 in 1994.[14] "In the past," one disillusioned party member
explains, "everyone thought that if they wanted to do anything sub-
stantial—if they wanted a position in society or in the government—
they had to be a member of the party. Most people no longer think

so." In addition, many party cells no longer bother to hold regular meetings. Local party units are supposed to meet at least once a month, but many get together only once every three months. "When they meet, they don't discuss party principles," one member noted, adding cynically, "They speak in Communist slogans, but they practice capitalist enrichment."

Now that the party is pursuing the free market, few Vietnamese fuss with trying to keep up with the tortured ideological deliberations of their aging leaders. "Socialism means hanging on to your chair," one of my Hanoi economist friends jokes, implying that socialism has more to do with clinging to power than with holding ideologically correct beliefs. If one asks a Vietnamese official today what socialism is, he often has trouble giving an intelligible answer, now that the notions of class struggle and dictatorship of the proletariat are passé. In 1991 the party daily defined socialism as "a society of people . . . which has a highly developed economy and advanced rich and national culture; in which everyone is fed and clothed, free and happy, with the requisites to pursue their individual fulfillment, social justice, and guaranteed democracy."[15] In other words, anything that furthers economic development is deemed socialist. This allows the central committee to run trading companies, the security police to operate hotels, and the army to set up property development projects with foreign capitalists.

Another challenge facing the Communist Party is the tension caused by uneven development between the south and north. The south, where many still remember life before Hanoi's victory, has developed most quickly during the past decade. Even many party members there are impatient for greater autonomy from northern control. Few Southerners, only 1 percent of whom have joined the 2.1-million member party, feel particularly beholden to the organization. In contrast, roughly 9 percent of the north's population belong to the party.

Furthermore, many xenophobic senior security officials seem to be convinced that Western countries have hatched "imperialist plots" to undermine Communist rule in Vietnam. Hanoi calls it *peaceful evolution*—the same term used by the Chinese Communists to describe their fear of subversion from abroad.

"The 'peaceful evolution' strategy of hostile forces is a counter-revolutionary strategy aimed at changing the political system of the remaining socialist countries without recourse to armed violence," a senior army officer wrote in a defense magazine in 1994. "To implement this strategy, all tricks, forms of action and measures are used, with special attention being given to taking advantage of religion to mislead, incite, and drag believers into struggling against the party and state."[16]

A pamphlet published by the party's culture and ideology department in 1994 provided a long list of forces allegedly aligned against the country's rulers: the U.S. government is using human rights to cover its attempts to intervene in Vietnam's politics; overseas Vietnamese are smuggling agents and literature into the country in an attempt to destabilize the government; and foreign relief organizations are imposing political conditions on their aid in an effort to push Vietnam to adopt capitalism.[17] Some observers see this rhetoric as an attempt by security officials to maintain a lid on dissent. Other analysts speculate that military leaders are using it to justify their requests for budget increases. "It goes with the turf," one foreign political scientist notes. "Military and security types always exaggerate threats."

In the longer term, the Communist Party's leading role will be challenged by a generational change. The top members in the ruling Politburo are all over age seventy and have worked together since the 1940s, but most are expected to step down at the Eighth Congress in 1996. "It is highly unlikely," says Vietnam specialist Bill Turley, "that succeeding generations will be as uniform in experience and outlook, or as consensual in leadership style, as the outgoing one."[18]

Development or Civil Rights?

The dread of arbitrary arrest and harsh labor camps that paralyzed many South Vietnamese in the years following the Communist victory has begun to pale as the country's rulers have launched their economic reforms. In 1992 Hanoi released the last batch of defeated Saigon regime officials and military personnel, some of whom had been held in reeducation camps without trial for seventeen years.

The Vietnamese government does not release figures on how many political prisoners it holds. In 1993 Amnesty International said there were "at least sixty," including monks, writers, and other intellectuals. Human Rights Watch/Asia estimated that the number of political detainees was in the "hundreds if not thousands." Vietnam may still be authoritarian, but it is no longer totalitarian. The human rights situation for most people has improved immensely under the reforms, even though the regime still crosses swords with Buddhist monks clamoring for greater religious freedom and democracy campaigners such as Doan Viet Hoat.

Vietnam's best-known political prisoner is Nguyen Dan Que, a fifty-four-year-old medical doctor. Like Hoat, Que chose to stay in Vietnam in 1975, even though his father had been killed by the Communists in Hanoi in the 1940s for his links to the anti-Communist Nationalist Party. In 1978 Que's criticisms of the new regime landed him in prison, where he was held for ten years without trial. Soon after his release, Que and some friends founded the nonviolent Movement for Human Rights in Vietnam and began to circulate documents calling for a multiparty system. He was promptly arrested and in late 1991 was sentenced to twenty years in prison for "trying to overthrow the people's government." There he remains, suffering from an untreated bleeding ulcer.[19]

Vietnam's 1992 constitution declares that human rights are "respected and protected under the law" but also insists that the Communist Party play a "leading role" in the country's politics. As Hoat and Que have discovered, there is little doubt which principle comes out on top if the two tenets collide. They also learned that Hanoi does not differentiate between an armed uprising and a call for non-violent change. In Vietnam, as in many other Asian countries, there is tension between economic development and civil rights. Like China, Hanoi considers economic progress to be the most basic human right. The non-Communist governments in Singapore and Indonesia also use economic arguments to justify authoritarian regimes. Over the years many Asian governments have insisted that the interests of the group take priority over those of the individual.

Vietnam's leaders, like many of their Confucian cousins, resent attempts by Western governments to push freedom of speech and open elections. Hanoi regularly lashes out at its human rights critics, arguing that their holier-than-thou proposals will cause political instability and make it impossible for the country's economy to move ahead. Vietnamese officials say the West focuses on civil and political rights without upholding economic and social rights such as food, housing, and education. Critics of Hanoi "over-emphasize individual rights and political rights of citizens, make absolute individual freedoms, and negate the [national] rights to independence, existence and development," the official Vietnam News Agency declared in a 1993 commentary. "We are determined not to let anyone turn these rights into instruments of propaganda to rally their forces, build counterrevolutionary organizations to threaten national security, jeopardize the peaceful life of the people, and infringe upon state law."[20]

The United States, which finally moved to exchange embassies with Hanoi in 1995, has said that progress on human rights will be an important consideration as Washington negotiates a raft of agreements on economic cooperation with Hanoi. "Western pressure on human rights is a good thing," a retired Hanoi official told me soon after Washington lifted its trade embargo a year earlier. "But we want the Americans to be more delicate." The official suggested that Western countries such as the United States, France, Britain, and Australia should coordinate their human rights campaigns. "The pressure must be delicate—don't let them lift the flag of nationalism," he said, alluding to Vietnam's conservatives. "Go softly, softly," he continued, suggesting that confrontation—like Washington's past clashes with China over most-favored-trading status— would not be effective in changing Hanoi's treatment of its dissidents.

"Too Little Government"

A visitor cannot spend much time in Vietnam before hearing about the "dark years," the decade after 1975 when the Communists launched their drive toward a socialist paradise. It was a time of hunger, forced farm collectives, nationalized factories, failed new economic zones, and the flight of a million refugees, including some of the country's best and brightest. The cost in wasted capital, human and financial, is immeasurable.

It was also during this time, however, that the Communists laid part of the foundation for Vietnam's current rapid growth. They provided political stability and unified the country for the first time in almost a century, making it possible for the north to "import" rice and consumer goods from the south and for the south to get cheap coal and surplus electricity for its factories from the north.

The Communists built up the country's human capital with literacy campaigns and public health drives. Illiterate adults went to school at night, and women for the first time began to receive at least a few years of primary school. Vietnam may still be desperately short of managers and lawyers, but its literacy rate of 88 percent remains impressive. Infant mortality rates plummeted from 156 per 1,000 live births in 1960 to 53 in 1992 as mass immunization campaigns stamped out such diseases as cholera and typhoid. Life expectancy in the north soared from fifty years in 1970 to sixty-five two decades later.[21] The Communists' "socialist transformation" and land redistribution programs were brutal, but they smashed vested interests and created a degree of equality needed for the country's economic cylinders to begin firing. Taiwan and South Korea also mounted land reform programs before their economies took off after World War II.

Vietnam today has "too much government" in some areas, however, causing "too much unnecessary and inefficient regulation or interference in market activities," the World Bank warns. It is still inclined to "try to micro-manage the economy in a way that is not feasible or desirable in a market economy." The bank's economists say that Vietnam needs to decentralize its cumbersome procedures for licensing foreign investment projects. In other areas, the World Bank says, Vietnam has "too little government," resulting in "insufficient protection of the public interest." For example, Hanoi has too few environmental regulations to protect the country's already overtaxed natural resources.[22]

Due to Vietnam's long, narrow geography, poor communications network, and years of war, the nation is surprisingly decentralized for a Communist country. Additional spontaneous decentralization under the reforms often allows local officials to ignore Hanoi's directives. Provinces in central Vietnam, for instance, have not bothered to stop logging, despite a government ban announced in 1992. Rivalry within the bureaucracy is widespread and hinders the coordination of economic policies and implementation of desperately needed infrastructure projects. "It's a misconception of a one-party state to think you're dealing with a monolith," says a foreign economic advisor working in Hanoi. "In a period of transition, there are many centers of power and influence."

Still, Vietnam has managed to escape the ideological battles that have plagued China. Since Ho Chi Minh died in 1969, Hanoi has avoided personality cults—such as those that emerged in China around Mao Zedong and Deng Xiaoping—by developing a collective leadership style. This collegial leadership, however, frequently paralyzes decision making, while the political and geographical factions in the Politburo wrangle over such issues as whether to privatize money-losing state enterprises. Often the compromise solution delays urgent economic decisions and ends up pleasing no one.

In addition, Hanoi needs to bolster its civil service if it hopes to close the gap between Vietnam and Asia's tigers. Despite its high literacy rate, Vietnam confronts a critical shortage of the skilled personnel needed to complete its transition from rigid planning to the free market. Besides managers, those with skills in law, banking, marketing, accounting, and administration are in particularly high demand. These shortages not only hold back business operations but also hobble the government's ability to resolve problems arising from the country's drive to the market economy. "For decades the criteria for promotion was politics, not skill," observes one foreign political scientist. "That means that tens of thousands of civil servants are exceeding their level of competence." Phan Ngoc Tuong, head of the government's Committee for Administration and Personnel, says that no more than 40 percent of Vietnam's nearly 170,000 administrative staff meet even "standard requirements."[23]

"We talk a lot about our economic achievements during the past four or five years," says Le Chi Hien, deputy director of the State Planning Committee's science and technology department. "But if we'd had better-trained civil servants we might have had even better results," Hien argues. "Most of our civil servants were trained in the old, centrally planned economics. They aren't suitable for working in the new free market system." To combat this problem, many government offices have launched retraining programs for their officials. Progress is slow, however. For example, only two out of five staff at the State Planning Committee, the government's economic umbrella organization (upgraded into the ministry of planning and investment in late 1995) have taken remedial courses in economics, administration, law, or computers. "Other offices might have even lower figures," Hien says, adding, "In the provinces, very few cadres enjoy retraining."

Attempts to improve the state bureaucracy is further hampered by the fact that many of the country's most talented civil servants are defecting to the private sector. To thwart a bigger drain, the government turns a blind eye when its employees find part-time jobs to supplement their poor salaries. The problem is that they are left with little energy for their primary jobs, and to make matters worse, those leaving government service are not merely competent, but essential to complete such economic reforms as overhauling the country's archaic banking system.

Better salaries are one obvious cause for defections to the private sector. Nguyen Manh Chuong more than tripled his take-home pay in 1994 when he became Hanoi manager for an Australian company involved in exporting Vietnamese garments, textiles, and shoes. Chuong, age fifty-six and fluent in English, had earned less than $100 a month in his previous job at the State Committee for Cooperation and Investment, the government's foreign investment watchdog. Chuong was also attracted by the fact that private sector jobs are more challenging. "There I did the same job every day," he says about his government post. "If you want to move ahead you need a lot of challenges to test your ability. . . . In my new job, I can still help Vietnam and also bring interest to the foreign company."

Red tape further stifles economic growth. "Cases of authoritarianism, oppression, personal retaliation, bureaucratism, disregard of law and discipline are serious in many places," the Communist Party admitted in a political report prepared for its midterm conference in 1994. "If you want to get permission to do something, you need ten stamps," editor Huu Tho adds, referring to the procedure ubiquitous in many Asian bureaucracies. "In order to get ten stamps, you have to overcome ten cases of trouble and corruption."

One of Vietnam's biggest challenges is to build a system of laws so the market economy can function smoothly. Vietnam is still too often run by the rule of individuals rather than by the rule of law. The National Assembly has promulgated scores of new laws in recent years to regulate the country's rush to the free market, yet perhaps no piece of legislation was more important than the new Civil Code passed in late 1995. The 834-article law, hammered out for more than a decade, spells out guidelines for every aspect of Vietnamese life from rules of copyright protection to mortgaging property and technology transfer. "It's a great step forward for protection of civil liberties," says Vo Tong Xuan, a parliamentarian from the Mekong delta. "It means people will be protected by law and not simply subject to administrative fiat."[24]

Laws in and of themselves are not enough to create the rule of law. The new code takes effect in mid-1996, but lawyers say the country will need even more laws and regulations before the code can regulate people's daily lives. Vietnam is finding that it needs independent courts, competent judges, and lawyers, as well as a general public aware of how the legal system works.

The Notebook Incident

In April 1994, several months before I was due to finish my stint in Vietnam, I was planning a short leave in the suburbs of Boston. Linda and my two children were studying there, and I wanted some time away from Vietnam to begin cobbling together ideas for a book. As I had done dozens of times before, I traveled to Hanoi's dilapidated Noi Bai airport to take a flight to Bangkok. I sailed through customs without a hitch until the officials X-rayed my luggage. Suddenly, a stern-looking official dressed in a crudely tailored, olive-green uniform without any markings indicating his affiliation pulled my bags off the conveyor belt and ordered me to follow him. "So you're the guy they've been waiting for," a customs bureaucrat mumbled as I was led to a dingy, windowless room off the airport's check-in area.

My "handler" told me to put all my luggage onto a beat-up wooden table, but he zeroed in on a black vinyl bag holding some seventy notebooks that I had accumulated during nearly four years in Vietnam. He soon was joined by four other officials dressed in similar uniforms. Several of them studied my notebooks, while two others began rummaging through the clothes, books, and files in my suitcases. After a few minutes the group's senior member asked the others to join him in the hallway. Moments later they filed back in, and the man said to me, "You can go, but you have to leave your notebooks here." I wasn't willing to leave my notebooks, but my appeals to the officials fell on deaf ears. "These are cultural materials," the leader insisted. "You need authorization from the ministry of culture to take them out." I soon realized that I had no alternative but to return to Hanoi and talk with the foreign ministry's press department, the office responsible for foreign journalists working in Vietnam. Looking back on it now, I should not have been surprised by what I now call the "notebook incident."

I had opened the Hanoi bureau of the *Far Eastern Economic Review* in 1990 when several news organizations received permission to set up offices. As it stepped up its economic reforms, the ruling Communist Party apparently wanted more international press coverage. My closest working relations were with the press department, to which I had to apply to get permission for most of my meetings and any trips outside of Hanoi.

My relations with this department were almost always cordial, even though its officials on several occasions had criticized my articles. One senior foreign ministry official reprimanded me to my editor for reporting complaints within the Communist Party about corruption in a government minister's family. "I wonder whether Murray is trying to disrupt renovation in Vietnam," the official said.

Three months before the notebook incident the deputy director of the press department called me in and read me a formal statement castigating three articles I had written about dissidents in Vietnam. He accused me of having "ill-intention toward Vietnam" and of having "exploited some personal opinions of hostile forces outside of the country to smear the political system of Vietnam." The statement charged me with "ruining the reputation" of my magazine and warned that "if you and the *Review* continue such nonobjective reporting we will have to take it into consideration."

This incident, however, was only my most recent run-in with the press department and other Vietnamese government offices, such as the secretive security apparatus of the interior ministry. Soon after I arrived in Hanoi in 1990 I was invited to have tea with a senior security official who told me that one of his office's main functions was to make sure that "no one harms you." Of course he did not mention that his staff kept tabs on the movements of foreigners and many Vietnamese suspected of troublemaking. The police also monitor telephone calls of foreign journalists. Once when a professor from Australia was interviewing me on the phone about the make-up of the Communist Party's Politburo, the line was cut three times. Realizing that this conversation was not going to be allowed, we abandoned the discussion. Most of my Vietnamese friends insisted on having only the most cursory conversations on the phone.

Every Friday afternoon, my minders from the security police called Tran Le Thuy, the *Review*'s assistant, to request a meeting. I never met them but after several years began to recognize their voices on the phone. They would ask Thuy where I had been during the week, to whom I had talked, and what stories I was working on. Every six months or so Binh, the boss of my minders (whose real name I cannot disclose), would ask for a lunch meeting. During these lunches Binh would ask who the sources were for certain bits of information that I had used in my stories. He began each of our meetings this way, even though I explained to him repeatedly that it was a fundamental principle of Western journalism not to divulge the names of sources. He would drop hints to let me know that he knew what I had been up to, to whom I had spoken, and so on.

The notebook incident took place on a Saturday and I was not able to meet anyone from the press department until Monday. By this time my deputy editor, Nayan Chanda, had sent a message to the foreign ministry expressing concern about the matter. The Canadian chargé d'affaires in Hanoi, Christopher Brown, had also filed a complaint.

The meeting with the press department's deputy director was friendly. He began by telling me that he too had had difficulty a few years earlier, when he was trying to take some notebooks to Japan where he had planned to do some research. He said that resolving my problem was *de qua*, very easy. I should type up a list of my interviews, including the dates and main subjects discussed. The press department would then attach a letter to this list requesting the ministry of culture to allow me to leave with the notes.

Putting together a list of nearly four years' worth of interviews took me several days, and resolving my problem did not turn out to be quite so easy. When I arrived at the culture ministry, officials insisted that they needed another two to seven days to vet my notebooks. The foreign ministry made several attempts to break the impasse but failed. On one of my numerous trips to the ministry of culture, I became impatient. "I don't understand why the foreign ministry says one thing and you say another," I protested. "They're responsible for foreign affairs; we're responsible for culture," a frustrated culture ministry official responded. Then almost whispering, "I'd like to help, but they're from A–15," pointing at two sets of legs visible beneath a room divider in the next room. A–15 is a unit of the security police and, as I was slowly beginning to understand, had ultimate jurisdiction over my notebooks.

After two weeks I finally realized that the standoff could continue indefinitely, so I put all my notebooks in a closet and headed for the airport. I had torn out all of the sensitive pages by then to make sure that the security police found nothing interesting if they went through them in my absence. Everything went smoothly until the final security check, when I asked to have my laptop computer hand-inspected. Out of nowhere the unidentified customs officials reappeared. One of them began frisking me, as if he were searching for drugs. Another told me to empty my pockets. He took my wallet and began pulling out my money, credit cards, and pictures of my children. A third official looked through my hand luggage and found a few notebooks I had used since the original ones were blocked a few weeks earlier. "You're trying to break the law," declared the man in charge. "You know you're not allowed to take out cultural materials." I protested that I had nothing of any cultural value, but he was prepared for any contingency. He pulled out a book of customs regulations and began reading a ruling which said that "handwritten materials" have cultural value and need a license before they can be exported.

I was the last passenger left in the security-check area and the plane was due to leave. While the official and I debated whether a journalist's notebooks have cultural value, an impatient young woman from Vietnam Airlines came over to ask the men detaining me whether I was going to be allowed to leave. Finally, the official declared, "You've been in Vietnam a long time and should be better informed about Vietnam's laws," and let me go.

Nearly two months later I returned to Hanoi to finish up my assignment and pack up my household. I submitted another letter to the foreign ministry asking for permission to take out the notebooks, even though I no longer needed them; I had found alternative ways to get the notes I needed out of the country. Three days before I was to leave I received a call from the ministry of foreign affairs telling me to show up the next morning at the culture ministry with my notebooks. A stocky, short-haired woman in her late forties stacked all of my notebooks on the table in front of her but took only a cursory look before sealing the books in a cardboard box.

When I got back to the office I had a message on my answering machine from Binh, the top minder who refused to return my calls since the notebook flap began. Binh wanted to meet to say good-bye. During drinks at an upscale new Hanoi bar Binh never once mentioned the notebooks or the government's dissatisfaction with some of my articles. He talked instead about the problems of the growing gap between rich and poor and about the investment activities of foreign companies in Vietnam. "I hope you remain a friend of Vietnam," Binh said as we parted. "Come back to visit us."

When I arrived at the airport the next morning, a young man whom I had never met approached and asked if I was the *Review* correspondent. He grabbed my customs form, plane ticket, and passport and began checking me in. He even asked Vietnam Airlines officials not to bill me for overweight baggage, making me feel a bit like a vanquished Chinese general. (Throughout history, whenever the Vietnamese army defeated invaders from China they would escort the retreating soldiers to the border with full regalia. Hanoi then sent an envoy to Beijing to pay tribute to the Chinese emperor.)

The notebook incident reminded me of the dangers of starry-eyed optimism about Vietnam. The country is likely to encounter pitfalls in its headlong pursuit of Asia's tigers. At the same time, these events showed that even Hanoi's most ardent keepers of orthodoxy have a healthy streak of pragmatism. As I boarded the plane to Bangkok, I realized that the Vietnam I was leaving in 1994 was different from the one in which I had arrived four years earlier. I couldn't help but feel optimistic about Vietnam's chances for ultimate success.

Hanging on to the Chair

Since the upheaval that toppled its former allies in Eastern Europe, pundits have pondered the future of the Vietnamese Communist Party. The party's *Nhan Dan* daily admitted in 1992 that "our party is no longer in its springtime, but only has old trees without any green sprouts. These worries are not unfounded." Regardless, even Hanoi's harshest critics doubt that the party will collapse any time soon. One reason is its deep roots in Vietnamese history. The party is widely respected, even by many anti-Communists, for its pivotal role in ousting France and the United States. Unlike their deposed counterparts in Eastern Europe installed by the former Soviet Union, the Vietnamese Communists seized power on their own. Rather than wait for discontent to explode, they defused popular dissatisfaction by admitting their mistakes and launching economic reforms in the mid-1980s.

The country remains desperately poor, however, and still lacks a large class of professionals and entrepreneurs clamoring for greater democracy, as happened in Eastern Europe. Unlike the Chinese Communists, the Vietnamese party has not had to resort to wide-scale violence to cling to control, and despite all of its troubles, it maintains full control of the security apparatus, the government bureaucracy, and the press.

"At least in the next five years, until the end of the century, I don't see the possibility of a big political change," observes Thanh, a savvy Hanoi intellectual. "But if China changes," he adds, alluding to possible upheaval across Vietnam's northern border after Deng Xiaoping dies, "change in Vietnam will be quite rapid. . . . The collapse in Eastern Europe and the Soviet Union caused a big psychological and moral impact on Vietnamese Communists," says Thanh, who is a member of the party and has spent several years studying in the West. "This was the cradle of communism and its collapse was the biggest challenge to the Vietnamese party since its founding. . . . Now China is the biggest remaining Communist country. If the Chinese party is still in power, the Vietnamese party will remain in power. If the Chinese Communists are out of power, the Vietnamese Communists will be out of power. Maybe there won't be chaos," he says, adding hopefully, "maybe the change will be gradual."

The Vietnamese party has bet its future on continued economic growth, but what will happen if there is an economic downturn? "In such circumstances the system may prove quite brittle, as there is no precedent for the management of such disputes short of forcibly silencing one's opponents," observes David Marr. "Vietnam faces the problem of new economic interests at work within an outdated political structure. Nevertheless," Marr continues, "Vietnam is not condemned to return to the violence and bloodshed of earlier decades. Everyone over twenty years of age remains mindful of past traumas and anxious to move onward peacefully. . . . People may not agree on what it means to 'catch up' with the rest of the world, but they want to be on the road, sharing the adventure."[25]

Many in the West assume that Vietnam will not be able to boost its economy without liberalizing its political system. But leaders in Vietnam, as in China, point to the Taiwan, South Korea, and Singapore of the 1970s to argue that Asian countries develop fastest in societies that couple free market economics with single-party politics. Soaring industrial output, surging savings rates, and legal protection for investors have been more important than political freedom in creating Asia's thriving economies. Democracies such as the Philippines have witnessed feeble growth. "Vietnam is evolving along tracks like that of almost every other state in East Asia," American Vietnam specialist William Turley observes, alluding to the fact that Vietnam's neighbors became economic high-flyers in the 1960s and

1970s while keeping a tight lid on politics. As these societies prospered and urbanized, however, the emerging middle class stepped up its demands for a more open political system. "Vietnam will do okay as long as it slowly loosens its grasp and co-opts its businessmen," continues Turley. "They don't care about politics as long as the government stays out of the market and maintains stability. . . . The rest of society is fairly passive, the Buddhists notwithstanding," Turley says. Most Vietnamese, except for a handful of religious leaders, are likely to tolerate the regime as long as the economy keeps performing, he argues.

Still, far-reaching change is inevitable. Thomas Vallely of Harvard's Institute for International Development states that Vietnam's future ultimately lies in the hands of its newly emerging middle class. Vallely, a frequent visitor to Vietnam, believes this elite is made up not only of the new breed of private businessmen and intellectuals but also includes representatives from the army, the Communist Party, provincial governments, and state-owned enterprises. Within this group, he argues, "are people who want to further open up the economy and also people who want to close the economy to keep their privileges. Those who want to maintain a monopoly have more control within the government as well as in the Communist Party. But the people who advocate more openness have a more solid intellectual framework for capturing the future." Vallely is convinced that the "constant chatter" among these elites, which the government can no longer control, will ultimately determine to what extent Vietnam opens its economic and political systems.

"The party can't stop change," adds Ly Quy Chung, a newspaper editor in Ho Chi Minh City, who also worked as a journalist in the old Saigon. "When it accepts the free market, more relations with its neighbors, and normalization with the United States, these factors automatically will create a new Vietnam," he insists. "They can't hold the country in its old line. The party and the government must prepare politically for this change." Chung and other observers believe that as Vietnam mingles more with the outside world, its economy grows, education levels increase, and the old-guard revolutionaries pass from the scene, the emerging middle class will demand wide-ranging liberalization of the country's political landscape. Of course, Vietnam will likely face disruptions along the way, but if the country continues to grow economically it could undergo a metamorphosis that not only bolsters the livelihood of its people but frees up their lives as well.

Some think that over the next few decades Vietnam will look much like Taiwan, South Korea, and Thailand, once impoverished authoritarian regimes that have been transformed into nascent democracies. Others believe that Vietnam will more likely evolve into a Singapore, Malaysia, or Indonesia, which have coupled impressive economic growth with more modest liberalization of a strong one-party rule.

It is doubtful that Communist ideology can be revived, but could a renamed Communist Party still play a role, perhaps similar to that played by the Kuomintang in Taiwan? "If the party is clear-sighted and has upright members it will survive," argues Tran Bach Dang, a Ho Chi Minh City intellectual who served as underground party boss in the city during the war. "If not, it will collapse. We don't have a right provided by God to stay in the leading chair forever."

10

Chasing the Tigers

◆ ◆ ◆

Can They Sing Karaoke?

The sultanate of Brunei Darussalam, the Abode of Peace, was an appropriate place to end Vietnam's international isolation. Until this day the tiny, oil-rich state had been the most recent member to join the Association of Southeast Asian Nations (ASEAN), and Brunei's sultan had never been a player in the group's disputes with Hanoi. Here, on July 28, 1995, at a modern convention center on a hill just outside Brunei's capital, ASEAN's six foreign ministers stood at attention next to their Vietnamese counterpart as an honor guard solemnly hoisted Hanoi's red-and-gold flag up a pole alongside the flags of its neighbors.

The ministers were commemorating Vietnam's admission as the seventh member of this club of high-flying Southeast Asian countries that includes Brunei, Indonesia, Malaysia, the Philippines, Singapore, and Thailand. Vietnam's decision to join the group marked a watershed in the country's history, putting an end to three decades of confrontation and polarization in Southeast Asia. "After many years of war, we have now earned the confidence of friends in our neighborhood who will jointly help chart . . . the course of economic development of our country," Vietnamese Foreign Minister Nguyen Manh Cam declared after signing documents ratifying his country's induction into ASEAN.

Vietnam's membership demonstrates just how much the landscape of Asia has shifted since the end of the cold war. Ironically, ASEAN had been established in 1967, at the height of the Vietnam War, to contain the spread of communism from Hanoi across Southeast Asia. Since World War II Vietnam had been the focal point of almost continuous rivalry between the world's major powers. With the collapse of the Soviet empire Hanoi lost its superpower patron but was handed a new opportunity to extricate itself from pariah status and begin to court foreign investors. Vietnam has launched a diplomatic offensive in recent years to mend its strained relations with most of the world, particularly with non-Communist Asia, China, and the United States—countries that had mounted a campaign to isolate Vietnam after its 1978 invasion of Cambodia.

"The Seventh Congress stressed that the top priority of our nation was to develop our economy," Deputy Foreign Minister Le Mai says, referring to a 1991 meeting of Communist Party leaders. This congress had jettisoned ideological considerations as the driving force in Hanoi's foreign policy. Diplomacy and reconciliation had replaced military might and a strategic alliance with Moscow as the main planks in Vietnam's national security. Mai emphasizes that "to achieve a favorable environment, we need to carry out a policy of diversifying our international relations."

Vietnam's induction into ASEAN completes its rehabilitation as a good-standing member of the world community. Two weeks earlier, on July 11, 1995, U.S. President Bill Clinton had formally ended the Vietnam War by granting full diplomatic recognition to Hanoi. "By helping bring Vietnam into the community of nations, normalization also serves our interest in working for a free and peaceful Vietnam in a stable and peaceful Asia," Clinton said.[1] "Ten years ago, if people had suggested that Vietnam would be joining ASEAN, they would have been laughed out of court," a senior Singaporean diplomat observed a few weeks before Hanoi's induction. "Vietnam has changed a lot. It isn't the same place it was ten years ago."

Vietnam's ASEAN membership intimately links the country's future with that of some of the world's most dynamic economies. Together they boast a population of four hundred and twenty million consumers, most of whose economies have been growing at over 7 percent a year since the late 1980s. "When it joins ASEAN, Vietnam is signaling to investors that it wants to be part of the free market," states Chan Heng Chee, head of the Institute for Southeast Asian Studies in Singapore and the country's former ambassador to the United Nations. "This will have a contagious effect on the economy." Even before Vietnam joined ASEAN, its members already accounted for more than a third of Vietnam's foreign trade and approximately one-fifth of its foreign investment. Singapore's former prime minister Lee Kuan Yew, who long campaigned to isolate Hanoi, has visited Vietnam several times to advise its leaders as they move from central planning to a market economy. Malaysia has provided help in developing Vietnam's rubber plantations.

Membership in ASEAN will have a long-term psychological impact on Vietnam. "The first thing we tell them is that there are three qualifications for joining ASEAN," a senior Southeast Asian diplomat jokes. "You have to play golf, sing karaoke, and eat durian." Mastering the "ASEAN way"—the art of consultation and consensus decision making—will mark a dramatic transformation of Vietnam, which for decades has been better known for its warriors than its diplomats. "They're fighters," another diplomat observes. "In ASEAN, we work on congeniality and personal ties. This will be a radical switch for the Vietnamese."

Affiliation with ASEAN is expected to attract additional investment from Japan, Taiwan, and Western countries, whose companies began moving their labor-intensive factories to Southeast Asia two decades ago as wages rose at home. Membership is also the first step to gaining entry into two other economic institutions that will play key roles in Vietnam's economic future: the World Trade Organization and the Asia Pacific Economic Cooperation forum.

Vietnam today is more secure from military threat than at any time since the 1930s, but several foreign policy challenges cloud the country's horizon and jeopardize its economic take-off. "Hanoi must somehow accommodate China without threatening other Southeast Asians, and it must strengthen ties with major powers like

Japan and the United States without antagonizing China," Vietnam specialist William Turley argues. "Vietnam also shares a disputed border on both land and sea with a prickly yet unstable Cambodia, and its rivalry with Thailand for influence in the states between them may be in abeyance rather than dead."[2] A top priority must be to avoid hostilities with China in the South China Sea, an area encompassing the potentially oil-rich Spratly archipelago. These scattered rocks—claimed in whole by Vietnam, China, and Taiwan, and in part by Malaysia, the Philippines, and Brunei—straddle some of the world's busiest shipping lanes (they carry 70 percent of Japan's oil) and most lucrative fishing grounds.

Relations with Beijing are Hanoi's most important foreign policy problem: China not only serves as an economic and political role model for Vietnam but also remains its biggest potential threat, as it has throughout Vietnam's history. "Vietnam lies in the direct path of China's growing power and assertiveness, and no other country has China's potential to manipulate Vietnam internally," Turley points out. He is alluding to China's links to Vietnam's ethnic Chinese residents and its ties to high-ranking members of the Vietnamese Communist Party and military who have worked or trained in China during the years of socialist solidarity. Because the Chinese border is only one hundred kilometers from Hanoi, no nation's domestic politics "reverberate" in Vietnam the way China's does. As Turley states, China's "phenomenal economic growth, military modernization, hegemonial ambitions, and political example constitute enduring threats." With the collapse of the Soviet Union Hanoi no longer can rely on a superpower to balance its relations with Beijing. "The alternative of bandwagoning with China also lacks appeal as it would place Vietnam in China's sphere of influence, compromise Vietnam's independence, and sour relations with other Asian states," Turley observes. "Finding a middle way with the Middle Kingdom is Vietnam's central strategic conundrum."[3]

Sino-Vietnamese relations had deteriorated sharply in the 1970s as Hanoi stepped up its alliance with the former Soviet Union. In 1979, following Vietnam's invasion of Cambodia, China retaliated by sending its troops to attack across its southern border. Vietnamese soldiers repelled the attackers, but Hanoi had a much harder time overcoming the international isolation resulting from its occupation of Cambodia. Once Vietnam withdrew from Cambodia a decade later, however, political and economic ties between the world's two largest surviving Communist countries normalized rapidly. Some Vietnamese Communists even began talking about reestablishing a socialist alliance with Beijing following the collapse of Soviet communism.

These romantic notions withered abruptly in early 1992, when China's National Assembly claimed sovereignty over 80 percent of the South China Sea (which the Vietnamese call the Eastern Sea). China's newly asserted ownership lines ran smack through several oil exploration blocks that Vietnam was preparing to award to foreign companies. A few months later Beijing granted exploration rights to Crestone Energy Corporation, a small Denver-based firm, to drill for oil in an area most observers consider to be on Vietnam's continental shelf. "China's behavior in the Eastern Sea has opened people's eyes," a Vietnamese diplomat told me at the time. Resolution of the dispute had long been difficult because China insisted that rival claims could only be discussed in bilateral talks with other claimants and refused to allow differences to be discussed in multilateral forums such as the World Court or the United Nations. However, in a meeting with ASEAN foreign ministers in Brunei in July 1995, Chinese Foreign Minister Qian Qichen announced that Beijing would be willing to recognize international laws, including the 1982 U.N. Convention on the Law of the Sea, as a basis for negotiating differences. China earlier had proposed shelving the differences and setting up a joint development scheme, but Hanoi had shown little interest in sharing what it felt belonged to Vietnam under international law.

Before this, in 1988, fighting broke out between China and Vietnam when the Chinese seized several barren atolls in the Spratlys long claimed by Vietnam. Nearly seventy Vietnamese sailors were killed in the clash. Since that time both sides have avoided armed encounters, yet there is always the danger of miscalculation; Beijing, Hanoi, and most of the other claimants have stationed troops in the archipelago. Both China and Vietnam have on occasion sent naval vessels into areas where the other was conducting oil exploration activities, causing tensions to erupt from time to time. If fighting resumes, the poorly equipped armed forces of Vietnam would hardly be a match even for China's antiquated navy and air force (which Beijing has sought to upgrade in recent years by buying sophisticated Russian SU-27 fighter aircraft, S-300 ground-to-air missiles, and submarines).

As China develops a blue-water navy, Vietnam calculates that its best defense is its membership in ASEAN. Even though the group's leaders have ruled out forming a united front against Beijing, Hanoi will be able to find some comfort through its formal alliance with six internationally respected neighbors. ASEAN has sought to ensure Beijing's responsible behavior in the future by seeking to integrate China's economy with that of its Southeast Asian neighbors through trade and investment links.

The United States poses a second challenge for Vietnamese policy makers. President Clinton's decision to exchange embassies with Hanoi is a clear signal that Washington at long last will stop punishing Vietnam for winning the war. The economies of Vietnam's neighbors only started booming when they began selling their products to the gigantic American market. Vietnam, however, cannot export much to the United States until the two countries negotiate an agreement exchanging most-favored-nation trading status, thereby assuring each other the lowest available tariffs. In the meantime American firms need access to risk insurance from the Overseas Private Investment Corporation and below-market financing from the Export-Import Bank before their sales to Vietnam can take off. In addition, the two governments must sign scores of other agreements covering trade, taxation, and investment protection, some of which could take a number of years to complete.

Emotional barriers as well could delay implementation of economic links between the two countries. Family members of missing servicemen, vocal veterans groups, and a handful of Republican congressmen opposed Clinton's decision to normalize diplomatic ties with Vietnam. The two governments have been working together for years on accounting for some 1,600 U.S. servicemen still missing from the Vietnam War, but critics of Hanoi insist that the Vietnamese continue to hold back remains and information. One of those who supports normalization is John McCain, a Republican senator from Arizona and a decorated war veteran who spent five years as a prisoner of war in Vietnam. McCain argues that closer relations are the best way to ensure that Hanoi provides Washington with the fullest possible accounting. The senator also says that the surest means to protect U.S. security interests in Southeast Asia is to support a strong and economically viable Vietnam.

Critics of Hanoi can delay the granting of most-favored-nation status, the prize Vietnam needs most to boost its exports. Vietnam, like China, is a Communist country, which means that its trade status must face annual review. Some members of Congress may insist that progress on Hanoi's accounting for missing servicemen be a condition for renewal. Others may focus on human rights, much as they did earlier in the case of China. Hanoi and Washington held several rounds of talks on human rights and narcotics control even before Clinton's announcement. The Communist Party's biggest fear of the United States, however, is "ideological contamination." President Clinton alarmed Vietnamese leaders when, while announcing normalization of relations with Hanoi, he declared that "increased contact between Americans and Vietnamese will advance the cause of freedom in Vietnam just as it did in Eastern Europe and the former Soviet Union"—exactly the kind of "peaceful evolution" Vietnamese leaders hope to avoid.

Hanoi is particularly concerned about the impact of growing numbers of Vietnamese-Americans returning to their native country following normalization. A month after Washington resumed ties with Hanoi in July 1995 a Ho Chi Minh City court sentenced nine people, including two Vietnamese-Americans, to up to fifteen years in prison for subversion after they tried to organize a conference on human rights. (Under pressure from Washington the two Vietnamese-Americans were freed and expelled from Vietnam four months later.) A few days after this trial another court sentenced Thich Quang Do, a leader of the dissident Unified Buddhist Church, and five of his followers to up to five years in prison for "sabotaging religious solidarity." Observers interpret both trials as a signal to Vietnamese dissidents and the United States that Hanoi has no intention of abandoning its hard line on dissent.

Cambodia is a third potential hurdle along Vietnam's path to tigerhood. Hanoi ended its costly, ten-year military occupation of Cambodia in 1989; two years later it signed an international peace agreement that helped Vietnam mend its fences with China, Japan, ASEAN members, and most Western countries. But Cambodia still poses potential dangers to Hanoi, one of which is possible territorial disputes. Many Cambodians believe Hanoi pressed its former client government in Phnom Penh to sign border agreements in the 1980s favoring Vietnam. Some observers worry that this could prompt a diplomatic row in the future. Another danger is the possible mistreatment or expulsion of Vietnamese nationals living in Cambodia. As many as half a million ethnic Vietnamese have lived in Cambodia since French colonial times. Dozens of Vietnamese were killed and thousands of others fled to Vietnam during U.N.-sponsored elections in Cambodia in 1993. A new wave of ethnic animosity could erupt in the future. Hanoi fears the possibility that Cambodia could slide back into civil war if the fragile coalition government in Phnom Penh unravels. Renewed chaos would prompt a flood of refugees across Cambodia's eastern border. Vietnam would lose valuable economic opportunities if fighting spilled across its frontier.

Relations with Thailand are a fourth challenge facing Hanoi's policy makers. Membership in ASEAN will not sweep aside all of the differences Vietnam faces with its non-Communist neighbors overnight. Thailand is the ASEAN country Vietnam trusts least. The two countries have a long history of rivalry over Cambodia and Laos, two small buffer countries separating these giants of mainland Southeast Asia. During the American war in Indochina Thailand served as a major base for U.S. bombers. Bangkok later supported Khmer guerrillas fighting Vietnamese troops occupying Cambodia during the 1980s. Future tensions between Vietnam and Thailand could be prompted by overlapping territorial waters that hold shrinking stocks of fish but potentially giant reserves of natural gas and oil. In mid-1995 Vietnamese and Thai sailors engaged in a half-hour machine-gun battle which killed a Thai fisherman and two Vietnamese. Thailand's plans to divert water from the upper reaches of the Mekong River are another possible irritant. Stepped-up Thai use of the river's water could cause salt water to flood the fertile rice fields of southern Vietnam's Mekong delta.

Despite these potential flashpoints, there has never been a time in recent memory when Vietnam's relations with its neighbors have been more cordial. Isolated incidents may erupt in the coming years, but most analysts believe Vietnam and its Chinese, Thai, and Cambodian neighbors are too preoccupied with developing their economies to be interested in conflict.

The "Second" Revolution

Vietnam is in the throes of its "second" revolution, one that is changing the country every bit as much as the one launched after the Communists first seized power. But will the changes be enough to propel Vietnam into the ranks of Asia's tigers? Will Vietnam follow in the footsteps of such prosperous, increasingly democratic East Asian neighbors as Taiwan and South Korea, where economic growth has created a burgeoning middle class demanding a bigger say in politics? Or is it possible that Vietnam will degenerate into political and economic chaos, much like its former Communist allies?

The Communist Party faces no immediate threat to its survival, unless its counterpart in China disintegrates or the Vietnamese economy plunges into a nosedive. Indeed, even the regime's harshest critics do not want the Communist Party to collapse. Many intellectuals wish for democracy but fear that too much political freedom introduced too quickly will bring chaos, upsetting economic gains achieved thus far. They recognize that economies stagnated in the countries of the former Soviet Union after their ruling Communist parties disintegrated, and they see that democracies such as the Philippines are among Asia's most economically backward. These lessons have convinced most of Vietnam's pro-democracy intellectuals to prefer a gradual, "peaceful evolution" from communism to one-party authoritarianism to a more politically open society. Intellectuals also recognize that Vietnam is still largely agrarian, lacking in industrial development and much poorer than most of its neighbors or former Eastern European allies. This means that Vietnam has few entrepreneurs, professionals, and managers to develop alternative policies or begin organizing an opposition political movement to challenge the ruling Communists.

As a result, the Communist Party may well stay in control, although many observers believe that Vietnam over the next decade or two will evolve along the lines of Singapore, Malaysia, and Indonesia, which have maintained strong one-party rule while achieving dynamic industrial growth. Some believe that in coming years the Vietnamese party will transform itself along the lines of the ruling People's Action Party in Singapore or GOLKAR in Indonesia.[4] But in the longer term, many thoughtful Vietnamese look to Taiwan and South Korea as political models. They point out that blossoming private enterprise in these two Confucian neighbors created a middle class that formed an independent power base outside of the ruling party and gradually began demanding a role in the country's decision-making process. This transformed Taiwan and South Korea from poor, repressive dictatorships in the 1950s into thriving democracies in just four decades. Thailand now appears to be evolving along a similar path. These countries, Vietnamese intellectuals point out, have demonstrated that political change is possible without the disruption that sent Eastern Europe into a tailspin.

The remarkable economic and social changes under way in Vietnam have prompted observers to ask whether it will be the next member of Asia's club of high-flyers. Some pundits are swept along blindly by the optimistic tiger-hype of fund managers; others look at the hurdles Vietnam must overcome and conclude that it cannot make it. I come out somewhere in the middle. The energy and determination, the Confucian emphasis on education and thrift, as well as the hard work of millions of youthful entrepreneurs, farmers, and workers convince me that Vietnam will eventually prove the pessimists wrong and blossom into a tiger in the long run. Much of my confidence about Vietnam's future is based on respect for the country's progress. Vietnam's recent economic achievements (although uneven) have been nothing short of spectacular. The Communist Party continues to rule but is now preoccupied with exporting rice and crude oil rather than socialist dogma and disgruntled refugees. After half a century of war and economic mismanagement the Communists have embraced free market ideology with a vengeance. The Vietnam I started reporting on for the *Far Eastern Economic Review* from Bangkok in 1986 was very different from the one I left in 1994.

Millions of Vietnamese live better than they did a decade ago, when they farmed in cooperatives and stood in queues to buy their rice from state shops. People cannot vote the Communist Party out of power, but their lives are much freer now that they are allowed to find their own jobs and travel freely within the country. The security police still round up dissidents, but people are less afraid. They have started speaking out when corrupt officials take their land or their houses. Karaoke bars, satellite dishes, and private hotels are sprouting everywhere, and more Vietnamese are studying and traveling abroad. Vietnam's infant mortality rates are dropping, while life expectancy for the country's citizens has risen sharply.

Vietnam's economy has surged some 8 percent a year since the Communist Party launched its reforms in the late 1980s. Private enterprise is booming, exports are soaring, hyperinflation has been reined in, and foreign investment has begun to take off. Growing incomes are pulling millions of peasants out of absolute poverty and have transformed the skyline of the country's cities. There is enthusiasm in the air as Vietnamese buy their first motorbikes, build new houses, open businesses, and begin experimenting with new ideas on how to get rich.

The conventional wisdom is that Vietnam will maintain 8 percent to 10 percent growth at least until the end of the decade, which means it will double its gross domestic product between 1993 and 2000. Even at that rate Vietnam still has a lot of catching up to do: China is already a decade ahead, and Malaysia is in front by roughly a generation.

Vietnam is still a long way from being a stockbroker's paradise, and many wonder if the country can maintain its recent economic success. Much depends on whether Hanoi continues to boost its productivity by pursuing pro-growth policies that bolster foreign investment and trade. For starters, the government will have to abandon its old notions of control and allow competitive markets to work relatively unfettered. The country needs to double domestic savings and increase spending on its decrepit ports, crumbling roads, and overtaxed power distribution network. Hanoi must provide jobs for millions of unemployed, overcome distribution bottlenecks, establish a stock market, and force state-owned enterprises to stand on their own.

Plenty of hurdles lurk along the path to tigerdom. The government must get rid of the layers of red tape, soaring corruption, a barely functioning legal system, confusion over frequently changing regulations, and conflicts between the central and local governments that continue to hobble foreign investors. Officials must reverse the declining standards of education and find ways to train the managers needed to complete the country's march from Marx to the market. The government must devise ways to absorb more of the money investors and donors have available for Asia's most fashionable emerging market.

Many investors say that working in Vietnam today is not much harder than it was in China in the early 1980s when that country began to open up. Cautious Western businessmen chronicle a list of woes, but bullish entrepreneurs from Taiwan, Japan, Singapore,

South Korea, and Hong Kong have no doubts that Vietnam will continue its dynamic growth. They paint a bright picture, convinced that pragmatism in Hanoi will beat out political impediments in the race to get rich. This, many Asian business leaders believe, over the next few decades will propel this longtime Spartan backwater into the ranks of the region's tigers.

Notes

◆ ◆ ◆

Introduction: Vietnam Awakes

1. Murray Hiebert, "Giant Steps: Shoe Maker Biti Is One of Vietnam's Most Able Firms," *Far Eastern Economic Review*, 8 July 1993, 52–53.

2. David G. Marr, *Vietnam Strives to Catch Up* (New York: Asia Society, 1995), p. 5.

3. Ibid.

4. Dwight H. Perkins, Introduction to *In Search of the Dragon's Trail: Economic Reform in Vietnam*, ed. David O. Dapice, Dwight H. Perkins, and Jonathan Haughton (Cambridge, Mass.: Harvard University Press, forthcoming).

5. World Bank, *Vietnam: Transition to the Market* (Washington, D.C., 1993), p. ii.

Chapter 1: Asia's Youngest Tiger Roars

1. Vietnam News Agency, 30 January 1994; and Murray Hiebert, "Corps Business: Vietnam's Military Is Learning to Turn Profits," *Far Eastern Economic Review*, 23 December 1993, 40-41.

2. For a detailed description of the events of March 24, 1978, see Nayan Chanda, *Brother Enemy: The War After the War* (New York: Collier Books, 1986), pp. 231ff.

3. This chapter draws from conversations with Vietnamese and foreign economists and several written sources, including *In Search of the Dragon's Trail: Economic Reform in Vietnam*, ed. David O. Dapice, Dwight H. Perkins, and Jonathan Haughton (Cambridge, Mass.: Harvard University Press, forthcoming); World Bank, *Vietnam: Transition to the Market* (Washington, D.C., 1993); Adam Fforde, *Vietnam: Economic Commentary and Analysis*, no. 5 (Canberra,

Australia: ADUKI Pty., 1994); *Vietnam: A Development Perspective* (Hanoi: n.p., November 1993).

4. Shada Islam, "A for Effort: Vietnam Earns High Marks at Donors' Meeting," *Far Eastern Economic Review*, 1 December 1994, 77.

5. *Vietnam: A Development Perspective*, p. 44.

6. Charles J. Johnson, "Vietnam's Energy Sector," in Dapice, Perkins, and Haughton, *In Search of the Dragon's Trail*.

7. World Bank, *Transition to the Market*, p. ii. See also Theo Panayotou, "Environmental Protection and Sustainable Development," in Dapice, Perkins, and Haughton, *In Search of the Dragon's Trail*.

8. World Bank, *The East Asian Miracle: Economic Growth and Public Policy* (New York: Oxford Press, 1993). For an earlier study of East Asia's economic success see Ezra F. Vogel, *The Four Little Dragons: The Spread of Industrialization in East Asia* (Cambridge, Mass.: Harvard University Press, 1991).

9. Dwight H. Perkins, Introduction to Dapice, Perkins, and Haughton, *In Search of the Dragon's Trail*.

10. Ibid.

11. World Bank, *Vietnam: Transition to the Market* (Washington, D.C., 1993), p. xii.

12. Fforde, *Economic Commentary and Analysis*, pp. 14–15.

Chapter 2: Roots of the Nation

This chapter draws from conversations with Vietnamese historians and several written sources, including Joseph Buttinger, *A Dragon Defiant: A Short History of Vietnam* (New York, Praeger, 1972); Nayan Chanda, *Brother Enemy: The War After the War* (New York: Collier Books, 1986); Neil L. Jamieson, *Understanding Vietnam* (Berkeley, Calif.: University of California Press, 1993); George M. Kahin, *Intervention: How America Became Involved in Vietnam* (New York: Alfred A. Knopf, 1986); Stanley Karnow, *Vietnam: A History* (New York: Viking, 1983); Gabriel Kolko, *Anatomy of a War* (New York: New Press, 1994); David G. Marr, Introduction to *Vietnam*, World Bibliographic Series (Santa Barbara, Calif.: ABC-CLIO Press, 1993); David G. Marr, *Vietnamese Anti-Colonialism, 1885–1925* (Berkeley, Calif.: University of California Press, 1971); David G. Marr, *Vietnamese Tradition on Trial, 1920–1945* (Berkeley, Calif.: University of California Press, 1981); John T. McAlister, Jr., *Vietnam: The Origins of Revolution* (New York: Doubleday, 1971); Ralph Smith, *Viet-Nam and the West* (Ithaca, New York: Cornell University Press, 1971); Keith Taylor, *The Birth of Vietnam* (Berkeley, Calif.: University of California Press, 1983); and Nguyen Khac Vien, *Vietnam: A Long History* (Hanoi: Foreign Languages Publishing House, 1987).

This chapter is a summary of what many Vietnamese and foreign scholars have long believed to be the main themes of Vietnam's history. Many of these beliefs are currently being questioned by a new generation of historians who argue that much of what the Vietnamese accept as history is a creation of intellectuals in the first four decades of the twentieth century. Because much of this work is just beginning and has not yet been published, my survey here was not able to benefit from this rethinking of Vietnam's past.

1. Ronald J. Cima, ed., *Vietnam: A Country Study* (Washington, D.C.: Library of Congress Federal Research Division, 1989), p. 33.

Chapter 3: The Vietnamese

1. Nguyen Huy Thiep, "Fired Gold," trans. Peter Zinoman, *The Viet Nam Forum: A Review of Vietnamese Culture and Society*, no. 14 (1994), 22.

2. Carlyle A. Thayer, "Recent Political Developments: Constitutional Change and the 1992 Elections," in *Vietnam and the Rule of Law*, ed. Carlyle A. Thayer and David G. Marr (Canberra: Australian National University, 1993), p. 75.

3. Adam Schwarz, "Guessing Game," *Far Eastern Economic Review*, 6 June 1996, 30, 31.

4. On the differences between the north and the south, see Murray Hiebert, "Vietnam's Dichotomy: North Dominates Politics, but South Drives Economy," *Far Eastern Economic Review*, 15 October 1992, 46–51.

Chapter 4: Red Capitalists

1. For profiles of Le Van Kiem's Huy Hoang company, see Adam Schwarz, "Capitalist Cadre," *Far Eastern Economic Review*, 29 February 1996, 42–44, and Murray Hiebert, "Home Front: Vietnamese Exporter Turns to Domestic Opportunities," *Far Eastern Economic Review*, 20 January 1994, 47; on Vietnam's entrepreneurs, see idem, "Do It Yourself," *Far Eastern Economic Review*, 31 March 1994, 62–64.

2. David O. Dapice and Rick Barichello, "Regulation and Trade Policy: Towards an Open Economy," in *In Search of the Dragon's Trail: Economic Reform in Vietnam*, ed. David O. Dapice, Dwight H. Perkins, and Jonathan Haughton (Cambridge, Mass.: Harvard University Press, forthcoming), chap. 5.

3. World Bank, *Viet Nam: Public Sector Management and Private Sector Incentives: An Economic Report* (Washington, D.C., September 1994), pp. x, xi.

4. Adam Schwarz, "Reality Check," *Far Eastern Economic Review*, 29 February 1996, 45.

5. Dapice and Barichello, "Regulation and Trade Policy."

6. I would like to thank David O. Dapice of the Harvard Institute of International Development for these figures.

7. International Monetary Fund, "Recent Economic Developments," unpublished report, 31 May 1994, p. 10.

8. Murray Hiebert, "Testing the Water: Vietnam's Privatization Efforts Start Gingerly," *Far Eastern Economic Review*, 3 February 1994, 45.

9. Ibid.

10. Ibid.

11. Adam Fforde, *Vietnam: Economic Commentary and Analysis*, no. 5 (Canberra, Australia: ADUKI Pty., 1994), pp. 57, 96.

12. Reginald Chua, "Vietnam May Shake Up Its Leadership," *The Asian Wall Street Journal,* 29 April 1996, 3; and Adam Schwarz, "Guessing Game," *Far Eastern Economic Review,* 6 June 1996, 30, 31.

13. For material relating to Nguyen Van Muoi Hai, I am indebted to Barry Wain, "Vietnam Gets a Bitter Taste of Reform: The Collapse of a Pyramid Scheme Scars Investors, Saps Credit Firms," the *Asian Wall Street Journal*, 10 May 1990, 1, 8.

14. *Lao Dong* [Labor], 6 March 1994.

15. Murray Hiebert, "Market Test: Cautious Re-emergence by Ethnic Chinese," *Far Eastern Economic Review*, 1 August 1991, 24–25.

16. Ibid.

17. This law does for domestic businesspeople what the foreign investment law does for foreign capitalists. Essentially, it spells out the principles that govern this form of investment, but the law by itself lacks teeth. It requires many accompanying laws (such as contract, land, company, and bankruptcy laws) before investors can be sure their investment is protected.

Chapter 5: The Hungry Earth

1. Prabhu L. Pingali and Vo Tong Xuan, "Vietnam: De-Collectivization and Rice Productivity Growth," paper presented at a symposium on "Priorities for Agriculture" at the annual meeting of the American Agricultural Economics Association, July 30–August 2, 1989, Baton Rouge, Louisiana, pp. 1–5; and David O. Dapice and Cao Duc Phat, "Rural Reforms, Poverty Alleviation, and Economic Growth," in *In Search of the Dragon's Trail: Economic Reform in Vietnam*, ed. David O. Dapice, Dwight H. Perkins, and Jonathan Haughton (Cambridge, Mass.: Harvard University Press, forthcoming), chap. 7.

2. Adam Schwarz, "Lending Support," *Far Eastern Economic Review,* 30 May 1996, 44–45. World Bank, *Viet Nam: Public Sector Management and Private*

Sector Incentives: An Economic Report (Washington, D.C., September 1994), p. 101.

3. World Bank, *Economic Report*, p. 128.

4. Adam Schwarz, "Problems in the Paddy," *Far Eastern Economic Review*, 21 September 1995, 66–67, 70.

5. Dapice and Phat, "Rural Reforms," chap.7.

6. Ha Van Dang, Vu Thi Phe, Nguyen Dang Kieu, and Pham Quoc Doanh, *Current Situation of Agricultural Land and Paddy Production of Farm Households* (Hanoi: n.p., April 1994), p. 18.

7. Vu Van Toan, Nguyen Quang Luyen, Ngyuen The Ba, Phan Thi Ngoc Ha, and Vu Duc Khanh, *Issues of Using Labour Force in Rural Areas of Vietnam* (Hanoi: n.p., April 1994), p. 10.

8. General Statistics Office, *Survey on Wealth and Poverty* (Hanoi, 1995), pp. 8–13.

9. Murray Hiebert, "In the Heartland: Vietnam's Red River Delta Awaits Aid Infusion," *Far Eastern Economic Review*, 17 June 1993, 58, 60.

10. Murray Hiebert, "Dynamics of Despair: Poverty Condemns Minorities to Margins of Society," *Far Eastern Economic Review*, 23 April 1992, 26, 27, 30, 32.

11. Ibid.

12. Adam Fforde, *Vietnam: Economic Commentary and Analysis*, no. 5 (Canberra, Australia: ADUKI Pty., 1994), pp. 73, 74; and Murray Hiebert, "Travelling Trash: Vietnam's Environment Under Attack from All Quarters," *Far Eastern Economic Review*, 3 February 1994, 21, 24.

13. *Vietnam: A Development Perspective* (Hanoi: n.p., November 1993), p. 58; and Murray Hiebert, "Stuck at the Bottom: Despite Vietnam's Reforms, Many Still Live in Poverty," *Far Eastern Economic Review*, 13 January 1994, 70, 71.

14. World Bank, *Vietnam: Poverty Assessment and Strategy* (Washington, D.C., 1995), pp. ii–iii; and World Bank, *Economic Report*, pp. 79–85.

15. World Bank, *Poverty Assessment*, p. iv.

16. Ibid., pp. ii, 3.

17. World Bank, *Economic Report*, p. 82; and idem, *Poverty Assessment*, p. iv.

18. World Bank, *Poverty Assessment*, p. 67; and Murray Hiebert, "Parading for Work: Vietnam's Farmers Seek Better Fortunes in the Cities," *Far Eastern Economic Review*, 27 May 1993, 60.

19. Michael Richardson, "The Baggage of Reform: Unemployment Looms in Vietnam," *International Herald Tribune*, 12 May 1995, 9.

20. Fforde, *Economic Commentary and Analysis*, p. 38.

21. Jonathan Haughton, "Overview of Economic Reform in Vietnam," in Dapice, Perkins, and Haughton, eds., *In Search of the Dragon's Trail.*

22. Dapice and Phat, "Rural Reforms."

23. World Bank, *Economic Report*, p. 86.

24. Dapice and Phat, "Rural Reforms."

25. World Bank, *Economic Report*, p. 86.

26. Ibid.

27. *Vietnam: A Development Perspective*, p. 60.

28. Murray Hiebert, "The Socialist Millionaire: Vietnamese Landowner Reconciles Wealth, Communism," *Far Eastern Economic Review*, 30 September 1993, 64.

Chapter 6: A Tale of Two Cities

1. World Bank, *Viet Nam: Public Sector Management and Private Sector Incentives: An Economic Report* (Washington, D.C., September 1994), 4.

2. *Vietnam News*, 5 January 1996.

3. The results of the survey are reported in Barbara Franklin, *The Risk of AIDS in Vietnam* (Hanoi: Care International, 1993); see also Murray Hiebert, "AIDS: Ambivalent Campaign," *Far Eastern Economic Review*, 8 July 1993, 34–35; and Murray Hiebert and Ginger Ladd, " 'Flower Sellers' Bloom," *Far Eastern Economic Review*, 8 July 1993, 36.

4. These figures are quoted in Reuters, "Ho Chi Minh City Becomes AIDS capital," *New Straits Times* (Kuala Lumpur, Malaysia), 8 January 1996.

5. Nayan Chanda, "War and Peace," *Far Eastern Economic Review*, 4 May 1995, 21.

6. "Memories of the Fall of Saigon," *New York Times*, reprinted in *New Straits Times*, 5 May 1995, 34.

7. Adam Schwarz, "Unruly Routes," *Far Eastern Economic Review*, 17 August 1995; see also Murray Hiebert, "Hanoi's Free-for-All Ways," *Far Eastern Economic Review*, 16 September 1993, 30.

8. On Hanoi's old quarter see Murray Hiebert, "Going Down the Tubes: Will New Money Destroy Buildings the Bombers Spared?" *Far Eastern Economic Review*, 8 August 1991, 44, 45.

9. See Murray Hiebert, "Travelling Trash: Vietnam's Environment Under Attack from All Quarters," *Far Eastern Economic Review*, 3 February 1994, 21, 24.

10. "Tallying Up 1995's Investment Figures," *Vietnam Investment Review*, 1–7 January 1996, 14.

Chapter 7: Reality Check

1. "Tallying Up 1995's Investment Figures," *Vietnam Investment Review,* 1–7 January 1996, 14.

2. *Report on the Performance of the Manufacturing Sector 1995* quoted in *The Star* (Kuala Lumpur, Malaysia), 23 January 1995, 2; *China Daily Business Weekly,* 28 January–3 February 1996, 1.

3. Michael Vatikiotis, "Romance Meets Reality," *Far Eastern Economic Review,* 22 September 1994, 75.

4. World Bank, *Viet Nam: Public Sector Management and Private Sector Incentives: An Economic Report* (Washington, D.C., September 1994), ii.

5. Erik Portanger, "Westralian Seeks to Halt Vietnam Venture," *The Asian Wall Street Journal,* 3–4 May 1996, 3. For a detailed description of the collapse of the Australian mining company's joint venture see Adam Schwarz, "The Honeymoon Is Over," *Far Eastern Economic Review,* 13 July 1995, 60–61, 64.

6. "P & O Pull-out," *Indochina Digest,* 22 September 1995, 1; Associated Press, "Hanoi Loses Another Investor," *International Herald Tribune,* 18 September 1995.

7. Murray Hiebert, "Industrial Disease: Strikes on the Rise at Foreign-Owned Factories," *Far Eastern Economic Review,* 2 September 1993, 16–17.

8. Adam Schwarz, "Proletarian Blues," *Far Eastern Economic Review,* 25 January 1996, 21–22.

9. Lawrence Ting, quoted in Julian Baum, "Taiwanese Takeover: Island's Entrepreneurs Are Leading the Way," *Far Eastern Economic Review,* 22 September 1994, 77, 80; and Murray Hiebert, "Open for Business: Vietnam's Economy Gets Big Lift from Taiwanese," *Far Eastern Economic Review,* 18 March 1993, 49–50.

10. Reginald Chua and Urban C. Lehner, "Investors Go the Extra Mile to Get a Foot in Vietnam," *The Asian Wall Street Journal,* 15–16 December 1995, 1, 12.

11. Murray Hiebert, "Last but Not Least," *Far Eastern Economic Review,* 31 March 1994, 68.

12. Murray Hiebert, "Do It Yourself," *Far Eastern Economic Review,* 31 March 1994, 62–64. For a longer interview with Truc see Barry Wain, "Even for a Native, Vietnam Is Tough," *The Asian Wall Street Journal,* 28 February 1994, 1, 6; see also Murray Hiebert, "Wooing Them Home: Overseas Vietnamese Cautious About Investment," *Far Eastern Economic Review,* 23 January 1992, 18–19.

Chapter 8: Dancing for Buddha

1. I am indebted to archaeologist-historian Tran Quoc Vuong for introducing me to the revival of folk festivals in northern Vietnam; see Murray Hiebert, "Folk Revival," *Far Eastern Economic Review*, 13 May 1993, 30–31.

2. Shaun Malarney, "Reconstructing the Public Domain: Changing Women's Roles and the Resurgence of Public Ritual in Contemporary Northern Viet Nam," paper presented at the annual meeting of the American Anthropological Association, Atlanta, Georgia, December 1994, pp. 32, 34; see also idem, "Ritual and Revolution in Vietnam" (Ph.D. diss., University of Michigan, 1993); and Hy V. Luong, "Economic Reform and the Intensification of Rituals in Two North Vietnamese Villages, 1980–1990," in *The Challenge of Reform in Indochina*, ed. Borje Ljunggren (Cambridge, Mass.: Harvard University Press, 1993), pp. 259ff. For descriptions of Vietnamese cosmology see Hue-Tam Ho Tai, "Religion in Vietnam: A World of Gods and Spirits," in Asia Society, ed., *Vietnam: Essays on History, Culture, and Society* (New York: Asia Society, 1985), pp. 22ff.; and Gerald Hickey, *Village in Vietnam* (New Haven, Conn.: Yale University Press, 1964).

3. Malarney, "Ritual and Revolution in Vietnam," pp. 391–92.

4. Shaun Malarney, "Creating Equality: The Reform of Marriage, the Wedding Ceremony and Its Consequences in Contemporary Northern Vietnamese Village Life," paper presented at the annual meeting of the Association for Asian Studies, Boston, March 1994, pp. 45–46.

5. Murray Hiebert, "Spiritual Renewal," *Far Eastern Economic Review*, 13 May 1993, pp. 30–31.

6. Shaun Malarney, "Buddhist Practices in Contemporary Northern Viet Nam," paper presented at the Harvard Buddhist Studies Forum, Boston, October 1993, p. 18; and Murray Hiebert, "Answered Prayers," *Far Eastern Economic Review*, 13 May 1993, pp. 26, 28, 29.

7. Puebla Institute, *Vietnam: Free Market, Captive Conscience* (Washington, D.C., 1994), p. 45.

8. On Hanoi's conflict with the Buddhists see Human Rights Watch/Asia, *Vietnam: The Suppression of the Unified Buddhist Church*, March 1995; Puebla Institute, *Free Market, Captive Conscience*; Amnesty International, *Socialist Republic of Vietnam: Buddhist Monks in Detention*, May 1994; "Buddhist Leaders Arrested in Vietnam," *Vietnam Journal: A Newsletter for Human Rights and Development*, 3, no. 1 (Spring 1995): 1ff.; Adam Schwarz, "Arrested Development: Crackdown at Home Follows Opening Abroad," *Far Eastern Economic Review*, 7 September 1995, 33, 36; and Murray Hiebert, "No Middle Path Here," *Far Eastern Economic Review*, 5 August 1993, 26.

9. The results of Le Thi Quy's survey at the Dong Xuan Textile Mill are

NOTES · **241**

reported in "*Doi Moi* and the Woman: Is Vietnam's Female Workforce Reaping the Benefits of Reform?" *Vietnam Investment Review*, 11–17 July 1994, 16.

10. Murray Hiebert, "Uneasy Riders: Young Thrill-Seekers Point to Changing Trends in Vietnamese Society," *Far Eastern Economic Review*, 1 September 1994, 54–55.

11. *Tap Chi Cong San* (Communist Review), October 1993, 3–6, translated in the BBC's *Summary of World Broadcasts*, 9 November 1993, B7–8; see also Murray Hiebert, "Opening a Pandora's Box," *Far Eastern Economic Review*, 29 July 1993, 24–25; and Barry Wain, "Vietnam's Market Reforms Distort Law and Morality," *Asian Wall Street Journal*, 19 October 1992, 1.

12. *Tap Chi Cong San,* October 1993, 3–6.

13. Michael Richardson, "The Baggage of Reform: Unemployment Looms in Vietnam, *International Herald Tribune*, 12 May 1995, 9.

14. *Tap Chi Cong San,* October 1993, 3–6.

15. Greg Lockhart, "Nguyen Huy Thiep and the Faces of Vietnamese Literature," in Nguyen Huy Thiep, *The General Retires and Other Stories*, trans. Greg Lockhart (Oxford: Oxford University Press, 1992), p. 8. This section draws from conversations with Vietnamese writers and literary critics, as well as several written sources, including Nguyen Ba Chung, "A Glance Through Modern Vietnamese Literature," *New Asia Review*, Fall 1994, 37–42; Philip Shenon, "Hanoi Novelist Skewers Party Officials," *The New York Times*, 12 April 1994, 4; Barry Wain, "What *Doi Moi* Has Done for, and to, Nguyen Huy Thiep," *Asian Wall Street Journal*, 26–27 February 1993, p. 6; Peter Zinoman, "Nguyen Huy Thiep's 'Vang Lua' and the Nature of Intellectual Dissent in Contemporary Vietnam," *The Viet Nam Forum: A Review of Vietnamese Culture and Society*, no. 14 (1994), 36–44.

Several prominent Vietnamese writers are now accessible in English: see esp. Bao Ninh, *The Sorrow of War*, ed. Frank Palmos, trans. Vo Bang Thanh and Phan Thanh Hao (London: Secker & Warburg, 1993); Huong Thu Huong, *Paradise of the Blind*, trans. Phan Huy Duong and Nina McPherson (New York: William Morrow, 1993); Huong Thu Huong, *Novel Without a Name*, trans. Phan Huy Duong and Nina McPherson (New York: William Morrow, 1995); Nguyen Huy Thiep, *The General Retires*. Several of Thiep's other stories, including "A Sharp Sword," "Fired Gold," and "Chastity," are translated by Peter Zinoman in *The Viet Nam Forum*, pp. 7–35.

16. Material on Bao Ninh's *The Sorrow of War* is adapted from Murray Hiebert, "Scars of the Jungle" (book review), *Far Eastern Economic Review*, 14 July 1994, 52–53.

17. Keith Taylor, "Locating and Crossing Boundaries in Nguyen Huy Thiep's Short Stories," unpublished paper, Cornell University, Ithaca, New York, p. 1.

18. Ibid., pp. 1–2.

19. Historian Ta Ngoc Lien quoted in Zinoman, "Nguyen Huy Thiep's 'Vang Lua,'" p. 36.

20. Lincoln C. Chen and Linda G. Hiebert, *From Socialism to Private Markets: Vietnam's Health in Rapid Transition*, Working Paper Series (Cambridge, Mass.: Harvard Center for Population and Development Studies, 1994), p. 4; see also Murray Hiebert, "Just What the Doctor Ordered," *Far Eastern Economic Review*, 10 January 1991, 16, 17.

21. World Bank, *Vietnam: Transition to the Market* (Washington, D.C., 1993), p. 183.

22. Ibid., p. 167.

23. Ibid., p. 159.

24. Murray Hiebert, "In the Family Way," *Far Eastern Economic Review*, 22 April 1993, 72.

25. World Bank, *Vietnam: Population, Health, and Nutrition Sector Review* (Washington, D.C., 1992), p. iii.

26. United Nations Educational, Scientific, and Cultural Organization (UNESCO), *Vietnam Educational and Human Resources Sector Analysis*, (mimeo, 1992), p. 40. For more background on education see Murray Hiebert, "Executive Search: Dearth of Managers Hinders Economic Reform," *Far Eastern Economic Review*, 23 June 1994, 17, 20; and idem, "The Drop-Out Factor: Education Crisis Follows Economic Reforms," *Far Eastern Economic Review*, 19 September 1991, 20–21. See also Ashley S. Pettus, "Vietnam's Learning Curve: Dwindling Subsidies Squeeze Teachers and Parents," *Far Eastern Economic Review*, 18 August 1994, 36, 37; and Amy Thanh Nguyen, "The Education Crisis in Vietnam," *The Bridge*, Summer 1994, 3–4, 10–11.

27. World Bank, *Transition to the Market*, pp. 188, 187.

28. Nguyen Chi Thanh, "Education System in Hanoi Trapped in Funding Crises," *Vietnam Investment Review*, 13–21 November 1993.

29. *Indochina Chronology*, 13, no. 3 (July–September 1994): 8; and *Tuoi Tre* (Youth) magazine, 3 October 1993.

Chapter 9: When Will the Party End?

1. Doan Viet Hoat's letter is reprinted in *Vietnam Journal*, 2, no. 2 (Fall–Winter 1993): 3.

2. Stein Tonnesson, "Democracy in Vietnam?" *NIAS Report*, no. 16 (Copenhagen, Denmark: Nordic Institute of Asian Studies, 1993), pp. 13, 15. This chapter draws from conversations with Vietnamese friends, foreign academics, and diplomats. I also benefitted from Borje Ljunggren, "Beyond Reform: On the Dynamics Between Economic and Political Change in Vietnam," paper presented at the conference, Democracy and Democratization

in Asia, University of Louvain, Belgium, 30 May–2 June 1994; Carlyle A. Thayer, "Mono-Organizational Socialism and the Vietnamese State," in *Rural Transformation and Economic Change in Vietnam*, ed. Ben Kerkvliet and Doug Porter (Boulder, Colo.: Westview Press, 1995); William S. Turley, "Political Renovation in Vietnam: Renewal and Adaption," in *The Challenge of Reform in Indochina*, ed. Borje Ljunggren (Cambridge, Mass.: Harvard University Press, 1993); William S. Turley and Mark Seldon, eds., *Reinventing Vietnamese Socialism: Doi Moi in Comparative Perspective* (Boulder, Colo.: Westview Press, 1993); and Barry Wain, "Vietnamese Find Political Taboos Fading," *Asian Wall Street Journal*, 13 June 1990, 1, 20.

3. Reginald Chua, "Hanoi Unveils Strict Rules to Control Internet Access," *The Asian Wall Street Journal*, 3 June 1996, 3.

4. Carlyle A. Thayer, "Recent Political Development: Constitutional Change and the 1992 Elections," in *Vietnam and the Rule of Law*, ed. Carlyle A. Thayer and David G. Marr (Canberra: Australian National University, 1993), pp. 60–61.

5. Murray Hiebert, "Letting Off Steam," *Far Eastern Economic Review*, 30 July 1992, 10.

6. David G. Marr, "The Vietnamese Communist Party and Civil Society," paper presented at the conference *Doi Moi, the State and Civil Society*, at the Australian National University, Canberra, 10–11 November 1994, p. 11.

7. Gabriel Kolko, *Anatomy of a War* (New York: New Press, 1994), p. 559.

8. Carlyle A. Thayer, "The Challenges Facing Vietnamese Communism," *Southeast Asian Affairs 1992* (Singapore: Institute of Southeast Asian Studies, 1992), pp. 355–356.

9. For a summary of views of several dissidents see Murray Hiebert, "Dissenting Voices: Criticisms Ahead of Party Conference Anger Government," *Far Eastern Economic Review*, 2 December 1993, 26.

10. Agence France-Presse, "Senior VN Journalist Calls for Democracy," *The Nation* (Bangkok), 4 March 1991.

11. *Tap Chi Cong San*, February 1990, in Turley, "Political Renovation in Vietnam," p. 337.

12. Linh quoted in Murray Hiebert, "Vietnam," in *Asia 1996* (Hong Kong: Far Eastern Economic Review, 1995), p. 220.

13. Murray Hiebert, "No Dong, No Deal: Corruption Spreading Rapidly in the North," *Far Eastern Economic Review*, 25 June 1992, 13.

14. Murray Hiebert, *Vietnam Notebook*, (Hong Kong: Far Eastern Economic Review, 1993), p. 194; "Party Birthday Party," *Indochina Digest*, 3 February 1995, 3.

15. This translation is from David W. P. Elliott, "Dilemmas of Reform in Vietnam," in Turley and Seldon, *Reinventing Vietnamese Socialism*, p. 65.

16. Tran Duy Huong, "Counter-measures Against 'Peaceful Evolution,' "

Tap Chi Quoc Phong Toan Dan (August 1994): 14, trans. in *Foreign Broadcast Information Service—Southeast Asia*, 8 November 1994, 99.

17. Marr, "Vietnamese Communist Party and Civil Society," p. 4.

18. Turley, "Political Renovation in Vietnam," p. 341.

19. Nguyen Quoc Quan, "The 5th Column: Prisoner of Conscience," *Far Eastern Economic Review*, 25 February 1993, 27.

20. Quoted in Hiebert, "Vietnam," p. 221.

21. World Bank, *Vietnam: Transition to Market* (Washington, D.C., 1993), p. 159.

22. Ibid., p. i.

23. *Lao Dong* (Labor), 5 March 1994. Material on the problems of the civil service adapted from Murray Hiebert, "Executive Search: Dearth of Managers Hinders Economic Reform," *Far Eastern Economic Review*, 23 June 1994, 17, 20.

24. Adam Schwarz, "Nation Builders: Assembly Lays Foundation for Rule of Law," *Far Eastern Economic Review*, 16 November 1995, 22. For a description of Vietnam's efforts to overhaul its legal system see Murray Hiebert, "Miles to Go: Despite Reform, Legal System Leaves Much to Be Desired," *Far Eastern Economic Review*, 29 July 1993, 24–26.

25. David G. Marr, *Vietnam Strives to Catch Up* (New York: Asia Society, 1995), p. 21.

Chapter 10: Chasing the Tigers

1. Nigel Holloway, "Winning the Peace," *Far Eastern Economic Review*, 20 July 1995, 16. The section on Vietnam's foreign relations challenges draws from conversations with Vietnamese and foreign diplomats in Hanoi and the following written materials: Carlyle A. Thayer, "Vietnam: Coping with China," *Southeast Asian Affairs 1994* (Singapore: Institute for Southeast Asian Studies, 1995); William Turley, "Vietnamese Security in Domestic and Regional Focus: The Political-Economic Nexus," unpublished paper, Carbondale, University of Southern Illinois, February 1995; Barry Wain, "China's Broken Line in the Sea," *Asian Wall Street Journal*, 3–4 March 1995; idem, "China's Spratly Claim Is All Wet," *Asian Wall Street Journal*, 15–16 April 1994; and Mark Valencia, "How to End the Spratly Spats," *Asian Wall Street Journal*, 17–18 February 1995.

2. Turley, "Vietnamese Security in Domestic and Regional Focus," p. 1.

3. Ibid., p. 4.

4. Ibid., p. 23.

Acknowledgments

◆ ◆ ◆

This book is the result of nearly four years of living and working in Vietnam, during which my perceptions were formed by the hundreds of writers, businesspeople, farmers, monks, *cyclo* drivers, students, factory workers, wheeler-dealers, parents, government officials, intellectuals, hawkers, soldiers, economists, dissidents, and teachers I met in my jaunts around the country. It is not possible to thank by name all those who helped me and became my friends without the risk that some will get into trouble with Hanoi's security operatives. Without their insights, I would have had precious little to say about this remarkable country.

I am also indebted to my editors at the *Far Eastern Economic Review*, the news weekly published in Hong Kong by Dow Jones & Company. Philip Bowring had the confidence to hire me to cover Vietnam from Bangkok in 1986 as the country launched its reforms and then assign me to open the magazine's first bureau in Hanoi in 1990. L. Gordon Crovitz and Nayan Chanda later provided encouragement and support when the going got rough. I have a special debt to Nayan, who first taught me the art of Vietnam watching.

Thanks to Tran Le Thuy, the *Review*'s cheerful and tenacious bureau assistant, who introduced me to much of what I learned about Vietnam and who struggled with the official bureaucracy to get me most of my interviews.

I am grateful to the Ford Foundation and the Christopher Reynolds Foundation, which provided grants that enabled me to take time off to complete a major chunk of the manuscript.

Thanks to the Mennonite Central Committee for first introducing me to Vietnam. This nongovernmental organization sent me there to work on its relief and development projects in the closing days of the war; I have never quite managed to get Vietnam out of my system since.

While reporting from Hanoi I profited enormously from my contact with fellow journalists, particularly Kathleen Callo and John Rogers of Reuters, Jean Claude Chapon and Andrew Sherry of Agence France-Presse, and Barry Wain, who parachuted in from Hong Kong for the *Asian Wall Street Journal*. Adam Schwarz, who replaced me as the *Review*'s correspondent in Hanoi, kept me abreast of major developments there after I moved on to Malaysia. I am indebted to the many overseas Vietnamese, foreign businessmen, aid workers, and diplomats, particularly those from Australia, Britain, Canada, France, Russia, and Sweden, who shared their insights with me.

Many scholars helped me during the time I was in Vietnam and while I was working on the book, including David Dapice, Dwight Perkins, and Thomas Vallely of the Harvard Institute for International Development, David Marr and Adam Fforde of Australian National University, Keith Taylor of Cornell University, William Turley of Southern Illinois University, Carlyle Thayer of Australian Defense Force Academy, and Shaun Malarney of Tokyo's International Christian University. Dapice, Malarney, Marr, Taylor, Turley, and Vallely read some of the book's chapters and provided valuable suggestions.

Loretta Barrett of Loretta Barrett Books is a marvelous agent. At Kodansha America, John Urda first believed in the book, and Joshua Sitzer had the vision and the red pen that helped mold it into existence.

I owe my greatest debt to my family. My wife, Linda, shared her insights and provided moral support; our children, Ann and Jonathan, pointed out many wonders of Vietnam that I had missed.

In the end, I assume responsibility for any distortions and oversimplifications that may have crept into this book.

Index

◆ ◆ ◆

Boat people, 7, 13, 42, 83, 112. *See also*
    Refugees
Boeing, 145
Boi Thuy village, 89
Brahman teachers, 36
Bribes, 76–81
Brinsden, John, 23, 143
Britain, 143, 195, 205
Brown, Christopher, 212
Brunei Darussalam, 219, 222–23
Buddhism, 10, 60, 152–85, 217;
    adoption of, by Vietnam's elite, 34;
    and Christianity, 160–65; and
    human rights, 226; under the Ly
    kings, 36; and the Ming dynasty,
    36–37
Buddhist Research Institute, 161
Buon, Bui Thai, 101

Callo, Kathleen, 49
Caloric requirements, 98, 99–100, 178
Cambodia, 9, 32–33, 59, 92, 163;
    border disputes with, 226; dry
    season in, 54; and French colonial-
    ism, 38, 41; invasion/occupation of,
    by Hanoi, 12, 21–22, 42, 192, 220,
    222, 227; Khmer Rouge in, 21, 42,
    227
Cambodian language, 33
Can, Le Thac, 181
Canada, 7, 52, 64, 148, 150, 185, 212
Cao Dai religion, 161–62
Capitalism, 20–26, 64–85, 113–16, 203;
    and Buddhism, 154; and ethnic
    Chinese, 81–85; and the first
    tycoons, 64–70; and illegal activity,
    76–81; and overseas Vietnamese,
    147–48; and regional differences,
    56–57; and state capitalists, 70–76
Capital punishment, 171
Care International, 120
Caterpillar, 145
Catholic church, 160–65. *See also*
    Christianity
Celli, Claudio, 164
Censorship, 46. *See also* Dissidents
Census (1989), 180
Center for Natural Resources
    Management and Environmental
    Studies, 97

Center for Women's Studies, 166
Central Trading & Development, 142–
    44
Chaebol, 73
Cham (ethnic group), 56
Chanda, Nayan, 122, 212
Chan Heng Chee, 221
"Chastity" (Thiep), 173
Chau, Pham Duong, 176–77
Chau, Phan Boi, 39–40
Chay long rong, 118
Chiang Kai-shek, 142
China, 9, 21, 24–25, 31–42; and
    ASEAN, 220–22, 224, 226; and
    Catholicism, 163; and the Co Loa
    festival, 156; economic growth in,
    vs. in Vietnam, 24; and endangered
    species, 96; face-saving in, 45; flight
    of refugees to, from Vietnam, 13;
    flour imports from, 64; foreign
    investment in, 133, 138, 144; gross
    domestic product of, 230; gross
    national product of, 106; health
    care in, 178; and human rights, 44,
    205–6, 225; ideological battles in,
    207; invasions by, 77, 93, 155, 214;
    living standards in, 100; migration
    in, 102–3; and most-favored-nation
    trading status, 206; occupation of
    Vietnam by, 155; pesticides from,
    96; and petroleum resources, 25,
    139; population of, 32, 179;
    possibility of political change in,
    215–16; protests by peasants in,
    101; rural work force in, absorption
    of, 105–6; smuggling of dogs into,
    125; and the South China Sea, 222,
    223–24; southern, Manchu
    conquest of, 83; and the Spratly
    archipelago, 222, 223–24;
    subjugation of women in, 44; and
    tariffs, 146; Tiananmen Square
    incident in, 199; and Vietnam's
    invasion of Cambodia, 222–23; and
    the Vietnam War, 41, 56, 108. *See
    also* Chinese language; Chinese,
    ethnic; Confucianism
Chinese, ethnic, 7, 13, 81–85, 95
Chinese Investment and Development
    Corporation, 139

99–100, 178; and malnutrition, 29, 98, 178

Dikes, building of, 92

Dinh, 157

Dinh, Nguyen Huu, 73–74

Diplomatic relations, normalization of, 133, 146, 220, 224–25

Directive 10 (Communist Party), 13

Discipline, Confucian emphasis on, 25

Dissidents, 61–62, 186–89, 203, 225–26. *See also* Human rights

Divorce, 169

DMZ (demilitarized zone), 19

Do, Thich Quang, 164, 165, 226

Doanh, Le Dang, 74, 146

Doi moi, 13–14, 200

Domino theory, 23–26

Dong, Pham Van, 56

Dong Da, 194

Dong Khoi Street, 111–13, 115–16, 118–20

Dong Xuan Textile Mill, 167

Dow Jones & Company, 51, 112

Drugs, illegal, 94, 171, 225

Du, Nguyen, 43–44

Duc, Le Dien, 97

Duc Tan Floor Tiles factory, 66–67, 68

Duong Vuong (emperor), 34

DuPont Company, 139

Duty, Confucian emphasis on, 44

"East Asian model" of development, 26

Eastern Europe, 112, 170, 176, 215–16, 225, 228

Eastern Sea (South China Sea), 32, 92, 222–23

Eating rituals, 45

Economic growth rates, 22, 24, 57, 100–101, 229–30

Education, 9, 14, 26, 101, 180–85; emphasis on, in Confucianism, 24–25, 229; and ethnic Chinese, 83, 84; foreign support for, 29; and women, status of, 169; World Bank data on, 180, 182, 185. *See also* Language; Literacy rates

Electrical power, 28, 29, 92, 97, 134

Embargos, 7, 21, 23, 117, 133, 144, 188

Emotions, expression of, 47–48

Endangered species, 96

English language, 9, 52, 116, 122, 183, 209

Environmental issues, 95–97, 128, 130–31; deforestation, 25, 26, 95–96; pollution, 96, 130

Equitization scheme, 72

Export-Import Bank, 224

Export-Import Bank of Japan, 144

Export-processing zones, 135, 143

Face-saving, 45, 46–47

Family groups, 44–45

Far Eastern Economic Review, 51, 126, 152, 211–12, 214, 229

Fatherland Front, 194

Fertility rates, 179. *See also* Population

Fforde, Adam, 29–30, 72

Firecrackers, 49

"Fired Gold" (Thiep), 43

Food: and cooking styles, 55; and eating rituals, 45. *See also* Diet

Food Technology Corporation, 64–65

Ford Foundation, 185

Foreign Trade College, 181

Forestry Inventory and Planning Institute, 95

France, 163, 171, 196, 205, 215; foreign investment by, 139, 150; overseas Vietnamese companies from, 150; Roman Catholic missionaries from, 38, 39; visit by the president of, to Vietnam (1993), 149; war with, 9, 99, 108–9, 128, 141, 154, 173. *See also* Colonialism

Franklin, Barbara, 120

Freedom: and crime, 170; and literature, 172, 176; religious, 164, 203; of speech, 10, 61, 205

Freedom Forum (newsletter), 186

Freedom Forum (organization), 61–62

Funeral ceremonies, 158–59

Garment industry, 7, 17, 26, 63, 65; and ethnic Chinese, 82–83; and foreign investment, 140, 143, 144; and labor disputes, 140; in the Red River delta, 93

General Forwarding & Agency Company, 70–71

"General Retires, The" (Thiep), 173

About the Author

◆ ◆ ◆

Murray Hiebert, a native of Manitoba, Canada, was first in Vietnam during the closing days of the Vietnam War, when he worked in the central coastal city of Nhatrang for a nongovernmental relief and development agency. From 1979–1986, he was an editor of the *Indochina Issues* monthly for the Center for International Policy in Washington, D.C., and from 1986–1990, he covered Indochina from Bangkok for Dow Jones & Company's *Far Eastern Economic Review* while also reporting for the *Washington Post* and National Public Radio's *All Things Considered*. One of the first foreign journalists to move to Vietnam after the ruling Communist Party launched its dramatic economic reforms in 1986, Hiebert opened the Hanoi bureau of the *Review* in 1990. He lived there with his family, covering Vietnam, until 1994.

He currently lives with his wife and two children in Kuala Lumpur, covering Singapore and Malaysia for the *Review*.